SOULFIRE

*Preaching the Church's Message in a
Secular, Postmodern World*

The Rev. Dr. Gary Nicolosi

WESTBOW
PRESS®

A DIVISION OF THOMAS NELSON
& ZONDERVAN

WestBow Press books may be ordered through booksellers or by contacting:

WestBow Press
A Division of Thomas Nelson & Zondervan
1663 Liberty Drive
Bloomington, IN 47403
www.westbowpress.com
844-714-3454

Scripture quotations are from New Revised Standard Version Bible, copyright © 1989 National Council of the Churches of Christ in the United States of America. Used by permission. All rights reserved worldwide.

ISBN: 978-1-6642-1305-0 (sc)
ISBN: 978-1-6642-1307-4 (hc)
ISBN: 978-1-6642-1306-7 (e)

Library of Congress Control Number: 2020922883

Print information available on the last page.

WestBow Press rev. date: 12/18/2020

CONTENTS

PREFACE

Why another book on preaching when there have been so many published on the subject? And why another book of sermons when over the course of Christian history hundreds of thousands if not millions of sermons have been preached and printed?

SoulFire addresses the issue of preaching in a secular, postmodern world – a world like none other in history – a new emerging world that has made proclaiming the Gospel of God's love in Jesus exceptionally challenging. Although technology allows us to share the Christian message on a global scale unimaginable just a few decades ago, the populations in the United States and Canada are becoming more secular and less religious. With each passing generation – from the Boomers, to Gen Xers, to the Millennials, to Generation Z – there are fewer believers and church members. This downward trajectory shows no indication of leveling off. Thus, there is a need for preachers to reimagine how we communicate in a culture where people may not know the Christian story or know it accurately.

While our method of preaching may need to change, our message remains unchanging – "Jesus Christ is the same yesterday, today and forever" (Heb. 13: 8, NRSV). I believe the Bible to be the inspired word of God. When I enter the pulpit, I believe that I am preaching God's word and not my own word. It is a word preached through my personality, knowledge, skills and experience to a specific congregation in a particular time and place. I have confidence in this word, even as I am a fallible and flawed human being preaching it. The "call from God" gives me the power and purpose to communicate God's word effectively.

Although *SoulFire* is not a book on church growth, I believe that an open and inclusive church with a solid biblical message grounded in Christian faith is best positioned to reach our secular, postmodern culture. Clergy need to preach the good news to people who desperately need to hear it, or as Bishop Lesslie Newbigin put it: "one beggar telling another beggar where to find bread." The Gospel is not about morality, church going or rule keeping. The Gospel is, "We fail miserably, but God loves us anyway." While none of us are good enough or worthy enough to receive that love, God still gives it. God's love claims us, everyone.

SoulFire is a book that combines how to preach in a secular, postmodern world with sermons on exploring faith, the spiritual journey, contemporary issues and church life. St. Augustine said that the task of a preacher is to edify, educate and entertain. The sermons in this book are designed to do all three – edify or inspire you to an encounter with God, educate or help you think through the meaning and implications of Christian faith, and entertain or hold your attention.

Although I take full responsibility for the contents, *SoulFire* could not have been compiled and written without the support and encouragement of dear friends who read the sermons, lectures, and introductions, and recommended changes and improvements.

Greg Thompson, Ken Andrews, Stephen Adams and John and Wendy Thorpe have been with me throughout this process of putting the book together. Their friendship and support has been a tremendous blessing to me. Stephen Adams deserves special thanks because he persuaded me to write this book.

Over the years several other dear friends urged me to write a book, including Prescott Crafts, and my mentor and colleague in

ministry, Bishop Samir Kafity. My assistants at St. Bartholomew's, Poway, California, the Rev. Mary White and the Rev. Carolyn Richardson always inspired me, sharing ideas, and encouraging me to preach the Bible in fresh ways. I also want to thank Dr. Peggy Roffey, the Parish Life Coordinator at St. James Westminster Church in London, Ontario for presenting me with a book of my sermons upon my retirement. Knowing Peggy, it was a labor of love. Some of the sermons in that book are included in this volume.

Dr. William Marra of Fordham University and The Rev. Dr. Eugene Fairweather of Trinity College, Faculty of Divinity, taught me to think philosophically and theologically about Christian faith. I am indebted to them for their influence on my life. They are God's good and faithful servants, both now with the Lord.

A special thanks to the Rev. Canon Robert Hulse who served as Rector of St. John's Anglican Church in Elora, Ontario for thirty-eight years. As a young divinity student, Bob was instrumental in shaping my ministry and preaching, and over the years I had the privilege of preaching at his church many times. Thank you, Bob, for being such a blessing to me.

I could not have written this book without the support of my wife Heather. She provided me with helpful research on culture and society, offered valuable advice, and gave a fresh perspective on the state of the church. Heather has been incredibly patient with me, especially as I spent so much time in my study apart from the family. Thank you, Heather, for being such a loving and supportive wife.

Finally, I want to thank my daughter Allison who has taught her father about God through her own trust, love, joy and gentleness. I would not be the priest I am today without Allison who keeps me grounded in knowing what matters most in life.

To all my readers, may you know the love of Jesus in your own life, find hope and courage to face the future with faith, and live joyfully and confidently that God reigns always and forever.

The Rev. Dr. Gary Nicolosi
All Saints Day
November 1, 2020

INTRODUCTION

For most of my life, I have had a love affair with Jesus. Though I love my wife and daughter, cherish friends, relatives and colleagues, Jesus has been the central figure in my life. He is the reason I became a priest, dedicated my life to the church, served parishes across North America, and have this passion to preach the Gospel. I have spent thirty-seven years of ordained ministry sharing Jesus with everyone who would listen, both within and outside the church. My commitment throughout this time has been to build up the church as a loving, faithful community witnessing to the risen Christ, helping people know how Jesus can make a transformational difference in their lives, and reaching out to those beyond the church with the same love and acceptance that our great God has for us.

After an early career as a New York attorney where I practiced criminal and labor law, I finally responded to the call of God to become a priest – a call I first felt in the sixth grade. It was a big risk to leave law practice and study divinity in Toronto, Canada, but it turned out to be the right move.

I was ordained in June 1983, retired in July 2016, and then returned to active parish ministry as an interim rector from September 2017 to June 2019. Throughout that time, I have served churches in two countries, the Episcopal Church in the United States and the Anglican Church of Canada. It has been a privilege to serve in both churches. I have met dedicated and faithful people, worked with talented and committed clergy, and experienced the best and worst of church life. Honestly, it has been an adventure with rarely a dull moment.

I do have one regret, though. Throughout my time in ordained ministry, both the Episcopal and Anglican Churches have declined dramatically in members. The decline began in the mid-1960s, and neither church shows any sign of a turnaround. There are many reasons for church decline and no one answer will tell the whole story. The culture is radically changing, to be sure, and the church has not done a good job of adapting in an effective way. However, there is more to it than that.

A friend of mine, a thoughtful Canadian Anglican, wrote me with his reflections on the church. He said that at least in Protestant churches, "What passes for institutional Christianity these days is not much more than a thin veneer of spirituality meant to provide a warm and familiar blanket and sense of purpose for navigating an essentially secular and material world."

My friend went on to say that churches have become places where "people can feel a vague kind of spirituality… not so much rooted in ancient church dogma handed down by the apostles and church fathers, grounded in our redemption through Christ's passion, resurrection and saving grace… but rather in feeling good about ourselves and being relevant in the world through celebrating diversity, equality, health and safety… Jesus is less God's Son than an ambassador for community improvement if not a warrior for social justice… Liturgy is reduced to going through the motions and not particularly rooted in holiness and communion with God, such that worship becomes casual, even facile and perfunctory."

He concluded by saying, "Thus there is frequently little sense of holiness, transcendence and piety in many churches, because church isn't grounded in the dogmas and centrality of faith but in fruitless attempts to be relevant to the prevailing secular and material world beyond it. Except that in the long run it's not a recipe for the church's relevance and continuing well-being, which is why churches are declining."

I quote my friend at length and with his permission because he is making an important point on why the Episcopal and Anglican Churches continue to decline. We have the form but lack the substance. We are all froth but no beer, all sizzle and no steak. There is a thin veneer of spirituality but we don't seem to grapple with the essential doctrines of our faith in a way that effectively communicates to a secular, postmodern world.

I remember a discussion in a church that was struggling to formulate a purpose statement. It was a very diverse congregation, and the members were having difficulty finding consensus. Finally, an old-time member not noted for subtly said, "My God, we are a church, for Christ's sake. We have to stand for something!"

We are a church, for Christ's sake, and we have to stand for something! The sermons and lectures in this book are my attempt to articulate what the church stands for, and how we believe in a loving God even in a world like this. My hope is that anyone who reads this book will find it helpful in their spiritual journey. However, I have written and compiled this book with three target audiences in mind.

First are clergy and seminary students who struggle with how to preach in a world no longer friendly to the church. This has resulted in enormous pressure on clergy to preach sermons that not only appeal to church members but are able to attract non-churchgoers and even non-Christians. And yet, there are clergy who do not feel prepared to produce such sermons, and the result is increased stress, depression and burnout.

A second intended readership are seekers, doubters, and non-believers. There are a growing number of people who are seeking a deeper meaning to life, or wondering how they can have a more fulfilled and satisfying life, living for someone or something greater than themselves that has lasting value and permanence. This book will challenge both seekers and inquirers to ponder the question: "What are the implications for my life if Christianity is true?"

Finally, committed Christians will benefit from this book, especially those concerned about the state of the church, the quality of preaching, or hunger for spiritual truth. Today we are all pilgrims in our own land.

SoulFire consists in a series of sermons and lectures that were delivered in the United States and Canada over the course of thirty-seven years of ordained ministry. The lectures and sermons were delivered in rural, suburban and urban churches, both small and large. I have edited most of the materials but have not updated the subject matter, since the sermons and lectures were addressed on specific topics and contexts. Still, I think they will prove relevant to the reader.

Part One, Building the Fire: Transforming Lives in Jesus shares my journey to preach effectively in a secular, postmodern world. I then share how I understand preaching and have gone about it these many years. Priests and pastors will have their own way of developing a sermon, and there certainly is no one right way for everyone. However, the method presented here has worked for me over the years, and I commend it to any aspiring preacher.

Part Two, Kindling the Fire: Exploring Faith is the intellectual or "head" side of Christianity – explaining Christian faith, why it makes sense and how to understand it. St. Anselm's maxim "faith seeking understanding" is the basis for the sermons in this section. There is an opening lecture on Christianity and the New Atheism and a closing lecture on The Case for Religion. There are sermons on the meaning and importance of the three central doctrines of Christianity: Incarnation, Redemption and Resurrection, understanding heaven, dealing with death, and how to respond to suffering. There also is a sermon that tackles the issue: Is Jesus the only way to heaven?

Part Three, Fanning the Fire: The Spiritual Journey is on drawing people into an experience of God. It is not enough to think through our faith; we have got to experience it. The sermons here are designed to help people reflect on their own encounters with God, even if they were not aware of it at the time. In some sense, we are all mystics. This section includes a wide variety of topics: experiencing and knowing God, prayer, mortality, earth spirituality, music, human potential, vocation and self-realization.

Part Four, The World on Fire: Contemporary Issues are sermons on current events and topics. When natural disasters or human tragedies shake us, sermons should be "teaching moments" on how faith and life come together. These sermons are examples of how Christian faith responds to crisis, whether it be terrorist attacks, school shootings, racism, economic disparity, corporate greed, the use of wealth, and our increasing lack of civility in our politics. It is possible for preachers to address social, political and economic issues without being polarizing. The key is to be Gospel-centered, framing the issue from a biblical perspective, and avoiding any partisan agenda.

Part Five, Home Fire: Church Life includes sermons on ordained and lay ministry, change, inclusivity, understanding the Eucharist, and celebrating the role of music in the church. There are sermons on the religious spirit and discipleship. The section concludes with a sermon preached shortly before my retirement, in which I shared three turning points in my life as a Christian, lawyer and priest.

Preaching on a weekly basis, or even three or more times a month, is one of the most challenging tasks that any human being can undertake. Litigating a law case before a judge and jury is perhaps equally demanding, but lawyers do not go to trial every week. Preachers, on the other hand, are expected to give well-crafted, thoughtful, incisive and life-changing sermons every week, or nearly every week. That is exhausting, draining work for the best of us, but that is our call as preachers. We are here to communicate a word from the Lord to our people. The sermon may not always be a homerun, but we give it our best. If even one out of three touches the hearts and minds of our listeners, that is a .333 average. In Major League Baseball, that would make us a star hitter. So, we don't berate ourselves if not every sermon is a homerun. If we have done our best, and given our best, we are God's faithful servants. St. Paul reminds us: "Therefore, since it is by God's mercy that we are engaged in this ministry, we do not lose heart. We have renounced the shameful things that one hides; we refuse to practice cunning or to falsify God's word; but by the open statement of the truth we commend ourselves to the conscience of everyone in the sight of God" (2 Cor. 4:1-2, NRSV).

Always we remember, the results of our labors are in God's hands. No one has said this better than John Venn, one of the founders of the Church Missionary Society in the Church of England. At a worship service in 1806 upon the anniversary of the departure of a young group of missionaries to Africa, John Venn preached:

> We must fix our hope of success chiefly upon God, on the nature of divine truth, and on the spirit and temper of the men who preach it. And although we have not met with immediate success, are we not laying a foundation on which may be successfully built hereafter? But what have we to do with success? Success as I say belongs to God – duty is our part. Shall we sit still and make no effort for the conversion of our fellow-creatures?

Can we acquit ourselves of guilt by waiting longer till we see a more favorable prospect? Our duty, our indispensable duty, is to endeavor; nor are our endeavors at all less acceptable to God, even though they may be unsuccessful.[1]

Of course, the work of the Church Missionary Society in Africa was not in vain. The Christian presence in Africa grew steadily, and today some of the most vibrant churches in the world are on that continent. We never know what God will do with the word preached – lives transformed and cultures changed. Our task is to preach as faithfully and effectively as our abilities and energy will allow and leave the rest to God.

PART ONE

BUILDING THE FIRE: TRANSFORMING LIVES IN JESUS

THE CHALLENGE: THE SECULAR, POSTMODERN WORLD

If you were growing up in the United States or Canada in the years following World War II, Sunday would have found you in church. Not everyone, of course but a large segment of the population attended church on a regular basis. Both the Episcopal Church in the United States and the Anglican Church of Canada thrived in a culture that was mostly friendly towards religion, and specifically Christianity. Some of the largest Episcopal churches today, for example, began as new church plants in the suburbs throughout the late 1940s and 1950s.

Mainline churches began to decline in the mid-1960s, and the downward trajectory has continued to the present day. While there are many reasons for church decline, the one that I want to focus on is preaching. Until the early 1960s, Sunday morning was for church – and worshippers regardless of denomination heard sermons that strengthened their faith and gave guidance for another week of living. The sermon, especially for Protestant Christians, was the heartbeat of the Sunday service. Even in liturgical churches such as the Episcopal Church and the Anglican Church of Canada, the sermon was an important part of the service since the Eucharist was usually celebrated only once a month at the main worship service. However, that would change.

When I entered divinity school forty years ago, there was an ongoing discussion about the importance of the sermon. By the 1970s the liturgical movement had made the Eucharist the central act of worship on Sunday morning. Gradually but steadily, almost every Episcopal and Anglican church began to celebrate the Eucharist every Sunday at every service. This was a major transformation in worship – with unintended consequences.

With the focus on the Eucharist came new liturgies, new expressions of worship that were designed not only to inspire parishioners to draw closer to God, but also to appeal to a wider audience beyond the church. The liturgy was seen as a way to form church members into disciples of Jesus as well as to speak to non-members in language and rituals that would touch their hearts and minds.

With this emphasis on Eucharist and new liturgies, what then would be the role of the sermon? Inevitably, it took on lesser importance.

In the 1960s, 70s, and 80s, counseling, pastoral care, and conversational preaching became common ways of ministering in a congregation. Preaching became more exploratory and less didactic, with the preacher more likely to pose questions than give answers. Instead of strengthening the faith of members, or at least helping them to better understand the faith, the preacher openly shared his or her own doubts about the most central issues of Christian faith, including the incarnation and resurrection, the virgin birth and miracles. The end result was that many Christians left church feeling spiritually dry, unprepared for another week in a world that could be brutal and harsh.

It is no coincidence that membership in the Episcopal and Anglican Churches began to decline in the mid-1960s, just as preaching began to be de-emphasized. Of course, one could justifiably claim there are many reasons for church decline, including a dominant theological and social liberalism that was unable to meet the felt needs of members in the pews who were struggling with personal issues, such as marriage, divorce, addictions, careers, raising children and having a purposeful life.

Members concluded the church was of no help to them in their daily lives. And so, they began drifting away, some to conservative churches that taught scripture in a literal or at least structured way. Others went to non-denominational seeker churches that were designed to meet the needs of specific demographic groups, such as middle-class suburbanites. Still others formed breakaway churches that were more traditional in their liturgy and doctrine. And finally, some joined the Roman Catholic or Orthodox Churches. Many stopped going to any church, identifying with what we now term "spiritual but not religious" or even "secular but spiritual."

While I value the Eucharist and support liturgical reform, I think preaching has a central role in church growth. Good preaching may not always result in church growth, but bad preaching will almost always result in church decline.

The issue is how to preach effectively in a twenty-first century world where attention spans are shorter, communication techniques are more sophisticated, and many people (including Christians) do not know the Christian story, or do not know it accurately or adequately. Moreover, preachers are more likely to be challenged for what they say in the pulpit than at any time since the Reformation. I learned this lesson early in my ministry.

As a newly ordained priest, I was preaching a sermon one Sunday evening in a little church on the Magdalene Islands in Quebec, Canada. In the middle of my sermon, a man who obviously had too much to drink, stood up and shouted, "Preacher, preacher, you don't really believe that stuff, do you? Where does it say that in the Bible?" Before I could respond, another man stood up and shouted at him, "Read the Book of Revelation!" Then began a heated argument between the two men, and I honestly thought there might be a fistfight in the church. Thankfully, though, the wife of the first man grabbed her husband by the arm and told him, "Sit down! Let the preacher finish the sermon." Well, the man did sit down, and I was able to finish my sermon, never quite sure what would happen next.

Take that story as a metaphor for what is happening with preachers today. We are preaching to people who may no longer believe or accept what we are saying, or even care about what we are saying. They may not stand up and begin shouting at us. More likely, they will stop attending church, go to another church, or even not go to church at all.

In our secular, postmodern culture, preachers need to recognize that sincere, smart, faithful believers struggle with how to embrace their Christian faith while maintaining intellectual integrity. The days of unwavering faith in any institution are gone. People expect thoughtful but heartfelt sermons that speak to them at their own level of need and understanding. Warm, fuzzy sermons or light, airy ones just will not do. Delivering a few reflections on the Sunday Gospel just won't cut it anymore.

After being ordained in the Diocese of Quebec in 1983, it did not take long for me to recognize that the good old days, when people packed the church and accepted what was taught with little questioning, were over. As a preacher, I could no longer presume that everyone in the pews knew or understood the Bible, or accepted the teachings of the church. The world was changing, the country was changing, the culture was changing, and so the church needed to change.

As a young priest I had no influence to change the institutional church, but I had the power to change my style of ministry, and that included preaching. I began to take seriously the cultural forces impinging on the church and its members. I resolved to preach sermons not just for believing Christians but for seekers, doubters, skeptics and even people hostile to Christianity. I wanted to build bridges between the sacred and the secular, the religious and the spiritual, the church and the culture.

I termed this style of preaching "bridge building" or connecting the church world to the secular, postmodern world.

By secular, I mean the tendency in humankind to do without religion or to try to do without religion, as church historian Owen Chadwick put it. Secularism values freedom, autonomy and choice. In the secular world there is a loss of transcendence and a religious frame of reference. Values are relative; belief is privatized; and religion is marginalized. Secularists do without God quite nicely, so why bother believing in anything?

Secularism squeezes out God from public life, leaving what Richard John Neuhaus termed a "naked public square." God is relegated to the private belief of individuals, with the world functioning without recourse to any grand narrative.

In the mid-twentieth century, secularism began to be challenged by postmodernism, a movement spearheaded by French intellectuals after the Second World War. Postmodernism rejects any objective truth because all explanations of reality are constructs. Pluralism and relativism are celebrated. Learning is endless. All authorities, whether church or state, are suspect. All systems, religious or any other, are viewed as alienating and repressive. Reality is kaleidoscopic, organic, multicultural and chaotic.

The good news of postmodernism (unlike secularism) is that there is an openness to mystery and even the supernatural. While postmodernism is notoriously difficult to describe – after all, it resists categorization – it does have several clear traits: a preference for experience over reason, heart over mind, intuition over thought, mystery over explanation, image over print, relationships over rules, change and transition over permanence and stability, and sacred moments over sacred space. Postmodernism is radically inclusive, preferring both/and to either/or thinking. It values open parameters over closed boundaries, exploration over inhabiting, journeying over dwelling, and ongoing learning and self-actualization. Postmodernists demand authenticity and integrity in their leaders, hate phonies, and are deeply suspicious of any absolute authority figure.

So, as a young priest, charged with preaching regularly to small Canadian congregations, I knew the history. I also knew our modern world. More than anything, I wanted to be authentic by being faithful to my calling and honest with my parishioners.

I concluded that in this secular, postmodern culture, the church would need to compete to be heard. The home field advantage Christianity had long enjoyed was gone. No longer could anyone presume that the church had a formative influence upon the political and social order, as it did prior to the 1960's.

As a result of immigration, globalization, and the technological revolution, we now take for granted that our neighbors and friends will be Buddhist, Hindu, Muslim, Shinto, New Age, atheists and agnostics, as well as Christians. People are exposed to a whole smorgasbord of options, from astrology to Zen Buddhism, and everything in between. There is no longer any grand narrative that holds everything together. Christianity is viewed as one story among many. Put simply, our culture no longer embraces Christianity's exclusive truth claim as the authoritative story. The world is diverse, the culture is fragmented, and the playing field is level. As the playwright Joan Didion put it, "When the ground starts shaking, all bets are off."

In 1997, I completed a doctorate in church growth from Pittsburgh Theological Seminary. I read the works of C. Peter Wagner and George Hunter III. Both men took on the subject of church growth with the rigor and objectivity of scientists but also with a passion for the church's mission. I became convinced that the one and only thing the church uniquely has to offer the world is a relationship with God in Jesus Christ. Everything else the secular world can do, and for the most part, does quite well. The purpose of the church, unlike any other institution, is to transform lives in Jesus.

After I became rector of a church in Lancaster, Pennsylvania in 1990, I wrote down seven shifts the church needed to make to respond effectively to the secular, postmodern culture. These seven shifts became the bedrock of my preaching and style of ministry in every church that I have since pastored.

1. From the church as depository of propositional truth to the church as embodied truth – Christians don't just proclaim the Gospel; we are the Gospel.
2. From the church as an institution to the church as a community of believers and seekers living the way of Jesus – a humble church not always having the right answers but witnessing to the right person.
3. From an emphasis on believing the right doctrines to living the right way – a community of love in action.
4. From "believing leads to belonging" to "belonging leads to believing" – inviting seekers to experience God, join in community and grow in faith – experience, community and faith, in that order.

5. From the church answering the question, "Is it true?" to the church living out the question, "Does it work?" – offering a practical, relevant but balanced Christianity of head and heart.

6. From the church defending faith to a church of connection, conversation and community – exploring the questions, recognizing the difficulties but trusting Jesus.

7. From "one size fits all" to meeting people at their own level of need and understanding – offering the good news in terms and forms that relate to their situation, that speak to them in their language and cultural style, addressing their existential questions.

It became clear to me that for the church to make these seven shifts demanded a new model of ministry – away from a pastoral, members-only model to a mission, outreach-oriented model that could reach out, engage and speak to the people beyond our church membership. I termed this model "The Open Church" – open because it is flexible, adaptable, and able to change its methods of ministry while remaining steadfast to an unchanging Gospel message.

Over the course of thirty-seven years, I have served as a parish priest in diverse places in North America: from the Gaspe Coast, Quebec to San Diego, California, from Lancaster County, Pennsylvania to Vancouver Island, British Columbia, and from London, Ontario to serving as Interim Rector in Scottsdale, Arizona. I have witnessed the impact of secularism and multiculturalism. These are not merely curious sociologic and demographic phenomena. They are the real world of today's church. These are the waters we swim in.

In 2007, I was invited to serve as Congregational Development Officer in the Diocese of British Columbia. This was a break from parish ministry, and I welcomed it as an opportunity to step back and think of the big picture. Well, the picture wasn't pretty.

Canada is a highly multicultural, secular country where churchgoing has declined dramatically since its peak in the 1950s. In British Columbia, for example, only about 7 percent of the population attend church on a regular basis. When the Diocese of British Columbia (which encompasses Vancouver Island and the Gulf Islands) had to close several churches, letters to the editor in the local Victoria newspaper actually celebrated the closures, claiming Christianity was bigoted and irrelevant.

It was in British Columbia that I came across Douglas Todd's book *Cascadia* which helped me understand how secularism was embedded in the culture. In the Pacific Northwest and British Columbia, Todd claimed that most people were not "spiritual but not religious." Rather they were "secular but spiritual." In other words, organized religion was not even an option. How, I wondered, do you communicate with people who know little about the Christian story, or may not know it accurately, or who are indifferent or even hostile to Christianity? Clearly, the kind of preaching that might work in the American South would not work in Vancouver Island or even London, Ontario.

Back in 2001, I was invited to give the keynote address to the Synod of the Diocese of Niagara, Canada. I began by sharing a story of a young man who came to the church office in Poway, California delivering a pizza. Which one of us had placed the order, he wanted to know. We looked at each other bewildered – none of the staff knew anything about a pizza. "But someone must have ordered a pizza!" the young man insisted. "After all, this is a church, isn't it? I am supposed to deliver this pizza to a church." We asked to look at the order form and it said, "Rancho Bernardo Presbyterian Church." The young man had the wrong church. "Well," he said, "all churches are the same, aren't they? I mean, a church is a church, what's the difference anyway? How was I supposed to know?"

This young man is not unusual, I went on to say. It is now common for people in much of North America to think and live without ever being substantially influenced by Christianity. We are living at a time in history when an increasing number of people have no Christian memory, no Christian background, no Christian vocabulary – where people possess no frame of reference for what Christians are talking about and what Christians believe – where people literally do not know the difference between one church and another, because they rarely, if ever, attend any church.

How are these people different from those of us who are Christians? They have their dreams, hopes, aspirations and visions of tomorrow. They value family, relationships and education. Many are not enamored by materialism. They express a personal commitment to the ideals of justice, democracy, equality and the environment. And yet, they largely reject organized religion. Instead, they prefer to construct their own definitions of spiritual meaning and pursue their own ideals of faith.

This is the challenge for the church today, and especially for every preacher. It is what keeps me up at night. It has been the central focus of my ministry since I was ordained. How does the church reach the different generations – the Baby Boomers, Gen Xers, Millennials, and Generation Z? With each passing generation, a lower percentage are members of any church. The downward trajectory seems irreversible.

The only way to address what is happening is to face it head on: to be willing to be led by the winds of the Spirit into unknown territory, and to step out in faith beyond our comfort zone, driven by an abiding commitment that the good news of God's love in Jesus is worth sharing.

I have been preaching for forty years, from my first year in divinity school until now. Over that time, I have become convinced that every human being yearns for wholeness, inner peace and an abiding satisfaction that comes when we focus on that which is beyond us but also within us. "Our hearts are restless until they rest in God," said St. Augustine. "The heart has reasons which are unknown to reason," wrote Pascal. Deep down in every human being is a yearning to receive divine blessing, to feel a holy touch, to experience peace beyond the ups and downs of life. At the core of our being we desire to experience total, unconditional love as precious children of God always and forever.

THE CHARGE: PREACHING IN A
SECULAR, POSTMODERN WORLD

The secular, postmodern world poses formidable challenges for any preacher. The Christian message may not be known or understood, not only by those outside the church, but even by our own members. Moreover, preaching in a culture that accepts relativism as normative makes it extremely challenging to proclaim Jesus as Lord and Savior without appearing to be a bigot. People think for themselves and evaluate truth claims on the basis of their experience more than reason. They tend to "feel" something as right rather than to go through a logical process that leads to an inevitable conclusion. And, as already indicated, people are increasingly skeptical of any authority figure telling them what to believe or how to act. As a Roman Catholic friend said to me, "Today, we are all Popes."

Given the challenges of preaching in this rapidly changing world where questions and doubts abound, church loyalty cannot be presumed. People now evaluate truth claims based on their own experiences. How then, do preachers communicate God's word when a growing number of people may dismiss what is being said as mere opinion? Here are my sixteen key points on effectively communicating the good news of Jesus. Taken together, these points consist of my method of preaching over the years, and I offer them to anyone rethinking how to preach today.

Basic Christianity. A competent preacher is someone who affirms what John Stott termed "basic Christianity" – the incarnation, redemption and resurrection of Jesus, the Holy Spirit in the life of the church, the reality of miracles, the power of the supernatural, the authority of the Bible, and God as Trinity: Father, Son and Holy Spirit. This is the Christianity that has been professed by most Christian Churches throughout the centuries.

Here is where mainline Protestant clergy need to take a hard look at themselves. Too often, preaching falls flat because there is little substance in the message. Perhaps preachers do not want to offend their congregants, or they do not want to be too bold lest they appear to be overly enthusiastic or emotional. Many Episcopal and Anglican clergy, for example, value reserve, understatement, open-endedness and restraint in making judgments or coming to conclusions. While this approach may maintain church unity, it also leaves people feeling spiritually empty.

I value biblical criticism and think it necessary for effective preaching. However, there is a kind of biblical criticism that is destructive rather than constructive. I remember a New Testament professor in divinity school comparing the study of the four Gospels to an onion. You peel the onion layer by layer, and you end up with what? When he was asked that question, he just remained silent.

That may well be the problem with mainline preachers today. Due to their seminary training, they may be preaching scripture which they do not believe to be true, at least literally true. Then in what sense is it true? Metaphorically, spiritually, inspirationally, much like a good fiction novel – is that what they believe? I think it was Ralph Waldo Emerson who said that he did not believe scripture was inspiring because it was inspired. Rather scripture was inspired because it was inspiring. In other words, scripture as great literature is what inspires us – and nothing more. I wonder if that isn't the problem with some preachers today. The content of what is being preached is not an inspired word of God but an inspiring word for human beings. Is that enough? I don't think so.

Preachers need to be convinced that what they preach is true, and not only true but vitally important to the lives of their listeners. Otherwise, they cannot expound it with conviction. A belief in basic Christianity is foundational to effective preaching.

An Open Spirit. Every preacher needs to combine a belief in basic Christianity with an open spirit. For some preachers, this may seem like a conflict, but actually the two complement one another. By an open spirit, I mean cultivating a mindset that affirms religious truth as an open process rather than a closed system. From birth to death, life is a journey in the awareness of God. That means living with mystery, ambiguity, and even the anxiety of asking hard questions rather than being satisfied with simplistic answers. Posing questions, stretching minds, having people reimagine their faith in ways that connect more meaningfully with the world is part of the preacher's task. We don't want to leave our people complacent, static and fixed in their faith that they are unprepared for the challenges of living in a rapidly changing world where human knowledge doubles every eighteen months.

It was the Canadian Jesuit Bernard Lonergan who opened his seminal work *Insight* by observing that when a dog has nothing to do, it goes to sleep; when a human being has nothing to do, he or she may ask a question.

Asking questions is part of being human. Rather than fear

questions, preachers should welcome them because through questions God may be giving us some new insight into his word or world. Admittedly, asking questions can increase our anxiety, disturb our complacency, and challenge our certainties. And yet, questions properly posed, are designed not to weaken the faith of church members but to strengthen it.

In Margaret Craven's *I Heard the Owl Call My Name*, a young priest is assigned to a remote First Nations village in northern British Columbia. One incident has the priest encounter a rather disgruntled and cynical teacher who is quite dissatisfied with the primitive living conditions in the village. As the teacher meets the priest for the first time and duly complains about conditions, he tells the priest that he is an atheist who considers Christianity a calamity and anyone who professed it to be terribly naïve. The story continues: "The young vicar grinned and agreed. There were two kinds of naivete, he said, quoting Schweitzer. One not even aware of the problems, and another which has knocked on all the doors of knowledge and knows that man can explain little and is still willing to follow his convictions into the unknown. 'This takes courage,' he said, and he thanked the teacher and returned to the vicarage."[1]

Preachers need to help their people be rooted in Christian faith but soaring into new horizons. One without the other will prove inadequate for Christians to live in this emerging world. We need Christians to have both roots and wings.

An Experience of God. Most people – especially Gen Xers, Millennials and Gen Z – are not so much interested in knowing about God as knowing God. They are not as interested in understanding as they are in experiencing. Think of car commercials, for example. Rarely does any commercial focus on the details of the car. Instead, it focuses on the experience of driving. Experience the drive and you sell the car.

Preachers should focus their sermons on the experience of God in the here and now. There are those sacred moments when it all becomes real to you, those moments that change you, challenge you, and lift you up from where you are to where God is. Call it an encounter with the Holy if you will.

The preacher needs to give people an experience of God, but focus on Jesus. It has often been observed that people like Jesus even if they do not like the church. People will read and talk about Jesus. They will listen to sermons about Jesus. Preachers are missing the boat if they do not focus on Jesus in their sermons – who he is, what he means to us, how he makes a difference in our lives, why we follow him, and his life, teachings, death and resurrection. Jesus is the main way the church connects with both Christians and non-Christians. And who better than to speak about Jesus than the preacher? Quite simply, we preachers have nothing to offer the world except Jesus, but in Jesus we have everything to offer.

A Work of Art. Preachers should think of themselves as artists and the sermon as a work of art. Painters, photographers, sculptors, graphic designers and music composers all create works of art. The sermon, too, is a work of art. Like any artist, you need to have the skills and creativity to fashion your creation. Language skills are crucial, acting skills help, a knowledge of the Bible is indispensable, and passion is imperative. You have to "feel" the sermon and not just think it through. It must become part of you, not as a subject to be taught but as a truth to be shared. What Bishop Lesslie Newbigin said of evangelism is equally true of preaching: "one beggar telling another beggar where to find bread."

The nineteenth century Episcopal Bishop of Massachusetts

Phillips Brooks gave a masterful description of preaching as "truth through personality." The preacher embodies the message of God's truth to the congregation. That is why you must feel what you preach. You have to believe that when you get into the pulpit, what you are about to say is a matter of life and death to your audience. The Baptist preacher Herschel Hobbs once wrote a book titled, *Thirty Minutes to Wake the Dead.* I am not sure that a preacher needs to speak for thirty minutes, but I agree with Hobbs: every sermon is an opportunity to transform lives in Jesus.

At Trinity Church, Boston, carved in the pulpit are these words from John 12:21: "Sir, we would see Jesus" (KJV) – a reminder of the preacher's purpose to give the congregation Jesus. Preachers should remind themselves that when they are in the pulpit, they are not there to give their political or social opinions, to share their personal tastes about this thing or that, or to recount their experiences during the week. They are in the pulpit to communicate the mystery and majesty of God, the redemptive love of Jesus for every human being, and the guidance and strength of the Holy Spirit in living faithful and fruitful lives. This is a high calling and we preachers have a solemn responsibility to be God's messengers.

Know Your Audience. Preachers cannot communicate effectively without knowing the people they want to reach. Knowing your audience is as important as knowing the Bible and church teaching. Know how they live, where they work, what they like and dislike, what music they listen to, what films they see, what is important to them, their beliefs, values, hopes and aspirations, their dreams for themselves and their families. Then we need to take Christ to these people, not on our terms but on theirs. The message needs to be tailored to the people we are seeking to reach. Preachers need to be flexible, adaptable, and willing to shape a message that resonates with their audience.

What works in one church may not work in another. Context is everything.

The effective preacher will be a priest and pastor, knowing church members with all their pains and struggles, their hopes and dreams, their joys and sorrows. The first priority of any new priest to a church is to get to know parishioners, and that means spending the first year attending house meetings, going to breakfasts, lunches and dinners, becoming familiar with the different ministries and ministers, and having ample one-on-one conversations with official and unofficial leaders, including longstanding members who know the history and dynamics of the parish. Developing a bond between priest and people is the beginning of good leadership – and good preaching.

Cardinal Newman took as his motto, *"Cor ad Cor loquitor"* – heart speaks to heart. That is a good definition of effective preaching. This presupposes that the preacher knows his or her people personally, visits them in their homes, cares for them in times of sickness, comforts them upon the death of a loved one, counsels them in times of crisis, prays for them and commends them to God.

Of course, no preacher can do everything, and many rectors and senior pastors will have a staff to assist in ministry. Still, every preacher must keep in mind the words of Jesus, "I am the good shepherd. I know my own and my own know me" (Jn. 10:14, NRSV). The sermons that best resonate with people are when they are delivered by a preacher who knows the members and the members know the preacher. John Maxwell gave wise advice at a clergy seminar when he said, "I don't care how much you know until I know how much you care." Caring for your members is a prerequisite to effective preaching.

Outward Focused. In Anglicanism, a parish is not simply a congregation of members but a geography. Every parish has geographical boundaries. This is the structure of the Church of England – an established church. The parish priest is responsible for everyone – not just active church members but all the people who live within the geographical boundaries of the parish. A parish priest, for example, might have four hundred church members but ten thousand members in the parish – the parish being the geography and the church being the congregation.

The United States and Canada do not have this structure, since neither country has an established church, though the Anglican Church of Canada does maintain parish boundaries. Still, the idea of thinking of the church as having parish boundaries is something preachers need to keep in mind in preparing their sermons. In some sense, they are preaching not just to committed Christians but to the people beyond their membership. To do this effectively, the preacher must know people outside the church. The problem is: many clergy know few, if any, non-Christians.

I remember a friend from divinity school getting ordained, doing a few years of parish ministry in British Columbia, and then deciding to get a doctorate in education at OISE – the Ontario Institute for Secondary Education in Toronto, Ontario. My friend said that his whole life had been spent within the church. He had grown up in the church, all of his friends were in the church, and then he became a priest and ministered to members of the church. He really didn't have any non-Christian friends. He wasn't part of any non-Christian world. That wasn't deliberate on his part, but that was the way it was for him, especially as a priest. He was surrounded by Christians living in a Christian world.

So, it was a shock when he went to OISE and discovered a world that he had never known before. Most of the people at the Institute were not Christians, or at least not practicing Christians. Religion was not on their radar screen. Church wasn't an option for them. For the first time in my friend's life, he was immersed in a secular world where God, religion and the church were on the margins. He said that it was one of the great wake-up calls in his life. It literally changed the focus of his ministry.

How many preachers are like that? We live, think, act and breathe in the world of the church, but there is a whole other world out there. Beyond the church is the mission field. In North American culture today, every preacher is, in some sense, a missionary. If we are to reach the people beyond our membership – speak their language, address their concerns, meet them at their point of need and understanding, then we need to know them. Knowing secular people is part of the preacher's work. The most effective preachers connect with two worlds, the sacred and the secular.

Passion. Archbishop William Temple observed that Christianity is the most materialist of the world's religions. By materialist Temple meant 'down to earth' – a religion of flesh and blood that deals with the details of life, that immerses itself in all the joys and pains of being human. Christianity is a religion where God enters into human experience, becomes one with us, knows what it is like to feel pain, to suffer, to experience loneliness and heartbreak but also to love, to sacrifice, and to show compassion and understanding to others.

Here is what that means for the preacher. The sermon should never be an esoteric exercise. The preacher is not in the pulpit to philosophize or lecture or give a theoretical talk disconnected from human experience. The sermon needs to address the human condition, to be concrete, experiential, and image laden. The effective preacher uses stories, illustrations, and anecdotes to bring the text to life in a way that connects with the lives of listeners. The audience should want to listen to the sermon because they sense that what is being said is what they need to hear.

Leaders in the secular business world understand this need to illustrate, perhaps better than we in the church. Think of Steve Jobs and his ability to market Apple. He did not simply speak about the product, whether it was a Mac, or iPad or iPhone. Instead he spoke of the difference the product made in people's lives and how it would change the world. It is no accident that patrons of Apple were as zealous for the company's products as most Christians are for their churches.

Perhaps the best illustration for a product was given by Roberto Goizueta, who at the time was the Chairman and CEO of Coca-Cola. Under his leadership Coca Cola was enormously successful, in part because of his articulate and passionate commitment to the product. In a speech delivered to the Executive Club of Chicago on November 20, 1996, Roberto Goizueta said: "A billion hours ago, human life appeared on Earth. A billion minutes ago, Christianity emerged. A billion seconds ago, the Beatles performed on The Ed Sullivan Show. A billion Coca-Colas ago was yesterday morning. And the question we are asking ourselves now is: What must we do to make a billion Coca-Colas ago be this morning?"

As his words indicate, Robert Goizueta was passionate about Coca-Cola. But what is Coca-Cola? It is soda water – flavoring, sugar or some other sweetener and carbonation. Imagine having that kind of passion for sugar water! Give him credit: Roberto Goizueta had that kind of passion for his product.

My question is: Do we preachers have that same passion for Jesus that Roberto Goizueta had for Coca-Cola? If not, why not?

The former President of Pittsburgh Theological Seminary, Carnegie Samuel Callian, would always ask: "Where is the passion in the church today?" I suggest the passion begins with the preacher in the pulpit. Preachers are called to speak about God in ways that educate, inspire and motivate listeners to be faithful followers of Jesus. Through their passion, their people become passionate in knowing, loving and serving God. Passion, bringing the Gospel home to people, making it down-to-earth, applying it to the lives of real flesh and blood people who know the joys and pains of being human, is the task of the preacher. At a minimum, preachers should be as passionate about God and Christ as any secular leader in business or politics. After all, preachers have a great God to proclaim – so let's get on with it.

Current and Contemporary. Preachers need to become cultural anthropologists. By that I mean that preachers need to know and study culture with as much diligence as they study the Bible and church tradition. Karl Barth famously observed that the preacher should have a Bible in one hand and a newspaper in the other. The preacher is there to connect the world of the Bible with the twenty-first century world of the audience. The task of the preacher is to be a bridge builder – connecting two worlds – the biblical world set in the distant past with a contemporary world that is largely secular and skeptical of any dogmatic claims.

Both the Bible and much of church teaching are premodern and pre-scientific, written in a world that presumed the miraculous and the existence of an interventionist God. The preacher needs to interpret that world to a postmodern culture that is far from accepting what the Bible or the church say. Preachers cannot presume that their audience understands or even agrees with what the Bible says or the church teaches. At the very least, many in the pews will have doubts or be highly skeptical of at least some portions of the Bible and church teaching. That makes the preacher's task doubly difficult: to proclaim the Gospel message effectively but also to persuade with the logic of faith. Robert Webber, a scholar on liturgical evangelism, suggested that what the church needs today is an "ancient-future faith" which is grounded in scripture and tradition, fresh and relevant to the present moment, and points forward to a hopeful future.

The preacher not only has to connect the biblical world with the present one, but also address current events, especially tragedies and crises, from a biblical and faith perspective. Every preacher, I presume, would have changed the planned sermon for the Sunday after 9/11. It would have been religious malpractice for any preacher to ignore that horrendous event.

Similarly, there are times when natural disasters so shake our lives, or human tragedies such as school shootings so shake our confidence, that the preacher must address these events both as pastor and spiritual guide. This does not mean that a preacher is bound to preach on every news story that grabs public attention. There are times, however, when certain significant issues should be addressed from the pulpit, and even on a more regular basis to use current news stories that illustrate a point in the sermon.

The bottom line is that preachers need to be well-read and know what is happening in the world, their country and community. Current events flow naturally into a sermon when the preacher stays informed of the news and subscribes to the many daily (and free) news and magazine services now available online. A well-informed preacher will be much more likely to write and deliver fresh, relevant sermons that will resonate with listeners.

Personality Types. The Myers Briggs Personality Type is a useful tool for the preacher. Myers Briggs has categorized personality according to introvert and extrovert, sensor and thinker, feeler and intuitive, judger and perceiver. Every person in the congregation has four letters that categorize their personality, with a total of thirty-two personality types. The preacher needs to be aware that most every type is likely present at a worship service.

That means some people appreciate concrete, story-oriented

sermons that come to a definite conclusion while others are quite content with mystery, ambiguity and open-ended sermons that explore questions more than give answers. The challenge for the preacher is to deliver sermons that reach both the head and the heart. The preacher needs to have a sermon of intellectual substance but deliver it with passion and believability, and always prodding listeners to think through the meaning of their faith. It is not a matter of just saying the right things but delivering the message in the right way – truth through personality, as Bishop Brooks put it.

An Economy of Words. As important as the sermon is in any worship service, it need not be long – and, in fact, it should not be long. A typical sermon should be between fifteen and twenty minutes. Depending on the topic, the sermon might be a bit longer or shorter, but normally any good preacher should be able to make the point in fifteen minutes – especially if the sermon is written out and the preacher knows the topic well. The French mathematician Blaise Pascal once apologized to a friend by saying, "If I had more time, I would have written you a shorter letter." Short, concise sermons take effort, time and discipline, but the finished product is almost always worth it. One thing the preacher does not want to do is ramble or constantly repeat oneself. That wastes time and shows ineptitude.

Finding Your Voice. Finding your voice is essential for any preacher. The way one person delivers a sermon will be different from another. No two people are alike, and no two sermon styles need be identical.

One of the great Canadian preachers was Dr. Leonard Griffith, who taught preaching at Wycliffe College, Toronto. He also was the principal preacher at St. Paul's, Bloor Street, the largest Anglican church in Canada. Many divinity students would attend St. Paul's on a Sunday morning just to hear Dr. Griffith preach. He usually gave a memorized twenty or twenty-five-minute sermon that held his listeners spellbound. When the service was ended, ushers distributed a transcript of his sermon at the doorways. Remarkably, the paper copy was exactly as he had preached it. Students marveled at Dr. Griffith's ability to memorize his sermon but despaired of ever doing the same thing. Not to worry, Dr. Griffith said. Find your own style of preaching – what works best for you. Do not copy me. Find your own voice.

Every preacher needs to find their own voice and style. Peter Drucker, the management scholar, said that each person learns best either by the written word or oral communication. Some learn best by reading, others by listening. Some communicate best by writing, others by speaking. Whatever your way of learning and communicating, you can preach to your strength. For some people, writing out the sermon is a prerequisite to effectively preaching it. For others, a written outline of the sermon is all that is required. Still others may have the sermon in their minds, and they may ruminate about it during the week, but hardly write anything down on paper. It all becomes a matter of finding your voice – your particular style of preaching.

From my experience, the best sermons are written out, even if the preacher does not take the manuscript into the pulpit. Writing out the sermon allows the preacher to have definition, structure and a focused theme that avoids rambling or wandering off topic. A wise priest once said to me that the best sermons were delivered from a manuscript, the second-best sermons had no manuscript, and the worst sermons were from notes. I cannot verify that as correct, but I offer it for consideration.

Today, many preachers speak without notes, often imitating the late-night talk show hosts who give an opening monologue.

What we forget is that these late-night hosts have teleprompters. They appear to be speaking extemporaneously but thanks to the teleprompter they have the script before them. Their talk appears natural, casual, and off-the-cuff, but it is structured and rigorously composed by a group of writers behind the scenes.

In any case, preachers are not late-night talk show hosts. They are communicators of the Gospel, messengers of God, or teaching elders as the Presbyterian tradition refers to them. They are not in the pulpit to entertain, though they do need to hold the attention of their audience. The Roman Catholic tradition has three questions for every preacher: What does the text mean? What does it mean to us today? What will we do about it? Good advice – to understand the text, to apply the text to our daily lives, and to discern a call to action of what the text would have us do.

Original Intent. Does every sermon need to be Christ-centered? Many preachers believe so, and they insist on interpreting every passage of the Old Testament in light of the New Testament. This is a standard way of preaching that goes back to the New Testament church and the Church Fathers of the first five or six centuries.

However, I am a proponent of interpreting scripture as the writer intended it and as the reader understood it at the time of composition. What did the writer mean when he wrote a particular passage or book? How would his readers have understood the message? I think preachers should be as faithful to a biblical text as they possibly can be. They need to maintain the integrity of the original message and not read into it more than the writer would have intended. This does not mean that the New Testament has no role in preaching on an Old Testament passage, only that we should not read more into a text than its original meaning.

If we preach, for example, on an Old Testament text that is

particularly violent – the destruction of the city and people of Jericho (Josh. 6:21), the slaughter of the people of Ai (Josh. 8:20-29), or the last verses of Psalm 137: 7-9, the preacher should not say that such texts justify the killing of infidels or the murder of infants. Obviously, the preacher would explain that the New Testament love ethic supersedes these texts. The preacher would also try to understand the rationale for these texts, the fear that the religion of infidels would infect the Hebrews, or the rage and anger against Israel's enemies. Whatever way the preacher handles the text, one needs to begin with the original meaning as understood by the author and reader.

The same is true in handling prophetic texts that the church now applies to the New Testament, such as "a young woman shall conceive and bear a son" (Isa. 7:14, NRSV) or many other texts that seem to point to Jesus and New Testament events. While the New Testament may interpret these texts in a way that points to Jesus, the preacher will want to be sure to read and understand these texts as the author and readers understood them – focusing on original intent.

Read, Read, Read. The preacher needs to read for two reasons. First, reading fosters ongoing learning and personal development. You have to constantly keep up with the culture or you will become quickly outdated. If you want to reach the culture, you need to know the culture – in the arts, entertainment, science, law, business, medicine, social issues and politics. The only way to reach people is to know how they think and experience reality, how they live and relate in the world, and what matters to them and defines them as human beings. One way to do this is to read books, magazines and journals from a wide variety of sources.

You can tell when a preacher has stopped reading by the type of sermons being delivered. They will be stale, irrelevant, more reflective of a previous era than the present time, with illustrations and stories that date back many years. I will never forget an outstanding Jesuit priest who was also a brilliant lawyer. His passion was law and politics, and in those two areas he excelled. But whenever he was asked to lead a retreat or give a sermon, his knowledge of scripture and church teaching stopped at the time he was ordained – pre-Vatican II thinking. As a lawyer, he was sharp and knowledgeable, but as a priest and preacher he was outdated and unable to bring faith to life.

The second reason the preacher needs to read is to gather articles, stories and illustrations for sermons. Almost any newspaper or magazine will have an article that could be saved for inclusion in a sermon. Some preachers have sermon files that categorize illustrations by topic or text. Others use one box – a shoe box, for example – that holds stories and articles that they review in preparing sermons. Still other preachers carry a small notebook and jot down a story that may come their way in reading or conversations. The smart phone has a notes app that is an excellent substitute for a notebook.

The Internet is now a source of unlimited information where preachers can access articles in a way that would have been unimaginable just thirty years ago. Of course, preachers will want to check the facts to ensure accuracy – not everything on the Internet is true. In addition, the preacher will want to be sure to note any copyrighted sources, and to give credit for whatever materials are used in the sermon.

Sermon Preparation Time. How long should sermon preparation take? For a young preacher out of seminary, the general rule is that a fifteen-minute sermon requires fifteen hours of preparation – an hour for each minute of delivery. As the preacher becomes more experienced, preparation time may shorten from seven to ten hours per week, but rarely should it be less. Effective communication demands adequate preparation time to structure a thought-provoking, inspiring sermon with an attention-getting beginning, a substantive and well-organized middle, and a memorable conclusion that drives the theme of the sermon home. All this takes time to prepare.

The preacher needs to schedule time from the weekly calendar and make sermon preparation a priority. After all, the fifteen minutes in the pulpit is the one time during the week when the preacher has the opportunity to address the entire congregation. It is time not to be wasted but used effectively to build up the church.

As part of my preparation time, praying the scripture lesson before preaching on it is essential. In the Episcopal Church, as in many churches, we have a three-year Sunday lectionary consisting of Old and New Testament lessons, Psalm and Gospel. I read the lessons, pray them, and then begin to formulate a sermon. Lectio Divina – a monastic way of reading and praying scripture – is an excellent method to pray the lessons. I encourage preachers to learn more about this method of reading and praying scripture. Often God will speak to us in unexpected ways and give us a fresh perspective when we ruminate on a text, reading it slowly, carefully and prayerfully several times, and allowing for intervals of silence. Whether a preacher chooses to use this or some other method, praying the lessons before planning the sermon is essential preparation for preaching.

Personal Stories. One of the hot topics when I was in divinity school is whether preachers should tell stories about themselves in the pulpit. I knew several professors of preaching who adamantly opposed any personal story by the preacher, no matter how apropos to the overall sermon. The fear was that by telling personal stories, preachers were drawing attention away from God and placing it on themselves.

These professors had a point. The danger is that in telling personal stories, the sermon will focus on the preacher rather than God. That said, I believe sharing a personal story is appropriate when the story relates to the theme of the sermon, does not replace the focus on God, and is used to illustrate or bring to life a key point of the sermon.

Properly used, a personal story "incarnates" the word being preached. The preacher may speak didactically or abstractly about a subject, but a personal story is a powerful and persuasive way to put flesh on the sermon – to bring it to life in a way that resonates with listeners. Especially when the congregation knows the preacher, a personal story can bring credibility to the sermon – that the preacher knows the topic because she has been there. The preacher is not speaking off the top of his head but from the depths of his heart. Personal stories give credibility and life to a sermon that otherwise might fall flat, and therefore they should be used as appropriate but without taking the focus away from God.

It's All About God. Every sermon should be an encounter with God. The sermon is not self-help advice or a motivational talk. While there is a place for "how to" sermons that offer practical advice in living the Christian life, the primary purpose of the sermon is to transform lives in Jesus. People come to church with a wide variety of needs, but the greatest need of every human being is to know, love and serve God. In God, all our needs find their place. People may not leave church having all their problems solved, but they can and should leave having experienced the mystery and majesty of God. They should feel drawn into communion with this God who sustains them in all their troubles, burdens and confusion, a God who lifts them up and gives them the courage and hope to live another week in an often harsh world.

Theologians may differ on what the worst sin a preacher can commit in the pulpit. Preaching heresy or false doctrine is certainly a serious matter. Attacking church members is never a wise move if the preacher wants to keep her job. However, I think the worst thing a preacher can do in the pulpit is to bore the audience. Making the good news of our salvation in Jesus Christ boring is almost unforgivable. How could preachers take such great good news and make it so boring that listeners keep looking at their watches or smart phones just waiting for the sermon to end? A preacher should begin the sermon with the attitude, "I have some fantastic news to share with you! The Lord has spoken and I am going to share that message and how it affects your life. What I am going to say is of the utmost importance. Listen carefully as if your lives depended on it because they do."

Perhaps you may think what I just said is too dramatic. However, God's love in Jesus Christ is not to be taken lightly. The Gospel is not just another news story that we can dismiss as unimportant. If it is true, then the Gospel is the most important thing in the world – nothing else comes close. Preachers need to prepare and deliver sermons with that kind of conviction – "For God so loved the world that he gave his only Son…" (Jn. 3:16, NRSV).

When I was in the sixth grade in parochial school, a gruff old Jesuit priest by the name of Father Duffy came into our classroom to talk about Jesus. He lifted up a crucifix – a cross with the body of Jesus on it – and said to us, "God loves you this much!" I have never forgotten that moment. God's love continues to amaze me. It fills me with deep humility but also with a passion to share that love with others. Every preacher should have that kind of passion with every sermon delivered. We preachers are on a mission to change the world – one life at a time, transforming lives in Jesus.

PART TWO

KINDLING THE FIRE: EXPLORING FAITH

Robert Runcie, a former Archbishop of Canterbury, coined the phrase "thoughtful holiness" – the enduring marriage of faith and reason. Thoughtful holiness implies that the church should never be afraid to ask the hard questions because part of mature Christian believing is to love God with our whole mind as well our heart and soul. Christians are on a pilgrimage, a lifelong search for God, convinced there is as much joy and integrity in living the questions as in finding the answers. In the supernatural life, God is always being pursued but never fully possessed, because to claim possession of God is idolatry.

How do we make sense of Christian faith with its strange teachings about a God who came to earth, died a criminal's death on a Friday, and by Sunday morning was raised from the dead? And what about heaven – we can only speculate about such a concept. And then, there are all those questions on which some Christians seem to stumble: Is Christianity the only true religion? How could a loving God make a world with so much suffering? And isn't religion the cause of much of the evil in the world? These and other questions are stumbling blocks for sincere seekers who may be open to Christianity but do not want to compromise their intellectual integrity.

The dominant mindset in Western culture is philosophical pluralism, which holds that the only authentic way to live harmoniously in diversity is to accept relativism – to believe that there is no such thing as universal truth. This view obviously is in conflict with Christianity and its claim that Jesus is the Way, the Truth and the Life. The task of the church is to find ways to communicate effectively in a culture where philosophical and religious pluralism are normative. How is it possible for Christians in a pluralistic culture to proclaim Jesus as Lord and Savior without appearing to be bigots? This is our challenge.

The church will need to chart a course beyond Christian triumphalism and cultural relativism in building bridges between the religious and secular worlds. We will need a renewed confidence in Jesus and the power of the good news of the kingdom of God. We also will need to demonstrate there is no conflict between being a thoughtful human being and a committed Christian. The sermons and lectures in this section attempt to make the intellectual case for Christianity, following the spirit of St. Paul who wrote: "Do not be conformed to this world, but be transformed by the renewing of your minds, so that you may discern what is the will of God – what is good and acceptable and perfect" (Rom. 12:2, NRSV).

God, Secularization and the New Atheism is the Smythe Lecture delivered at St. John's Anglican Church in Elora, Ontario. It tackles the twin issues of the rising secularization in the West, including Canada, and the popularity of the New Atheism spearheaded by Richard Dawkins and other scientists and philosophers. I offer my response to both trends and how the church might go about engaging in a dialogue with secular-minded persons who are open to spirituality.

The Most Important Question in the World is an Easter sermon written in light of the 2020 COVID-19 pandemic. What does it mean to live as an Easter people in a virus-infested world? In this sermon I give examples of people who held onto their Easter faith even with the imminent threat of death. They died believing that because Jesus lives, so shall they.

Sight and Insight was first preached at the Cathedral Church of the Nativity in Bethlehem, Pennsylvania back in 1988 on the Second Sunday of Easter – commonly called Low Sunday. I think this is an ideal Sunday to grapple with the resurrection in a way the preacher would not do on Easter Sunday – to deal with the details of the resurrection and how to make sense of it.

Understanding Heaven was preached on All Saints Day 2011 but revised in 2020. Heaven is not an easy concept to understand because we who live in time/space cannot imagine eternity. All we can say for certain is that heaven is where God is, and where God is, there we shall be. That should be enough for any of us.

Into the Dark was an All Souls Day reflection when Christians remember their deceased loved ones. All Souls Day is an appropriate time to preach about the resurrection. In this sermon I cite the German theologian Oscar Cullmann who distinguished immortality (Greek) from resurrection (Hebrew). Immortality is philosophical speculation, but resurrection is grounded on Jesus being raised from the dead.

The God of Messiness, Mud and Dirt could have been a sermon for the Christmas season, but it was preached on the Feast of Christ the King at the end of the liturgical year in late November. The sermon deals with understanding the incarnation – God becoming one with us, experiencing our joys and pains, and in the end sacrificing himself to save us.

Rising above Your Pain deals with responding to suffering and tragedy in our personal lives and in our world. We all have our pains and sorrows. None of us are immune from suffering. We may never know why human beings suffer, but our challenge is to move beyond the "Why?" question – Why is this happening to me or the ones I love? and ask instead "How?" – How can I be an agent of healing in a hurting world?

Salvation in No One Else deals with a thorny issue in our secular, pluralistic culture: How can we say Jesus is Lord without condemning the vast majority of people who have ever lived on the planet to hell or annihilation? St. Peter in the Book of Acts claims that in Jesus salvation is found in no one else. I examine three options on how to respond to this issue.

The Case for Religion was a lecture delivered in response to the accusations brought against religion by the New Atheist movement. Richard Dawkins and others charged that religion was not simply false or untrue but evil, something not even to be tolerated because of its destructive effect to people and the planet. While admitting there is bad religion in the world, the lecture argues that on the whole, the case for religion, and particularly Christianity, is more compelling than the case against it.

GOD, SECULARIZATION AND THE NEW ATHEISM

THE SMYTHE LECTURE

Christendom is at an end, and secularism and postmodernism are now the dominant forces in society. The church is being pushed to the margins, and belief in God is more a matter of private opinion than public discourse. Even holidays, such as Christmas and Easter, are now secularized, and there is a growing number of people who do not know the Christian story or do not know it accurately. How do we speak about God in this kind of world, where people are more likely to be "secular but spiritual" rather than "spiritual but not religious"? This lecture is my attempt to bring together secular, spiritual and religious elements in a common quest to embrace the meaning and mystery of life.

THE RISING TIDE OF SECULARIZATION

In my third year of divinity school, I accepted a position as Incumbent of five small churches on the Gaspe Coast in the Diocese of Quebec. I had never been to Quebec, so this was an act of faith on my part. My fiancé, now my wife, had been to

Montreal several times, but beyond that she knew little about the province.

As we drove to my new parish from Hamilton, Ontario, we stopped in Montreal to visit relatives. While in the city I got to see many of the tourist sites, including several beautiful churches. In fact, what impressed me about Montreal was the grandeur of the churches, convents and religious academies that seemed to be everywhere.

After leaving Montreal to continue our journey to the Gaspe, we noticed that every village had an imposing church at its center. Crosses and shrines dotted the landscape. This was a culture saturated in Christendom. The symbols of faith were everywhere.

When we got to Quebec City, there were many historic churches in the old town, but we noticed that several of them were no longer churches. They were museums, tourist centers, theaters and office complexes. There were vacated church buildings for sale or rent. Christendom, we realized, was only a façade, much like a movie set of a medieval town. As I would learn in my time in Quebec, beneath the surface of Quebec Christendom was a passionate secularism. With the advent of the Quiet Revolution in the early 1960s, Quebec almost overnight transformed from one of the most religious regions in North America to one of the most secular.

Today only a small percentage of the population in Quebec attend church, and those who do attend are mainly the elderly. Church buildings now serve as theaters, antique shops, social service, community or senior centers, with worship provided on Sunday if a priest is available.

It was the nineteenth century German philosopher Friedrich Nietzsche who first proclaimed that "God is dead" because "belief in the Christian god [had] become unbelievable." We might want to take issue with Nietzsche, but there is little doubt that in

Quebec and other parts of North America secularism has replaced Christianity as the dominant influence in the culture.

According to a July 7, 2008 report in *MacLean's* magazine, only 2 percent of Canadians say religion is very important to them.[1] Secularization has taken hold of Canada, expanding its influence and tightening its squeeze on the population.

By secularization I mean the growing tendency of humankind to do without religion, or to try to do without religion, as church historian Owen Chadwick put it. In the world of secularization, there is loss of a religious frame of reference, a loss of religious relevance to the issues of the day, and a loss of transcendence beyond the here and now. Secularization happens when one grand narrative – say, the Christian story – no longer holds society together. Pluralized beliefs make inevitable privatized faith, marginalized religion and relativized values. Today we live in a secular vacuum, what Richard John Neuhaus has termed "the naked public square."

All this makes evangelization increasingly difficult. The Canada before Quebec's Quiet Revolution was solidly Christian, not just in Quebec but in much of the country. The nation had a higher churchgoing rate than the United States. If you lived in Quebec, for example, your whole life was centered on Christianity and the church. You went to Mass regularly, made your confession to a priest, and prayed with the Cardinal of Montreal as he led the rosary on the radio. You could not conceive of yourself as anything but a Christian.

After the Quiet Revolution, however, things radically changed in Quebec – and to a slower extent – in all Canada. Church attendance began to drop dramatically. People felt no need for the church which seemed increasingly irrelevant to their lives. Most people in Canada now function perfectly well without religion.

Since the Quiet Revolution, a new world has emerged in

Canada – a world that has gone from the great medieval synthesis of faith and reason to a modern world that has squeezed faith out of everyday life. In this emerging world, a growing number of people have no Christian memory, no Christian background, and no Christian vocabulary. They are familiar with neither the rituals nor the etiquette of the church. Quite simply, "the God question" is not a question many people are asking or even feel a need to ask.

Remember the Marquis de Laplace in his famous reply to Napoleon regarding what role God had in his conception of the universe. Laplace remarked, "I have no need of that hypothesis." Today, many people seem to have no need for God. They work out in the gym, meditate, practice yoga, focus on their careers, eat organic foods, play golf, watch hockey, go to pubs, shop and enjoy themselves, and perhaps even marry and raise a family, but God does not figure in their lives.

THE ASSAULT ON RELIGIOUS FAITH

How did we get to this state of affairs? We could go back to the period after the Thirty Years War (1618 – 1648) when European leaders determined that faith could no longer unite the continent. In its place they substituted reason. People of differing faiths could come together, unite in common purpose and work for common goals in a rational and harmonious way apart from their personal faith convictions. Think of John Locke, David Hume, Jean Jacques Rosseau, Voltaire and Immanuel Kant, and you begin to see a new vision for the modern state take hold in Europe. In this new world order, faith was tolerated only so long as it remained private opinion.

The French rationalist philosopher Rene Descartes echoed the sentiments of many in Europe when he wrote: "That nothing ought to be admitted as True, but that which has been proved by good and solid reasons."[2]

The Dutch philosopher Baruch Spinoza went further and postulated a universe ruled by the cause and effect of natural laws, without purpose and without design. For Spinoza, a pantheist, God was Nature and Nature was God.

The Scottish philosopher David Hume made a persuasive case that anything that could not be empirically verified should be relegated to the flames as the worst kind of sophistry. He put the existence of God and the immortality of the soul in doubt.

The German philosopher Immanuel Kant attempted to defend the existence of God and the immortality of the soul, but even he wrote a book titled *Religion within the Limits of Reason Alone* which argued that faith must be subordinate to reason to avoid superstition and fanaticism. Kant reversed St. Anselm's maxim that faith seeks understanding by insisting that understanding must shape faith. Take, for example, God's command to Abraham that he kill his son Isaac. Kant responded to such a command this way: "Abraham would have to answer this supposedly divine voice: 'That I ought not to kill my good son, that is, wholly certain; but that you, who appear to me, are God, of that I am not certain and never can become certain even if it should resound from the (visible) heavens.'"[3]

Kant wrote his work in the last decade of the eighteenth century. In his own mind he was attempting to save religion from its critics. However, by the end of the nineteenth century, organized religion had suffered severe blows from Karl Marx, Charles Darwin and Sigmund Freud. Darwin's theory of evolution was an enormous challenge for believers not because Christians believed in a literal six-day account of creation or that God could not create the world through some process taking billions of years. No, Darwin's picture of evolution, involving natural selection, cast doubt on the goodness and beneficence of God creating a process that seemed cruel, heartless and relentless – what Herbert Spencer would term "survival of the fittest."

It was G.K. Chesterton who said that Christianity is Europe and Europe Christianity. He meant that the intellectual foundation of much of the Christian faith originated in Europe. Whatever the truth of that assertion, by the end of the nineteenth century it was obvious that Christianity was waning over much of the continent. The English poet Matthew Arnold, the son of the famous Anglican clergyman Thomas Arnold of Rugby, wrote the poem *Dover Beach* that compared the waning of Christianity in Europe to the tide withdrawing from Dover Beach.

> *The sea of faith*
> *Was once, too, at the full and round earth's shore*
> *Lay like the folds of a bright girdle furl'd;*
> *But now I only hear*
> *Its melancholy, long, withdrawing roar,*
> *Retreating to the breath*
> *Of the night-wind down to the vast edges drear*
> *And naked shingles of the world.*[4]

Let me offer a case study of how traumatic nineteenth century British Victorian society was for Christian believers. The poet Christina Rossetti wrote that lovely Christmas carol *In the Bleak Midwinter*. Singing that carol, you would not know that it really is a cry of faith in a God who was increasingly marginalized by the secular, scientific world of Victorian England. Although we may not realize it, "the nineteenth century was easily the best-documented moment of widespread doubt in human history," as historian Jennifer Michael Hecht put it.[5]

Christina Rossetti wrote her poem at a time when Darwin's theory of evolution had become popular, and philosophers and scientists were increasingly rejecting the idea of revealed religion, and especially the truth claims of Christianity. The romance of faith was giving way to the bleak, barren landscape of a world without God, where there was nothing but blind chance. And so, she writes:

> *In the bleak midwinter, frosty wind made moan,*
> *earth stood hard as iron, water like a stone;*
> *snow had fallen, snow on snow, snow on snow,*
> *in the bleak midwinter, long ago.*

Can you sense the quiet desperation of those words? "Snow upon snow, snow upon snow" falls to the ground, transforming the landscape of Europe into cold, barren tundra, relentlessly extinguishing the flame of faith. It is a difficult time to believe in God when the best and the brightest have relegated religious belief to the margins of intellectual discourse. There is the novelist Thomas Hardy throwing down the gauntlet in his poem, "God's Funeral." There is Jeremy Bentham, John Stuart Mill, Thomas Carlyle, Thomas Huxley, Herbert Spencer and George Eliot, all with a word that no longer believes in the "Word made flesh."

Can you sense the heaviness of soul in Christina Rossetti's words? She is writing about Christmas in a world that does not believe in Christmas. She doesn't know how to respond to this unbelief, much less feel adequate to give a response. All she can do is fall back on faith – the simple, heartfelt faith in Jesus. And so, she concludes:

> *What can I give him, poor as I am?*
> *If I were a shepherd, I would bring a lamb;*
> *If I were a wise man, I would do my part;*
> *Yet, what I can I give him – give my heart.*[6]

You give your heart when you can no longer give your mind. Faith, for Christina Rossetti, is to believe in the mystery of God even when rational explanations fail us.

And yet, since the time of the Enlightenment, the arguments against God's existence have been relentless, with perhaps none more poignant than the one made by the eighteenth-century French philosopher Voltaire. On November 1, 1755, the Lisbon earthquake struck without warning, destroying much of the city and killing countless thousands, many of whom died while attending Mass on All Saints Day. Voltaire asked: How could a gracious God allow such an awful tragedy to happen to the people who believed in him? Is God really in control of things? If God is in control, then what kind of God would allow such tragic suffering to happen?

Voltaire was echoing the question raised by the fifth century philosopher Boethius: If God is righteous, why evil? Boethius answered: Either God wishes to prevent evil but cannot, in which case God is just but not omnipotent. Or God can prevent evil but does not want to, in which case God is omnipotent but not just.

We all have seen people suffer terribly, and not just adults but children and infants, and we wonder how could a loving God allow such things to happen. We have seen natural disasters devastate communities, and we ask, "Why did not God make a better job of creating the world?" It rather looks, as David Hume once mockingly suggested, as if it had been badly bungled, or were the work of a committee.

Life raises all the questions we can handle regarding God's existence. There are doubts enough a plenty. If we are honest, we have to admit there is always an area of darkness in life hinting that God may not exist.

The twentieth century saw a forceful challenge to Christian faith from philosophers of the British school of logical positivism.

A.J. Ayer dismissed all religious faith as absurd. For Ayer and his fellow logical positivists, truth is to be found only by the scientific method that formulates hypotheses about phenomena on the basis of physical observations that can be tested over and over. Since religious claims are not subject to empirical verification (or falsification), rational inquiry requires that they disown them. Ayer showed his contempt for Christianity when he wrote that, "one reason for not believing in Christianity is that there is not the slightest evidence in its favor."[7]

By the end of the twentieth century, the relentless assault on religious belief had pushed Christian faith to the margins of intellectual respectability among the major universities of Europe and North America. Universities that were founded as religious institutions now replaced their theology departments with religious studies departments – for while the scientific study of religion was permissible, the study of theology was not. Gradually but persistently Christianity among academics moved from the mainline to the sideline of scholarly legitimacy, fading gently into the night.

THE NEW ATHEISM

As the twenty-first century began, religious belief in Europe and Canada seemed harmless enough. It existed on the intellectual margins of society, not very prominent and not at all important. That changed with the events of 9/11. The world saw the horror of Islamic terrorists shouting, "God is Great!" as they crashed their hijacked planes into the twin towers of the World Trade Center and Pentagon. Religious belief, so it now seemed, was neither safe nor harmless but deadly. From the ashes of 9/11 came to prominence what been termed the New Atheists: Richard Dawkins, Sam Harris, Christopher Hitchens, and others.[8]

In his book *God is Not Great*, Hitchens argued that religion is fundamentally toxic to human society and must be directly challenged and eradicated where possible. Religion "poisons everything," he wrote, and religious morality amounts to psychological abuse. Needless to say, Hitchens found nothing worthwhile in Christianity, and even Mother Teresa was lambasted.

Sam Harris, author of *The End of Faith* wrote that there would come a time when we will acknowledge the obvious: theology is now little more than a branch of human ignorance. Indeed, it is "ignorance with wings." It is not surprising then, that Harris yearns for a time when faith will be banished from public life and from our own minds.

The socio-biologist Richard Dawkins described religion as a "virus," and in his book *The God Delusion* proclaimed that monotheism is "the great unmentionable evil at the center of our culture." For Dawkins, faith in God is not just an error in judgment. It is sheer madness. He quotes approvingly Robert Pirsig's book, *Zen and the Art of Motorcycle Maintenance*: "When one person suffers from a delusion, it is called insanity. When many people suffer from a delusion, it is called religion."[9]

The intellectual foundation of this New Atheism is not new. It is a worldview known as "scientific naturalism" – a label first used by Thomas Huxley in the nineteenth century to emphasize the principle that science must never appeal to supernatural explanations. The New Atheists expand this concept and assert that the natural world is literally all that exists. There is no divine creator, no cosmic purpose, no soul, and no possibility of life after death. They believe that lifeless and mindless physical stuff, evolving by impersonal natural processes over billions of years, is the ultimate origin and destiny of everything, including living and thinking beings. This materialist worldview is itself the offspring of "scientism" – the assumption that the modern scientific method is the only way for reasonable, truth-seeking people to gain knowledge of the real world.

Dawkins, Hitchens and Harris are passionate about their cause – zealous as any fundamentalist believers. Their arguments are couched in the rhetorical violence they spurn in others, and their use of ridicule to disparage religious faith shows their contempt. They are reminiscent of a central character in Graham Greene's *The Power and the Glory*. In that novel, a priest on the run from an atheist regime in Mexico is finally captured by government soldiers. The lieutenant responsible for his capture has a conversation with the man he is planning to execute in order to deprive the local population of its last active priest.

"You're a danger," the lieutenant tells him. "That's why we kill you. I have nothing against you, you understand, as a man."

"Of course not," the priest replies. "It's God you're up against."

"No," says the lieutenant, "I do not fight against a fiction."[10]

Well then, who is he fighting against? If God is a fiction, why is he so angry? Dawkins, as I have just cited, comes out fighting, ready to do battle, with a "take no prisoners" mindset. All religious faith is destructive to human existence, and therefore no accommodation is possible. As Harris candidly acknowledged, tolerance should end where religious faith begins. The goal of the New Atheists is nothing less than the eradication of God and religious faith from every facet of human life both public and private.

A RESPONSE TO THE NEW ATHEISM

There are many ways to respond to the New Atheists. One thing is clear: the scientific method can neither prove nor disprove the existence of God. Neither can the theory of evolution adjudicate the matter one way or the other. Science may be able to answer the "How" question – How did the universe come into existence?

However, it cannot answer the "Why" question – Why did the universe come into existence? Or the "What" question – What is the meaning of human existence?

Here is where the church should focus its energies in connecting with a secular, postmodern culture – on four basic questions I learned in a college introductory philosophy course that go to the heart of human existence.

Who am I? The biologist tells me that about 99 percent of the mass of my body is made up of six elements: oxygen, carbon, hydrogen, nitrogen, calcium and phosphorous. Then there are another five elements that make up less than one percent of my body. And that's it. Every human being is a combination of chemicals. But am I more than this? Who am I?

Where am I? The astronomer tells me that the universe spans a diameter of about 150 billion light years from the earth. The sheer scale of the universe is impossible to imagine, and even harder to put an accurate figure on. When I think of the immensity of the universe, I feel small. I feel lonely. I feel insignificant. Where am I?

Why am I? Martin Heidegger's question, "Why is there something rather than nothing?" seems unanswerable. Philosophers dispute why human beings exist at all. They can't agree if there is a purpose to life – a reason for living – or if life is absurd, as the French existentialist Jean Paul Sartre claimed. Why am I?

Who am I? Where am I? Why am I? These are the questions that press themselves upon us with urgency. We cannot answer these questions until we answer a still more basic question: Is there a God? If God does not exist, then there is no ultimate meaning to life and we have no reason for existing. If God does not exist, how can any of us commit ourselves to rational inquiry, or the pursuit of truth, or even reliance on our own intellectual prowess? How can we take seriously conscience, and with it, any instinctive sense of right and wrong? Without conscience, anything goes, and every judgment is arbitrary and subjective.

It is important to understand the logical implications of a world without God. Ultimately, atheism leads to nihilism where there is no objective truth, or justice, or even love, just the will to make my own world and be my own god. After all, how could I be fair or unfair, just or unjust in a godless world? If human beings are simply products of evolutionist materialism, then why be concerned about political or social issues at all? Why engage in the pursuit of truth if "truth" itself is a fiction? If there is no justice, if there are no rights and wrongs, and if there are no safeguards of any kind; then what kind of world are we left with, except one where the strong dominate the weak and self-interest and expedience determine every action?

If Karl Marx's dictum is true that, "the material world to which we belong is the only reality," then all human values – love, justice, loyalty and friendship – are at bottom empty pursuits in a meaningless world. Life has no purpose, no meaning, except what we arbitrarily give it. We are simply accidents on a remote speck of cosmic dust destined eventually to be drawn into the nothingness of a black hole.

We can speculate about the existence of God. We can disagree on whether the world is creation or accident, but both standpoints require faith. It may take faith to believe God created the universe, but perhaps it takes even more to believe that the whole of existence – the intricacy of life, the harmony of nature, the beauty of the world, and the mystery of love – are all meaningless chance.

And yet, the order of our world almost compels us to believe in God. It is hard to believe that everything that exists is by chance. William Paley's teleological argument for the existence of God makes sense, even if some question the logic of it. With a clock the parts do not come together by themselves – someone had to put the pieces together in just the right way and with almost infallible precision for the clock to operate properly. Or, with a book the words do not happen to land in the right order. Someone must put it together to make sense.

So, a clock must have a clockmaker – someone to put the pieces together. Similarly, a book must have an author – someone to write it. A painting must have an artist – someone to paint it. A building must have an architect – someone to plan it. Could we not say the same thing about the world? That it did not happen by chance. Someone had to plan it, put it together, and organize it. This great Planner, Designer, Architect, Creator, we call God.

Today the Big Bang is the accepted scientific theory for the beginning of the universe, but who or what created the Big Bang? How did it "just" happen, or was there a First Mover or First Cause that initiated the creative process from beyond time and space? My college philosophy professor would often say that God does not exist, but God makes existence possible. In other words, a supernatural force beyond time and space is the source of all that exists.

Whether you agree with this logic or not, the universe is put together with ingenuity so astonishing that it seems highly unlikely to be a purposeless accident. While this view does not necessitate a personal God, it does lead us to a certain reverence and awe for the mystery that is the universe. Here, I believe, is where many believers and non-believers can find common ground: in their shared reverence for the grandeur of nature.

Bishop John Coburn, a former Episcopal bishop of the Diocese of Massachusetts, wrote a marvelous little book titled *Grace in All Things*. He tells about being on a battleship in the Pacific Ocean during World War II. Evening was falling after a long and grueling day on patrol. As the sun set over a calm sea, there was this thrilling tropical color that engulfed the ship. It was a moment of indescribable peace. God was around us, Bishop Coburn recalled. No one spoke – for amid war there was the wonder of eternity, written in the gentle waves, the glory of the sky, the peace of that quiet moment.

Here is the religious spirit at its best: reverence, awe and humility about the mystery of life and the grandeur of the universe.

To reiterate: science cannot prove or disprove God's existence; but as the priest-scientist John Polkinghorne noted: "Science creates the feeling that there is more to the world than meets the eye."[11] What this "more" is; is the great spiritual quest of our time. From the New Age to Eastern sages to Christian mystics, from Deepak Chopra to David Suzuki to Eckhart Tolle to the Dalai Lama to Father Thomas Keating to Pope John Paul II, there is a search for more than meets the eye.

A MISSION STRATEGY FOR A SECULARIZED CULTURE

I think this is where the church has enormous opportunity to tap into the spiritual yearnings of people in our secularized culture, whether they are religious or not, believe in God or not. Rationalism can take us only so far, but it cannot help us to appreciate a Mozart symphony or a Bach fugue. To be human, truly human, we need to see reality as awe-inspiring and life-giving and nurturing, beyond all our explanations, to which the appropriate response is praise and thanks.

Several years ago, Harold Mumma published his remarkable book *Albert Camus and the Minister*, which reported on the conversations the French existentialist had with an American Methodist minister. Camus, who by this time had become famous for such novels as *The Plague* and *The Stranger*, admitted to his minister friend that he was searching for something he did not have and could not define.

Whether Camus ever found that something is problematic, but the book suggests that in his last years Camus came close to becoming a Christian He admitted to his minister friend that he was searching for something that the world was not giving him.

We can call that something "mystery." People today are open to mystery, even if they cannot explicitly believe in the existence of God. They are searching for that something more, something they cannot define or describe, but they feel in their hearts. Call it the quest for harmony or wholeness or oneness with the world around us. Deep down at its roots it is a quest for the transcendent source of their being. As St. Augustine put it, "Our hearts are restless until they rest in God."

Do you ever feel that there is more to your life than you can really name? When my daughter was born, and I held Allison for the first time in my arms, the gift of life took on new meaning for me. I had preached on the gift of life several times, but now I held her in my arms. Unimaginable love had touched my heart. I would never view life the same again.

When your baby is born, or you find the strength to carry on after your spouse dies, I believe it is God working in your life, manifesting his presence, sustaining you, and drawing you into his embrace. God, or whatever name you want to call the holy presence in each of us, is with us. I believe God's love is for everyone – and it is already yours – whether you know it or not – whether you believe it or not.

Even the New Atheists have restless hearts. Take Sam Harris, for example. His book *The End of Faith* is an indictment against God and organized religion. And yet, this committed atheist seems to be drawn to the mystical. In an address to the Atheist Alliance International last October, Harris said that he did not like being categorized as an atheist because to him it "seems more or less synonymous with not being interested in what someone like the Buddha or Jesus may have actually experienced… yet these experiences often constitute the most important and transforming moments in a person's life." Harris went on to express his admiration for deep meditation and for the cultivation of silence and solitude. Such a person discovers a "universe of mystery" and a place where "selfhood is relaxed" and "negative social emotions such as hatred, envy and spite" are replaced by emotions "such as love and compassion."[12]

What is Harris looking for, if not a kind of spirituality that may indeed lead to a joyous, compassionate, loving, powerful, boundless, light-filled reality that Christians call God?

Then there is Woody Allen. In January 2008 he was interviewed by *Maclean's* magazine. He was asked about the paradox of making meaningful films but believing in a meaninglessness existence. Here is how he responded: "My own personal conclusion concurs with what seems to be the everyday finding of our physicists, that [the world] was an accident, that it will end, and it was just an odd little phenomenon that has no meaning, that [it] wasn't created by any super-being or with any design, it's just a chance phenomenon and a micro-speck in an overwhelming, violent universe, and it will end… every planet will be gone, and every star will be gone… out of nothing to nothing."[13]

And yet, despite what appears to be his completely nihilistic philosophy, Allen refuses to give up on life. He went on to say, "And yet the trick, to me, seems to be to find, not meaning, but to be able to live with that and enjoy life."

Yes, life is still to be affirmed and valued and cherished. I ask: how can the church speak to Woody Allen and the many like him in Canada who love life – beauty, love, goodness – even as they believe that in the end life will be sucked up into a black hole of nothingness? What good news does the church have for Woody Allen and people who think like him?

Christians believe God created the world, but God did not simply go away and leave everything to its own devices. God is involved in the world. God holds the world together. God sustains it and keeps it going. God cares about it. So, if there is a God who made us and cares about us, it stands to reason that God would not leave us in the dark about himself – or even to grope our way to him. Christians believe that God has shown us who he is in Jesus Christ.

To believe in the God of Jesus is to know that I am no accident in this world. I have a purpose, a reason for existence. The God who created the universe also created me. I live and move and have my being because God made me. I am no insignificant thing. I matter.

To believe in the God of Jesus is to know that I am loved. St. Paul says Jesus "loved me and gave himself for me" (Eph. 2:20, NRSV). Although Paul was referring to himself, Martin Luther suggested we should personalize that statement and imagine God giving himself for each and every one of us individually. We should never doubt that we are loved totally and unconditionally.

To believe in the God of Jesus is to know there really are such things as right and wrong, good and evil, truth and falsehood. God has shown us where he stands and what he wants from us in the way we live. I find this a great comfort – because in a world of myriad choices, not all of them good, true happiness is only found by living according to God's way.

To believe in the God of Jesus is to be a good steward of the earth. Ecology is the science that recognizes the world as a delicate, precision system that needs looking after. But I learn this from the opening pages of the Bible: "In the beginning when God created the heavens and the earth... God saw everything that he had made, and indeed, it was very good" (Gen. 1:1,31, NRSV). God created not a garbage-dump but a garden. I have a responsibility to preserve the earth, which in its turn, preserves me.

To believe in the God of Jesus is to have confidence that what is right will win in the end. The eternal God made a good world and a just God is working in that world now. I will readily admit there is a great deal of madness in our world. People do evil things. Still, as a Christian I believe what is good and right will eventually triumph over what is evil and wrong. So, I am not too depressed at the many terrible things I see around me (and in me). Rather I affirm in the words of the old hymn: "This is my Father's world, / Oh, let me ne'er forget / That though the wrong seems oft so strong, / God is the Ruler yet."[14]

Francis B. Sayre, Jr. was for many years the Dean of the National Cathedral in Washington, D.C. In one of his sermons after he retired, Francis Sayre told a story about a woman on Martha's Vineyard. She had been twice widowed, and now spent much of her time and energy as an artist. She attended church now and then, but she admitted to Dean Sayre that she could no longer believe in the teachings of her youth: that Jesus was God, or that his birth was from a virgin, or that he was resurrected after he died. "Do you believe these things?" she asked him.

"Yes," Dean Sayre told her gently, "I do believe all those Christian things, and so do you! For they are not literal, logical, fact statements like two plus two equals four. Rather, they are symbolical, allegorical, poetical descriptions of realities far deeper than two plus two. They express the reality of life, of this spirit and its kinship with eternal truth: miracle and mystery in all ages and climes."[15]

We all know this God, including Woody Allen, Sam Harris, Richard Dawkins, Christopher Hitchens, Europeans and Canadians. As you gaze upon the stars and see the immensity of space, as you ponder the complexity of life, the miracle of birth, the mystery of love, you walk among the trees or along the lake, as you experience the surf on the beach, or climb the mountains and gaze upon the vistas, as you give the gift of love and receive that love from another person, you have an intuitive sense that life is miracle and mystery, and that upholding it all is a divine presence we call God.

Every human being, I believe, has this heartfelt suspicion that just beneath the apparent contradictions, brokenness and discord of this everyday world lays a hidden unity that gives our lives meaning, purpose and significance. When we embrace God, or more accurately, when God embraces us, we have a sense that our individual lives are caught in a great cosmic story that is headed somewhere wonderful. We are not alone. We journey in the company of a Divine Companion whose inexhaustible energy will ceaselessly work to bring ultimate love to every relationship and situation. In the end, we are not destined to be swallowed up by a black hole into nothingness but to experience the eternal embrace of the One who gives us life, sustains our life, and offers us abundant life.

Believing in God will not solve all your problems or answer all your questions. And yet, at the heart of Christian faith is the belief that the power and wisdom behind the universe is love, and that this love will triumph against all the evil and suffering that come our way. Believing in God may not remove the ache from your heart, but it can give you the comfort of knowing that even in the worst of times, love is at center of the universe.

Thornton Wilder's *Our Town* is a magnificent presentation of the drama of everyday life. It expresses the basic idea that if we live with the proper perspective, then every moment of living is sacred. Seen from an over-arching view, all of life can be lifted from the ordinary to the extraordinary, from the sight of the commonplace to the scene of creation.

Nothing sums up this philosophy better than a scene in *Our Town* in which a letter is sent to a Grover's Corners girl by a minister who is a humorist but also a very wise human being. The letter is addressed as follows: "June Crofut; the Crofut Farm; Grover's Corners; Sutton County; New Hampshire; United States of America; …Continent of North America; Western Hemisphere; the Earth; the Solar System; the Universe; the Mind of God…"[16]

Yes, you and I are in the mind of God. We are created by God, sustained by God and loved by God. We live in God's world and our destiny is to be with God forever. In the mystery and wonder of life, we catch glimpses of this God, a God fully revealed in Jesus. This is a God whom we can know, love and adore, a God who never abandons or forsakes us, a God who constantly cares for us and is with us always.

October 26, 2008
St. John the Evangelist Anglican Church, Elora, Ontario

THE MOST IMPORTANT QUESTION IN THE WORLD

1 CORINTHIANS 15:12-19
MATTHEW 28:1-10

The resurrection of Jesus is not so much about an empty tomb or even his appearances to the disciples. Throughout the ages, the testimony of Christians in their living and dying is to the risen Christ. Christians do not believe in Jesus in the same way they might study Plato or Socrates. Jesus is not a dead figure of the past but a living, personal, powerful presence. Because Jesus lives, so shall we.

"If you could meet any person of the past and ask just one question, whom would you meet and what question would you ask?" That question was asked to a British philosopher who did not believe in God. Surprisingly, the philosopher responded by saying that he would like to meet Jesus and ask him if he really rose from the dead. If he did, the philosopher said, that would change everything.

That philosopher got it right. The most important question in the world is whether Jesus rose from the dead and is alive today. In other words, did Easter really happen?

The resurrection of Jesus is the very heart of Christian faith. It is impossible to talk about the good news of Jesus Christ without referring to the resurrection. No resurrection means no good news. St. Paul makes this clear in his understanding of the resurrection in 1 Corinthians 15:12-19. Apparently, some Corinthians had doubts or even were beginning to disbelieve in the resurrection. Paul responded forthrightly. He wrote: "If there is no resurrection of the dead, then Christ has not been raised; and if Christ has not been raised, then our proclamation has been in vain and your faith has been in vain" (1 Cor. 15:13-14, NRSV). Paul goes on to say: "If Christ has not been raised, your faith is futile, and you are still in your sins. Then those who have died in Christ have perished. If for this life only we have hoped in Christ, we are of all people most to be pitied" (1 Cor. 15:17-19, NRSV).

The good news of Christ's resurrection was the farthest thing from the disciples' minds that first Good Friday. Everything had gone horribly wrong. Jesus entered Jerusalem in triumph, but events quickly turned to tragedy. In a few hurried hours Jesus was arrested, tried, condemned and executed. Now that he was dead, the disciples were frightened that what had happened to Jesus might happen to them.

Then came that remarkable Sunday that changed everything. Matthew's Gospel tells us that two women by the name of Mary (Mary Magdalene and the other Mary) went to look at the tomb. When they got there, there was a violent earthquake. An angel of the Lord had come down and rolled back the stone and sat on it. The guards shook with fear and froze into a catatonic state.

The angel said to the women: "Do not be afraid; I know that you are looking for Jesus who was crucified. He is not here; for he has been raised, as he said. Come, see the place where he lay. Then go quickly and tell his disciples, 'He has been raised from the dead, and indeed he is going ahead of you to Galilee; there you will see him'" (Mt. 28: 5-7, NRSV).

As the women hurried from the tomb, running to tell his disciples, Jesus meets them on the way. "Greetings!" he says to them. "Do not be afraid; go and tell my brothers to go to Galilee; there they will see me" (Mt. 28:9-10, NRSV).

When you look at all the accounts of the resurrection in the New Testament, you get a sense of the excitement of the moment. Something happened which had thrown the day into turmoil. There is a picture of confusion and chaos, of people running everywhere, of coming and going, trying to come to terms with an incredible event. The four Gospels do not agree on the details of the resurrection, but at the heart of every account is the proclamation that Jesus lives – not simply lives in the hearts of the disciples but lives as an objective reality.

Take the time to read the sermons in the Book of Acts and you will find that every one of them is an Easter sermon. In his Pentecost sermon, Peter sums up the Easter message when he says: "This Jesus God raised up, and of that all of us are witnesses" (Acts 2:32, NRSV). The resurrection is mentioned more than one hundred times in the New Testament, and nearly every book refers to it. It is the key factor that changed the seeming defeat of Jesus on the cross into a great victory over death.

I attended a church meeting in which a Canadian Anglican bishop complained that there were too many clergy in the diocese who found preaching on Easter Sunday to be the most difficult day of the year. I asked him, "Why?" He said the clergy had no idea on how to preach about the resurrection. The idea was beyond them.

How sad that there are Christian clergy who don't know what to make of the resurrection! I realize that churches tend to get more worshippers on Christmas Eve than Easter morning, but Easter is the main event. Without Easter there is no church, no faith, no good news. It's easy to sing Christmas carols, but to shout and believe that "Christ is risen" takes faith. If Easter isn't at the heart of our faith, then we have no faith. Jesus is still dead and we might as well pack it up as a church.

Christianity stands or falls on the reality of the resurrection. If Jesus rose from the dead, everything else in the New Testament makes sense. If he did not, then nothing makes sense. As the English Jesuit John Coventry put it: "The church is the community of the resurrection." On the resurrection depends how we live and even how we die.

Do you believe in the resurrection, believe it in such a way that you refuse to let death have the last word in your life? Many of us know all about death. In 2020, as the world deals with the coronavirus, death and dying are very much on our minds right now. Only a tiny percentage of the population will likely die from the virus, and yet even the threat of death makes us pause. It reminds us we are mortal, all too mortal, and that someday we will die, if not of a virus, then of something else. The truth is: no one lives forever.

Italy has suffered more deaths than any other European country due to COVID-19. In the midst of what only can be termed a modern-day plague, there were news reports of an eighty-four-year-old priest who decided to put himself in harms-way and minister to the victims of the coronavirus, knowing full well that he was in the high-risk category for dying if he got the virus. He was determined to care for the sick and dying, and to ensure they had the last rites of the Church. As it turned out, this priest did indeed get the virus and died. However, he died doing God's work, caring for God's people, staying true to his vocation, and living and believing that in life and death God would be with him. Because Jesus lives, so would he.

Another Italian priest who gave his life was seventy-two-year old Don Giuseppe Berardelli. He ministered in a town about 50 miles from Milan and died sometime between March 15 and 16. When Don Giuseppe got the virus, he was brought to a hospital for treatment. As his condition worsened, he was given a ventilator, but he refused it so that someone who was younger than him could use it. In an area of Italy where ventilators were in short supply, Don Giuseppe chose to give the gift of life to a stranger at the cost of his own life.

Why would he do such a thing? Why not hold on to life at all cost even if someone else had to die? After all, by all accounts he was a man who loved life, enjoyed his motorbike, and cared deeply for his people. Don Giuseppe did not want to die, but he knew that death was not the end of life; it was the beginning of new life with God. Because Jesus lives, so would he.

I suppose what motivated that eighty-four-year-old priest and Don Giuseppe Berardelli to give their lives on behalf of virus victims is what has prompted saints throughout the ages to do the same thing. I think of Father Damien of Molokai, the Belgium priest who volunteered to serve the leper colony on the island of Molokai in Hawaii. He was supposed to work at the colony only a short time, and then be replaced by three volunteers. Instead he chose to stay on the island where he eventually contracted leprosy. After sixteen years on Molokai, Father Damien died on April 15, 1889. In 2009, Pope Benedict XVI declared him a saint.

Then there were the Martyrs of Memphis – four Episcopal sisters of the Community of St. Mary – who died in an epidemic of yellow fever that swept through the city of Memphis, Tennessee in 1878. Almost everyone who could afford to do so left the city and fled to higher ground away from the river. The four nuns had the opportunity of leaving but chose to stay and nurse the sick. All four Episcopal nuns and two Episcopal priests died. They chose to remain in the city and care for the sick and dying even at the cost of their own lives.

Why did they do it? Why did an 84-year-old priest risk his life to care for coronavirus victims? Why did Don Giuseppe Berardelli refuse a ventilator so that another person could use it? Why did Father Damien choose to go to Molokai, minister to lepers until he himself became one and died? What did Episcopal nuns and priests remain in a yellow fever infested city when they had every opportunity to save their lives, but chose instead to care for the sick and dying?

Here is the greatest proof for the resurrection of Jesus. It's not the empty tomb or even the post-resurrection appearances of Jesus to his disciples. It is the fact that Christians throughout history have been willing to live and die for Jesus, to battle sickness and suffering even at the cost of their own lives, to stand up against evil and oppression, to accept death courageously, to live life boldly, and to face whatever may come their way in the power of God's love. In the resurrection of Jesus ordinary human beings find the power to rise above their own self-centeredness and instinct for survival and do noble things because they believe in a great God. They know that life can sometimes involve heartbreak and suffering, but that in all our troubles and trials, Jesus is with us still and will bring us home to heaven.

The resurrection of Jesus is not something that can be proved by logic. It has to be experienced, lived out, and acted in the world. You step out in faith and surrender your life to the God who has given his life for you. Two Italian priests have shown us the power of resurrection quite recently, but it happens all the time when Christians live, act and follow in the way of Jesus.

So, to the philosopher's question put to Jesus: "Did you or did you not really rise from the dead?" I would respond by saying: "Look around you. Christians are living and dying for Jesus today." The living Christ is no fiction to them, but a present, powerful, personal presence in their lives, strengthening them, sustaining them, and giving them the courage and perseverance to do what they can't.

Take courage, dear people. The coronavirus does not have the last word in your lives; God does. Live as people of the resurrection. Live as if death does not have the last word. Live as if love is at the heart of the universe. Live as if the darkness will never overwhelm the light. Because Jesus lives, so shall you.

April 12, 2020
Online, Peoria, AZ

SIGHT AND INSIGHT

JOHN 20:19-31

The only way to know the risen Christ is through a personal relationship with him. Relationship precedes knowledge. The risen Christ can never be known by the scientific method, as if he were an object for analysis. Rather he is known in the same way we get to know a friend or the person we eventually marry – through personal knowledge that comes in relationship. We know the risen Christ personally, or we never know him at all. St. Anselm put it like this: "I seek not to understand in order that I may believe; rather, I believe in order that I may understand."

I have an attorney friend who is an agnostic, though he likes Jesus very much. He also happens to be a successful trial lawyer. One day we were having coffee together and I asked him why he did not believe in Christianity. His answer did not surprise me. He simply said that, as far as he could determine, there simply was not enough evidence for him to believe in the resurrection. Too many unanswered questions, too many "holes" in the story, too many discrepancies in the four Gospel accounts – he simply could not reach a verdict that the resurrection really happened.

Not enough evidence – that is the cry of Thomas when he was

told by the other apostles that they had seen the Lord. The very assertion must have seemed nonsense to him. Dead people do not come back to life. He knew that. And so, he makes a statement that could be said by any skeptic today: "Unless I see the mark of the nails in his hands and put my finger in the mark of the nails and my hand in his side, I will not believe" (Jn. 20:25, NRSV). In other words, Thomas is saying, unless he sees it, he will not believe it. What cannot be seen, touched or verified physically through the senses is not real to him. He demands sight, but what he really needs is insight.

To appreciate the difference between sight and insight, let me focus on a hypothetical. What if a camera had been placed in the tomb where Jesus was buried? The camera runs from the time Jesus is laid in the tomb on Good Friday night until Easter Sunday morning when the women arrive. About the resurrection, what do you think we would see on the film? Would we see a corpse come back to life, like Lazarus who was called from the tomb? I do not think so. Lazarus was brought back to life, only to die again. His was the resuscitation of a corpse, not the resurrection of the body.

The resurrection of Jesus is not a corpse come back to life. In the resurrection, St. Paul tells us, we take on a "spiritual body" (1 Cor. 15:44, NRSV). A spiritual body is not an earthly body, but an embodied personality in a state of glory. It is full of splendor beyond any earthly limitations, imperishable and immortal.

When Jesus rose from the dead, he had a spiritual body. Here is the resurrection of an embodied personality – life in all its fullness without end. If the Gospels have difficulty in describing the resurrection, the explanation is simple enough: how do we describe the indescribable except in broken words and partial images? To see a spiritual body, one needs more than sight; one needs insight.

The Jesuit theologian Gus Weigel used to remark to his

students that if the risen Christ had appeared to Pilate or Herod they probably would not have recognized him. To see the risen Christ as he really is, one must see him by faith, or not at all. Faith, Weigel claimed, is never a cut and dry matter, and for good reason. God is not some cosmic bully compelling us to believe. There is always ambiguity in the evidence – enough evidence to allow us to believe but never enough to compel us to believe. God knows that sight without insight is compulsion, and this God refuses to do.

In the thirteenth century St. Thomas Aquinas wrote some of the most majestic Eucharistic hymns, affirming that the bread and wine of Holy Communion are really and truly the body and blood of Christ to those who have faith – "faith, our outward sense befriending, makes our inward vision clear." In the Eucharist faith sees the Christ where the unbeliever only sees bread and wine.

Anyone who wears glasses knows what a difference they make in how we perceive the world. Without glasses the world is blurred; people and things are only shapes and sizes. When we wear our glasses, the world comes into focus. We see things clearly, as they really are. Faith is like wearing a pair of glasses. Without faith, we see, but only dimly. Without faith, the risen Christ could have appeared to his enemies, and they would not have recognized him. Without faith, the disciples would not have seen the Lord.

That is why intellectual acumen is no substitute for faith. Knowing Christ is not a matter of the mind. It is a matter of the heart – experiencing God through personal relationship.

Relationship precedes knowledge. That is how people come to know each other, and it is the way we come to know Jesus. Developing a personal relationship with Jesus is the only way to know him – know him not objectively off the top of our mind but personally from the depths of our heart.

St. Augustine said, "Faith is to believe what you do not see; the reward of this faith is to see what you believe." Along the same lines, the eleventh century Archbishop of Canterbury St. Anselm declared, "I believe that I may understand." Only where there is faith or trust *in* God is there real knowledge *about* God. Faith transforms sight into insight. Faith allows us to believe when we do not see. It provides us with the certainty that evades the senses.

Take St. Paul, for example. He suffered enormous hardships on behalf of Jesus, yet he never wavered in his faith. Why is that? Paul had an encounter with the risen Lord on the road to Damascus. That encounter changed his life and he went from a persecutor of the church to the church's most effective advocate. Paul was not transformed by information about Jesus but by personal encounter. He knew Jesus loved him and even died for him; therefore he would love Jesus, and even die for him. He wrote: "I have been crucified with Christ; and it is no longer I who live, but it is Christ who lives in me. And the life I now live in the flesh I live by faith in the Son of God, who loved me and gave himself for me" (Gal. 2:19b-20, NRSV).

St. Paul lived not by sight but insight. He didn't simply have head knowledge; he had heart knowledge. Knowing the risen Christ did not simply inform his mind; it transformed his life. He was sure, absolutely sure to the moment of his death, that Jesus was his living Lord in this life and the life to come.

Christianity is not an academic system, a philosophy of life, or even a religion – it is, as the German theologian Dietrich Bonhoeffer put it, "to be caught up in the way of Jesus Christ" – knowing Jesus, loving Jesus, serving Jesus, becoming more Jesus-centered and living more Jesus-like. If we try to know Jesus off the top of our head rather than from the depths of our heart, our faith will remain superficial.

So, let us go back to my attorney friend's claim that there is simply not enough evidence to believe in the resurrection. If by "evidence" he means proof beyond a reasonable doubt, then such evidence God refuses to give us. If God wanted to compel us to believe by force of evidence, then Jesus would have come down from the cross when challenged by the crowd: "Let the Messiah, the King of Israel, come down from the cross now, so that we may see and believe" (Mk. 15:32, NRSV). To this, the risen Christ responds in our Gospel, "Blessed are those who have not seen and yet have come to believe" (Jn. 20:29, NRSV). Faith gives us the spiritual sight – the insight – to see God when the senses prove inadequate and logic takes us only so far.

On this Doubting Thomas Sunday, focus on Jesus. Enter the life of Jesus. Follow in the way of Jesus. Move from sight to insight, so that even if you have not seen you may yet believe and confess with Thomas and the saints of every age: Jesus, "My Lord and my God" (Jn. 20:28, NRSV).

April 10, 1988
Cathedral Church of the Nativity, Bethlehem, PA

KNOWING GOD PERSONALLY

JOHN 17:1-11

God is not primarily known by the mind but experienced in the heart. We seek to understand what we believe, but we believe what we experience. Knowing God is not an intellectual exercise as if studying an object by the scientific method. Rather God is known in relationship as we would know a lover or friend. Christian mystics almost always speak of God in personal terms as if being with a dear companion. We don't have to struggle to find this God, since God already is with us. St. Augustine prayed: "Lord Jesus, let me know myself and know you and desire nothing save only you."

My friend had been telling me why she did not believe in God. She was raised an Episcopalian, attended Sunday school and sang in the children's choir. She studied the Prayer Book and memorized the catechism in preparation for Confirmation. She still loved the language of the 1928 Prayer Book even though she did not believe a word of it.

So, what happened? Why had this successful attorney become an agnostic?

"Well," she said, "I knew a lot about God, but I really never knew God. I knew the language and the ritual, but I never experienced the reality. I could recite the Apostles' Creed from memory, but I didn't have the foggiest notion how that affected my life. Then one day, I was alone in my room saying the Lord's Prayer – "Our Father, who art in heaven…" As I said that prayer, I came to the realization that no one was listening because no one was there. I was in college at the time. It was the craziest thing. I just stopped believing in God."

Sound familiar? Maybe you know people like my friend, people who grew up in the church but no longer believe in God, or if they do believe in God, it does not seem to matter very much. These people know about the church, know its doctrines, rituals and practices, but they do not know God.

Do you know God? Let me draw out the implications of that question. Can you and I really have communion with God, as we would with an earthly friend? Can we know personally that same Jesus whose words and actions are recorded in the New Testament, who walked the roads in Galilee, Samaria and Judea two thousand years ago? I don't mean can we treasure his words or try to follow his example or imagine him in our minds. I mean, can he be really present to us? Can we actually meet him, commune with him, ask his help for our everyday affairs? Can we know this God personally?

"Yes!" says today's Gospel. Here is an astounding claim. The God who created you and me, who walked this earth to save us from ourselves, whose Spirit fills the whole world – this God we can know in the very depths of our being. We can be as certain of this God as we can be of our own selves. That is the promise of the Gospel: "And this is eternal life, that they may know you, the only true God, and Jesus Christ whom you have sent" (Jn. 17:3, NRSV).

To know God, in the biblical sense, is much like knowing a lover. In Genesis, for example, Adam "knew" his wife, and she conceived and bore Cain (Gen. 4:1, NRSV). In Matthew's Gospel, Joseph awakes from his dream, obeys the angel and marries Mary, but "knew her not" her until she had given birth to Jesus (Mt. 1:25, KJV).

Knowing God in this biblical sense is more than fact or observation. That kind of objective or scientific knowledge is Greek rather than Hebrew. In the Bible knowledge about God, just like knowing a lover comes through personal relationship. It is not an act of the intellect but a response from the heart. It is to know God from the depths of our being rather than off the top of our head. Cardinal Newman put it succinctly in his motto: *Cor ad Cor loquitur* – "heart speaks to heart."

St. Paul wrote in Romans: "If you confess with your mouth that Jesus is Lord and believe in your heart that God raised him from the dead, you will be saved. For one believes with the heart and so is justified, and one confesses with the mouth and so is saved" (Rom. 10: 9-10, NRSV). Believing is more a matter of the heart than the mind. It is not so much about acknowledging articles of faith as it is about trust in a person – being willing to enter the life of that person and allowing that person to enter your life.

So much of Christian education used to be a matter of memorizing the catechism, the creeds and the Prayer Book, as if knowing God could be attained by rote. The more we memorized, the more it was presumed we knew God.

Of course, there is a place for knowing the substance of our faith – too many Episcopalians know too little about the Bible, Christianity and our Anglican heritage. However, right answers about God are no substitute for a right relationship with God. "For God so loved the world that he gave his only Son" (Jn. 3:16, NRSV) – not to inform our minds but to transform our lives.

When I was in graduate school at Georgetown University, a

visiting professor of religious studies gave a public lecture. His lecture was a brilliant and fair elucidation of Christian faith. I was impressed by the breath of his knowledge. He spoke with authority. He cited the New Testament. He quoted St. Augustine and St. Thomas Aquinas. He was familiar with the three key philosophical arguments for the existence of God.

At a reception after the lecture, I went up to the professor to share my appreciation for his talk. Then I asked casually, "By the way, are you a Roman Catholic?"

The professor smiled and said, "I am not a member of any church. In fact, I am quite undecided on whether I believe in God."

"But how can you *not* believe in God?" I asked. "You know Christianity so well."

The professor replied, "There's a difference between knowing a subject and believing in it."

He was right. It takes more than head knowledge to be a Christian; it takes heart knowledge. If mastering the facts of Christianity made a person a Christian, then computers would be the new saints.

Think of the people who have touched your life for Christ. Perhaps it was a parent or relative. Perhaps it was a friend, a teacher, or a priest. What made these people so attractive to you? No doubt they witnessed Christ effectively in their words because they radiated Christ in their lives. They spoke as people who didn't simply know about God – God as speculation or abstract concept – but they knew God personally as friend and even lover.

I will never forget a conversation I had with Brother Robert when I was a young priest in upstate New York. Brother Robert was a Trappist monk at the Abbey of the Genesee. While doing what monks do, which in his case was baking bread, he meditated on the psalms.

On this day, I could see by an open Bible on his desk that he was reading Psalm 19. That has always been one of my favorite psalms. I studied the psalms under a respected Canadian Jesuit scholar. So, I thought I would enlighten Brother Robert with what I knew about Psalm 19. As I talked, he seemed overwhelmed. So, I asked him what he thought it meant. As he spoke, I felt as if the heavens were opening and God's voice was speaking through this simple monk.

After he finished, I asked him how he knew so much about it. He said, "I asked God what it means." Brother Robert knew God personally, and it showed by how he read and prayed the Bible.

"And this is eternal life, that they may know you, the only true God, and Jesus Christ whom you have sent" (Jn. 17:3, NRSV).

Knowing God personally is something akin to knowing your spouse in marriage. You meet, get to know each other, become friends, fall in love, get engaged and eventually married. On your wedding day, you are sure you know all there is to know about the other person, but you have just touched the surface. As the years go by and your relationship deepens, your knowledge of each other grows. You come to know the person in ways you never imagined when you first met.

Now that is the way it is in our relationship with God. In deepening our relationship with God, we come to know the God who already knows us. "It is a fearful thing to fall into the hands of the living God" (Heb. 10:31, NRSV) says the author of Hebrews. Fearful – because no one can remain the same who enters a relationship with God, just as we can never be the same when we enter a relationship with someone we love. Relationship – any deep, mutual relationship – will always change us.

We know God in a personal relationship, but that relationship needs to be sustained by discipline. No discipline, no relationship. Just as a marriage requires a lifetime of discipline to sustain the vows, so too does our relationship with God. It takes a moment in baptism to become a Christian, but it takes a lifetime to grow as a Christian. It takes frequent reception of Holy Communion. It takes the support of a loving church. It takes the fellowship of Christian friends. It takes regular Bible reading and service to others. It takes the practice of good stewardship.

And it takes prayer, because we cannot know God personally unless we are willing to spend time with God each day. After all, how can you possibly get to know a person unless you are willing to spend time with that person? Relationship demands discipline.

"And this is eternal life, that they may know you, the only true God, and Jesus Christ whom you have sent" (Jn. 17:3, NRSV).

Would it surprise you to know that every Christian can experience eternal life in the here and now? That every Christian can know God personally? That every Christian can have the assurance that God is here, that God is with us, that God is by our side in all the joys and pains of being human?

If you are struggling with whether you believe in God, I want you to know that God is right now, right here, by your side, and in your life. The God you struggle to know already knows you, loves you, and embraces you as his own.

The French philosopher Henri Bergson came to join a church late in life after living most of his life as an agnostic. A friend asked him, "How did you find God?" Bergson thought for a moment and then said, "Perhaps it was God who found me."

Isn't that the truth? You search for God but it is God who finds you. God comes to you, loves you, embraces you, and brings you home. God never gives up on you, even when you give up on yourself. No matter how lost you are or how much pain you may feel, God still loves you and searches for you, and finds you and carries you home. To your surprise, when you think God is absent from your life, you discover that he is right beside you.

It is like the woman who imagined that a high, impenetrable

wall separated her from God. She cried out, "God, where are you?" And then she heard a quiet voice respond, "Don't you know there is nothing between us?"

We may think that God is far away, distant and unapproachable, when all the while God is standing beside us. Once we find God, we will discover to our surprise that God has already found us.

This day, this moment, think of God. Think of God's presence. Know that God is near. Close your eyes, and with all the faith that you have, even if it be very little, tell God that you believe. If we let God take our life, we will find to our surprise that God gives us back our life – our life for his life. What a relationship of exhilaration and peace!

Yes, we can know God personally. We can enter into a relationship with this God where he is ours and we are his. That, dear people, is the greatest truth in the whole world: that we are called into relationship with God, in this life and forever.

"And this is eternal life, that they may know you, the only true God, and Jesus Christ whom you have sent" (Jn. 17:3, NRSV).

March 7, 1990
Cathedral Church of the Nativity, Bethlehem, PA

UNDERSTANDING HEAVEN

REVELATION 21:2-7; JOHN 11:32-44

Heaven is more difficult to comprehend than we may at first think. After all, how can we who exist in time and space comprehend eternity? We can speculate about heaven but not fully understand it. The Bible uses symbol and metaphor to describe heaven but all our words and images are inadequate for so great a mystery. Perhaps it is enough to say that where God is, there we shall be also.

Steve Jobs struggled with his pending death. He thought it was an incredible waste of our lives that we end in annihilation. Walter Isaacson recounts Jobs saying, "It's strange to think that you accumulate all this experience, and maybe a little wisdom, and it just goes away. So, I really want to believe that something survives, that maybe your consciousness endures."[1]

In his final months before his death, Steve Jobs wanted to believe in an afterlife. He was no different from any of us. We all want to believe that our essence or soul does not die but somehow lives on.

As I get older, I find myself thinking more and more about death. Friends and relatives die, and someday I will die. Every ache and pain, every cough and cold, reminds me that I am not going to live forever. Someday this body will fail, and I will take my last breath on earth. That is not being morbid, just realistic. My wife and I are now revising our estate plan to ensure our daughter's care when we die. It is not easy to think about a time when you will no longer be alive, but it is necessary, especially for parents with a Down syndrome child.

I accept the fact that I am going to die, but I do wonder about heaven. The Bible talks about heaven, but all the images, especially in the Book of Revelation, are figurative and symbolic.

I struggle with understanding heaven. Human beings are creatures of time and space. We cannot imagine any kind of reality apart from time (past, present and future) and space (forward, backward, upward, downward). And yet, God is eternal, and when we die, we enter eternity – a sort of "eternal now" without time or space. Eternity is impossible for us to contemplate – the only way we can think about it is through the categories of space and time – but that is precisely what eternity is not.

Some theologians speculate that after death we continue to exist in time and space, but in a different way from this life. I am not sure about that. Other theologians speculate that at death we get absorbed into God. The problem with absorption is that we lose our identity, our sense of self. St. Paul tells us in First Corinthians 15 that at death we will have a "spiritual body" (1 Cor. 15:44, NRSV) and retain our identity. So, the idea of being absorbed into God does not seem biblical to me.

Then there is reincarnation which is not a Christian concept. The prospect of coming back to earth as a cow or bug is even less attractive than being absorbed. In any case, at some point the earth will cease, so does that mean we will cease with it?

Atheists, of course, dismiss the whole idea of an afterlife, and stoically accept their annihilation, that at death they will cease to exist. I admire their forthrightness to face the consequences of this belief, but they are wrong.

That said, I must admit it is futile and even impossible for us to have any accurate picture of heaven or eternity with God. The Bible is filled with symbolic imagery of heaven, but the gap between time/space and eternity is too great for us to know anything much about what awaits us.

Jewish people understand this better than Christians. Orthodox Jews, who believe in an afterlife, refuse to speculate about it. They accept the fact that after death they will be with God without trying to describe what it will be like. Christians, on the other hand, seem to want to know all the details about heaven, and so we have all sorts of fantastic accounts describing it. But again, all these accounts use time/space to describe eternity.

If we cannot talk about heaven or eternity in any concrete, detailed way, what can we say?

We need to get away from thinking of heaven as a place, as if, when you die, you travel to another planet. Heaven is not a place but a state of being with God. That in itself is an indescribable experience, beyond human comprehension.

Imagine, for example, that you are blind from birth. You have never seen the beauty of the world, the yellow sun, the blue sky, the green grass, the trees and flowers in all their splendor. People have tried to describe the beauty of the world to you, but their descriptions have never taken hold of your mind. You cannot imagine what the world must really look like.

By the miracle of science, an operation gives you the sight you never had before. When the bandages come off your eyes, for the first time in your life you see the world as it is. You look out your hospital window and are amazed by the brightness, the colors, the shapes of everything that you see. People tried to tell you how beautiful the world was, but their words just could not describe the reality.

That is what we need to acknowledge about heaven because all our words and categories defy any adequate description. Poetry, symbol, and metaphor help us imagine the unimaginable. In the end, it does us no good to think about heaven as a place. Rather than ask "what" – what is heaven like? – we should instead ask "who" – who is in heaven? The answer, of course, is God and Jesus.

For me, the prospect of meeting Jesus face to face and being with him forever is the hope that keeps me going, no matter what life may throw at me. Yes, I do not know much about heaven, but there are ample passages in the New Testament that promise eternal life with God. I won't go through them all, but we read these passages from the New Revised Standard Version at funerals: John 11: 21-27 ("I am the resurrection and the life..."), John 14:1-6 ("In my Father's house there are many dwelling places..."), 1 Corinthians 15 where Paul gives the most extensive account of resurrection and eternal life. So, if nothing else, we have the scriptural promise that we will be with God when we die – that should be enough for any of us.

I do not think we should speculate about heaven, but we can take comfort that where God is, there we shall be also. No less an authority than Jesus tells us that he is preparing a place for us. "In my Father's house there are many dwelling places. If it were not so, would I have told you that I go to prepare a place for you? And if I go and prepare a place for you, I will come again and will take you to myself, so that where I am, there you will be also" (Jn. 14:2-3, NRSV)).

We don't know what heaven is like, but we do know that Jesus is there. And because he is there, everything is going to be all right.

That is the great comfort for you and me in time of death.

Heaven is where God is. That is all any of us need to know. In heaven we will experience love as we have never known it. We will know joy, peace, contentment and happiness as we have never experienced them. I cannot explain it or describe it satisfactorily, but I believe where God is, there I shall be also. That is enough for me. I simply rest on the promise of Jesus "that where I am, there you will be also" (Jn. 14:3, NRSV).

If heaven is where God is, will we know our loved ones there? I hope so. The resurrected Jesus, with a little prodding on his part, was still recognizable to his disciples, and I hope that we will be recognizable to one another. In heaven we shall truly be who God means us to be. Persons with Alzheimer's shall be in their right mind. People with mental illness will no longer live in the dark shadows. People physically disabled will be made whole. Those who suffer depression shall finally know joy. Yes, in heaven you and I shall be the ones God means us to be. We shall experience fullness of life as we have never known it.

Several years ago, I saw a play about an aristocratic but dysfunctional family struggling with many painful issues. There was a sister who was mentally ill and eventually had to be put into an institution. There was a brother who was a success at business but a failure in his personal life, struggling with alcoholism and alienated from his wife and children. There was a husband and wife who outwardly modeled the perfect marriage, when their love for each other had long since died. This family seemed to have everything when they were living on empty.

There is no happy ending to this story. They struggle and carry on as best they can but are never able to change their lives. The play gives us a vivid image of the weakness and frailty of human beings who hope for the best but often fall short. Most of us, to one degree or another, are like that.

And yet, the last scene of the play brought everyone in the

theater to tears. Miraculously, we see the mentally ill daughter in her right mind, the brother reconciled with his wife and children, and the father and mother in a loving embrace. And we know... we are seeing a picture of heaven where broken lives are made whole, bitterness is changed into forgiveness, hate is transformed into love, and our yearnings, hopes and dreams for a better life come to fruition.

No matter our pains and problems in this life, in heaven we will be one with ourselves, one with each other, and one with God. Heaven is our hope when all else fails. There we shall enjoy the presence of God. There we shall be embraced and loved by God forever. There we shall be our own true selves with those we love and who have loved us.

So, take hope, dear people. No matter your condition or situation, the best is yet to come.

November 4, 2011
St. James Westminster Church, London, ON

INTO THE DARK

1 CORINTHIANS 15:50-58

There is a finality about death that makes us feel ill at ease. Death is the end of everything we cherish in life or about ourselves. So, it should not surprise us that even people who do not believe in Christianity may believe in immortality – that the soul or the essence of who they are continues to exist after their physical death. Christians do not stake their faith on immortality but in the resurrection of Jesus. Unlike immortality, resurrection means that when we die, we really die. We go the way of all flesh, all life on earth. Death means the end of our existence. Resurrection is God's great reversal of the natural end of life. Christians believe that we don't live to die but we die to live. Death is not the end of life but the beginning of new life in God. Christ's resurrection is the first fruit of our resurrection. Death, our natural inevitability, is reversed by God's supernatural intervention. No wonder St. Paul writes: "But thanks be to God, who gives us the victory through our Lord Jesus Christ" (1 Cor. 15:57, NRSV)).

I have been hesitant to share this experience with anyone since it happened on that fateful day on August 17, 2015. On that day I went to the hospital to have my prostate removed. I thought I was emotionally and spiritually prepared for the surgery. The parish was in good care, my estate was in order, and I had even given my wife a list of all my passwords and accounts. I was ready for the surgery… but not ready. The truth is: I was nervous, frightened, and deeply aware of my mortality.

That Monday morning Heather and I awoke well before dawn to arrive at the hospital by 6:00 a.m. I did not have to wait long before my name was called, and I was escorted to a preparation room. The curtains were pulled around the bed and I was asked to take off all my clothes, put on a hospital gown, and lay down. Not long after, an orderly wheeled me to the operating room.

I found myself in this cold bright room with medical staff surrounding me. I was moved from the gurney to the operating table where I lay naked. The anesthesiologist approached me, introduced herself, and told me she was going to place a breathing mask on my face. She said to breathe normally; it was only oxygen. After a few moments, she said I would be receiving the anesthesia to put me to sleep. She told me to count to ten backwards. I counted… ten… nine… eight…. seven. And that is it. I completely blacked out and did not know or feel anything until I awoke in the recovery room several hours later.

So, what is the point of this story? Well, being theologically curious, I wondered as I was being wheeled into the operating room whether I would have some sort of divine experience on the operating table. You read about people having an out-of-body experience during surgery, claiming to see heaven, or feel a tremendous sense of warmth, or being engulfed by bright light. But alas, when I got to my room after the surgery, I realized that I had no such experience. When I was put to sleep by the anesthesiologist, I entered a state of complete darkness where I had no self-awareness whatsoever.

Now here is what I have been reluctant to share with anyone

until now.... During my recovery in the hospital, I kept wondering, "Is this, what death is like?" Your life suddenly stops, and you enter the darkness of annihilation where there is no self-awareness, no ego, no pain, or joy.... nothing. You just cease to be.

I also realized that if I had died on the operating table, I would not have known it. My death would have happened without the slightest awareness on my part.

I began to realize that if death is like entering the darkness of annihilation, then I will simply cease to exist. I will not know anything or feel anything. I will not cry or grieve or feel pain. Neither will I laugh or love or have any sense of self. I will simply cease to be. The darkness will have swallowed my life into oblivion.

If you are an atheist, then you have already accepted this reality. You know that at some point in the future you will cease to exist. The atheist philosopher Bertrand Russell had no problem with death, though he did not want his dying to be too painful. Similarly, the Canadian naturalist David Suzuki said that while he did not believe in God or an afterlife, he took comfort that his dead body would be used to fertilize the earth, helping to grow new life.

Richard Dawkins has tried to transform atheistic evolution into a secular spirituality. And yet, as the British physicist and priest-scientist John Polkinghorne has noted, the story of atheistic evolution ends in death – for us and for the universe. Eventually the whole universe dies and returns to nothingness.

One of the most unnerving images in science is the black hole. You may know that a black hole is a collapsed star so dense that nothing, not even light, can escape its gravitational field. Some scientists think a black hole lies at the very center of the Milky Way. From my perspective that is not a very comforting thought – to think that everything at the center of our corner of the universe collapses into intense and voracious darkness.

The fearful thing about a black hole is that once you are sucked into it, there is no escaping out of it. And yet, in my own way, after my surgery I felt as if I had escaped a black hole. I feel blessed that on the operating table I made this journey into the darkness, but also out of it. When I first reflected on what had happened, I was shaken. Perhaps there is no life after death, I thought. Perhaps the yearnings and desires that we have for heaven have no basis in fact. Perhaps we are deceiving ourselves in believing there is anything beyond this life. Perhaps, in the end, we all go into the darkness that drains the life right out of us.

Do any of us remember reading T.S. Eliot's *Four Quartets* – the third part on East Cocker? I read that poem as I was recovering at home, and it startled me in how it responded to my doubts.

> *O dark, dark, dark. They all go into the dark,*
> *The vacant stellar spaces, the vacant into the vacant,*
> *The captains, merchant bankers, eminent men of letters.*
> *The patrons of art, the statesmen and the rulers,*
> *Distinguished civil servants, chairmen of many committees,*
> *Industrial lords and petty contractors, all go into the dark,*
> ....
> *I said to my soul, be still, and let the dark come upon you*
> *Which shall be the darkness of God.*[1]

Reading Eliot's words changed my perspective on the darkness of death. I came to realize that even in the darkness there is God. In our living and dying, and even in our death, there is God. Yes, we cannot escape the darkness, but we do not enter the darkness alone. God is with us every step of the way.

And so, I remain committed to "the resurrection of the dead and the life of the world to come," as the Nicene Creed puts it.

How can I say this considering my journey into the darkness on the operating table?

When I was a university student, I remember taking a course on the New Testament in which an important distinction was made between "immortality" and the "resurrection of the dead." Oscar Cullmann, a German theologian, had written a journal article back in 1956 titled, "Immortality of the Soul or Resurrection of the Dead?" Cullmann argued that immortality was a Greek view that the soul lives forever even when the body dies. In fact, at death the soul is liberated, set free, because it is no longer confined by the body. Death, in this view, is the ultimate liberation of the soul. And so, death, far from being feared, is to be welcomed.

Philosophers such as Socrates and Plato argued for such a view, and Socrates was so convinced of its truth that when sentenced to death by an Athenian court, he willingly drank the hemlock and died. Plato in his *Phaedo* describes how Socrates goes to his death in complete peace and composure. Socrates does not fear death; in fact, he welcomes it because by it he is set free from the constraints of his body.

I remember being at a memorial service conducted in the backyard of the family's house. The mother who died had turned away from her Christian faith, though she was a good and sincere human being. Hers was a long drawn out death, and quite painful both for her and her family. The service consisted of words of remembrance and thanks for the woman's life, but there were no prayers or any mention of God. As the service concluded, family members released balloons into the sky as a symbol of new life – a stubborn belief that their mother was not really dead. Though family members did not believe in resurrection, they wanted to believe in immortality.

The trouble is, as Cullmann effectively argues, immortality is not a New Testament concept, and at best, is only philosophical speculation. You can believe in immortality if you want, but there is no way of proving it true.

Cullmann argues that the Christian faith is not based on the immortality of the soul. It is based on the resurrection of the body. In Christianity, we really die because the soul is not intrinsically immortal. We enter the blackness of annihilation. We cease to exist. Nothing within us survives beyond our death. We die as surely as our body gets cold and decays.

In Christianity death is not our friend but an enemy. It is not something to be embraced; it is something to be conquered. In the Gospel story, Jesus does not welcome death like Socrates. Mark says that in the Garden of Gethsemane he was "distressed and agitated" (Mk. 14:33, NRSV). He was anxious, fearful, to the point where Luke says, "his sweat became like great drops of blood" (Lk. 22:44, NRSV). The author of Hebrews goes so far as to say that at his passion and death Jesus offered up "loud cries and tears" (Heb. 5:7, NRSV) to the one who could save him from death.

Jesus really died and entered the darkness of death. He did not shirk or escape it; rather he entered it with all its horror. Only by entering death could he conquer it. Thus the Creed goes on to say: "On the third day he rose again…" Death is not the end for Jesus because God raised him from the dead. And death is not the end for us because God will raise us as well. We all die, but God lifts us up to his presence in heaven. We die and yet we live. We descend into the darkness and by the power of God we ascend into the light. Death is like a dead end, but God makes a way where there is no way. Love, light, and life have the last word, because God is greater than all the powers of darkness. The death we die in our bodies transforms into the life we live with God.

This is our Christian hope. It is not based on any philosophical speculation. It is based on the reality of the resurrection of Jesus from the dead. Because death no longer has the final word in the life of Jesus, it no longer has the final word in our lives. And so, we can enter the darkness in perfect trust that God will raise us up and bring us home to heaven.

Several years ago my Aunt Gloria died. I spoke on the phone with her son, my cousin James, who is a year older than me. I mentioned to James that with the death of his mother, all my aunts and uncles are now dead. James replied that he knew how I was feeling. He was feeling the same way. Then he said, "You know, Gary, we're moving to the front of the bus, and soon enough we're going to get off."

The passing years remind us of our mortality, don't they? Whether it is sickness, or surgery, or just getting old, we know that someday we will die. So, what happens when we get off the bus? As I see it, we have three options. First, we can opt for the way of atheistic evolution and accept the reality that at the end of life there is only annihilation. Our body may be used as fertilizer to grow new life on earth, but I do not find this very comforting. Second, we can speculate about immortality. The body dies but something within us continues to live. Frankly, I do not find this option very convincing or even appealing. All immortality says is that the soul does not die, but simply lives on – in what way or manner one can only speculate.

There is, however, a third option: to place our trust in Jesus Christ, who by his death destroyed death and by his life gives us eternal life. In Jesus, the powers of darkness do not have the last word in our lives. Life does not end with death, but death ends with life. We will pass through the valley of the shadow of death, but God will be with us every step of way to bring us to heaven. Yes, we really die, but all that God has created, and death has annihilated are recalled to life in a new act of creation by God.

St. Paul puts it like this: "For the perishable body must put on imperishability, and the mortal body must put on immortality, When this perishable body puts on imperishability, and this mortal body puts on immortality, then the saying that is written will be fulfilled: 'Death has been swallowed up in victory.' 'Where, O death is your victory? Where, O death, is your sting?' The sting of death is sin, and the power of sin is the law. But thanks be to God, who gives us the victory through our Lord Jesus Christ" (1 Cor. 15: 54-57, NRSV).

When the pain of our mortality becomes apparent, and our body fails, and our strength weakens, and we feel like we are sliding into a black hole, take heart and know that Jesus your Savior will save you from the death from which you cannot save yourself.

November 2, 2016
Online, Peoria, AZ

THE GOD OF MESSINESS, MUD AND DIRT

COLOSSIANS 1:11-20; LUKE 23:33-43

God has a passionate love affair with us. St. Catherine of Siena wrote, "Dear God, it seems that you are so madly in love with your creatures that you could not live without us. So you created us; and then, when we turned away from you, you redeemed us. ...It is love, and love alone, which moves you." This is no indifferent or apathetic God who couldn't care less about us. The God of Jesus cares so much about us that he became one with us, experiencing all the joys and pains of being human. This God in Jesus even sacrifices himself for us, doing for us what we cannot do for ourselves – saving us from sin and death. No wonder St. Paul writes: "But God proved his love for us in that while we still were sinners Christ died for us" (Rom. 5:8, NRSV).

I was speaking with a young woman in Starbucks. We were both putting cream in our coffees, when she noticed that I was wearing my clerical collar. "Are you a priest?" she asked me. When I said yes, she began to tell me how pessimistic she felt about the state of America, race relations, climate change, the general direction of the country. She was depressed by what was happening. She graduated from college several years ago and is looking for a full-time position. Right now she has to settle for working multiple jobs simultaneously just to pay her bills.

Her name is Mia. She doesn't attend any church. Mia was raised Roman Catholic, but she stopped attending Mass in high school because she could never figure out God – too distant, too abstract, too meaningless for her everyday life. She now finds spiritual satisfaction elsewhere: hiking, music concerts and just being with friends.

Mia's story is not all that uncommon for an increasing number of young adults. If they think of God at all, it is as a remote being, detached from the world, maintaining a dignified distance from the rough and tumble of human life. God is out there, far removed from our daily struggles. This is the kind of God who, if you fainted on the street, would say "too bad" and walk by without even calling emergency.

This God will not do much for us. It makes no sense to pray to this God when we are sick, or alone, or in trouble. This God is not interested in us and not of much help to us. You cannot blame Mia if she does not believe in such a God. Why should she? Why should any of us believe in a God who is indifferent to our lives?

However, there is another way to think about God. In his letter to the Colossians, St. Paul says that Jesus is "the image of the invisible God" (Col. 1:15, NRSV). Paul is saying that we cannot think of God without thinking of Jesus, and we cannot think of Jesus without thinking of God. Do you want to know God? Look to Jesus. When we look to Jesus, we see as much of God as we ever hope to see. That is why I like Bishop John Robinson's insight that Jesus is the human face of God. To see Jesus is to see God.

Jesus is God with a human face. He is most clearly recognizable as God when he takes upon himself our sin, dying our death, bearing upon himself the world's evil and pain. Jesus is the sinless one who dies for sinners, the innocent one suffering for the guilty. Jesus is the God who cries out from the cross, "Father, forgive them, for they do not know what they are doing" Lk. 23:34, NRSV) – witnessing to us that love is stronger than hate and forgiveness stronger than vengeance. This is the God who recognizes that no human being is beyond redemption, not the two criminals crucified with him or even the Roman soldiers who nailed him to the cross.

The God of Jesus is not a non-interventionist God who turns his back on us when we get into trouble. He is not a God who shrugs when we are in pain, or is indifferent to our cries for help. The God of Jesus is One that saw our dire situation, rolled up his sleeves and got to work – a God who is not too proud to get right down in the mud, dirt and general messiness of our lives.

One of the most beautiful communities in all of North America is La Jolla, California. When I lived in the San Diego region, I was always struck by the enormous wealth that exists in that community. Even the older, more modest homes sell for well over a million dollars; and newer more opulent homes sell in the many millions.

Now think of a different community – Tijuana, Mexico. Hundreds of families live in the Tijuana dump amid mounds of trash, and every day they send their children to find garbage to eat. The poverty and deprivation south of the border is staggering, especially around the dump.

Now imagine the distance from the opulent homes in La Jolla to the shacks by the garbage dump in Tijuana. That distance is nothing compared to the journey God made to reach us in Jesus. Could you possibly conceive of someone giving up his or her beautiful home overlooking the cliffs of La Jolla to live in a shack by a garbage dump in Tijuana? Unthinkable, you say. However,

God did more than that when Jesus came from the glory and splendor of heaven into the poverty and misery of earth.

Why did God do it? Because God loves us enough to be one with us, to suffer and die for us. This God does not give up on us even when we give up on ourselves. He enters into our distress to bring us to heaven.

The God of Jesus is no distant, uncaring, unfeeling, indifferent God. This God willingly stoops to the level of our existence and becomes one with us, fully human in every way that we are, except without sin. This God is not a vaguely beneficial spirit or a nebulous force beyond our imagining. This God wears a human face, crowned with thorns, scourged, beaten and crucified. This God is flesh-and-blood, putting love into practice wherever human beings are in need.

However, God does more than just enter our world. In Jesus God sacrifices himself for us. The essence of sacrifice is God doing for us what we cannot do for ourselves – save us from our own sin. If sin separates us from God, Jesus became our sin offering to reconcile us to God. Jesus not only took our place on the cross. He took our sin. He died our death. He gave his life so that we might live.

Nothing better illustrates the sacrifice of Jesus for us than two true stories, both coming out of the old Soviet Union.

Some of us may have seen the movie *K-19 The Widowmaker* starring Harrison Ford. The film is the story of a poorly built Soviet nuclear submarine out on initial maneuvers. The nuclear reactor on the submarine runs amok, requiring volunteers to enter the radioactive chamber to fix the reactor. The trouble is, entering the chamber means almost certain death because of the high levels of nuclear radiation. One by one, seven men volunteer to enter the chamber to work at half hour intervals. As each one exits the chamber, they suffer severe radiation burns throughout their entire body as well as radiation poisoning. Still, as one exits, another enters until the reactor is finally fixed. However, within days all seven men are dead. They took all that radiation upon themselves to save the crew and sub.

In a way, that is what Jesus did for us. He literally entered into the god-forsakenness of our existence to redeem it. He endured the agony of human sin and the separation it brought because in no other way could he identify himself with our humanity and make it possible for us to be forgiven and accepted by God. In the sacrifice of Jesus, we are saved from sin and death. He died so that we might live.

God had to sacrifice himself for us. There was no other way for God's justice and mercy to come together. God's justice demanded punishment for sin, but God's mercy demanded life for the sinner. In Jesus we see the justice of God become the mercy of God. He pays the price for our sins, thus fulfilling the demand for justice. In taking our place and dying our death, he shows us mercy. This is the sacrifice of God – paying the price for our sins but showing mercy to sinners.

Sacrifice always demands something from us. It is never "cheap grace" as Bonhoeffer put it. God can't just wave a magic wand and make everything right. There is a cost to our salvation, a price that has to be paid. Justice and mercy must come together, and they do in Jesus. His sacrifice on the cross shows the depths of God's love for us. God would do anything for us, even die for us.

This leads to the second true story, one that you recently may have seen on television. It is the HBO series *Chernobyl*, which is the story of the 1986 explosion and after-effects of the Soviet nuclear reactor at *Chernobyl* in the Ukraine. The series dramatizes two sides of the crisis. On the one hand, there are the cover-ups, misinformation, incompetence, fear to speak the truth and punishment for those who do – all intent on deflecting responsibility from the corrupt Soviet system.

There is, however, another side to Chernobyl – a heroic side, of people willing to speak truth to power even at the cost of their safety and careers, people willing to sacrifice their lives to save others, people willing to die so that others might live.

When the explosion happened, no one realized how serious the situation was, how even being near the site doomed anyone to certain death. And yet, Soviet firefighters called to the site desperately tried to put out the nuclear fire. They came dangerously close to the reactor. They entered into buildings and came out with their skin burnt. They worked tirelessly doing an impossible task. In the end, they fell sick, were taken to a special hospital ward where they eventually died from radiation poisoning.

In recognition of their sacrifice, the Russian newspaper *Pravda* published this poem:

> *God is a man who walked into a radiated complex,*
> *Put out the fire, burned his skin and clothes,*
> *Who didn't save himself,*
> *But saved Odessa and Kiev,*
> *A man who simply acted like a human being.*

Here is a picture of God – descending into the depths of our hell, battling a nuclear catastrophe, and trying to restore order to a chaotic world. In a way, that is a picture of Jesus: God who enters our world, born into poverty and oppression, takes upon himself our suffering and sin, and redeems it, so that you and I can live full and faithful lives.

In light of all the people who say they no longer believe in God or are unsure if there is a God or do not know what to think of God, I would tell them to look to Jesus. He is the human face of God. He is the one who enters into the world of a garbage dump community to bring the residents to a pristine and beautiful place. He is the crewmember who enters into a deadly radioactive chamber to save the lives of his comrades. He is the firefighter who draws near to a burning nuclear reactor to save those who know nothing of his sacrifice. Jesus is the Son of God who enters into the messiness, mud and dirt of our world because he loves us, and even dies for us.

So, if you are having trouble believing in God, look to Jesus. He is the fullness of God on earth. What other type of God would you possibly want? In Jesus we have a God who would even die for you – he loves you that much!

November 24, 2019
Church of the Advent, Sun City West, AZ

RISING ABOVE YOUR PAIN

LUKE 13:1-9

When suffering comes our way, we naturally ask, "Why did this happen to me?" That is the wrong question. Instead we should ask, "How do I live in a world where suffering and pain simply happen?" Suffering is a mystery. Philosophers and theologians can speculate on the problem of suffering, but no adequate answer has yet been given. We are not here on this earth to speculate about suffering but to fight it. We are here to relieve suffering, not accept it. In Christ's victory on the cross, death has been defeated once and for all. St. Paul exhorts us: "Therefore, my beloved, be steadfast, immovable, always excelling in the work of the Lord, because you know that in the Lord your labor is not in vain" (1 Cor. 15:58, NRSV).

When I was studying preaching in divinity school, I found that one of the difficulties in writing a sermon was that there was no congregation. The sermon was more an academic exercise than a pastoral response to the real needs of people. I was writing the sermon for my professor and preaching it to classmates, but the real flesh and blood people in the pews were absent.

That changed when I got into a parish. Here were real people with real joys and sorrows, real problems and pains, people with spiritual needs, physical needs, and emotional needs together in one congregation.

Anglicans usually sit in the same pew each week, and therefore as I wrote my sermon, I would picture in my mind the people I would be preaching to that Sunday. Who were these people? What were they experiencing in their lives? How were they coping with the ups and downs of daily life?

What I came to realize is that almost every person in any congregation has a burden of some kind. Some people are going through enormous suffering. Others are facing the prospect of death. Others are transitioning from their home to an apartment or even to a care facility. Some are just struggling to survive without going hungry or homeless.

There's the man in the back who is still mourning the loss of his wife who died of Alzheimer's. He's so lonely that he doesn't know what to live for anymore. There's the heartbreak of the young, divorced woman with three children. She wonders how she is going to keep her house without going bankrupt. There's the father struggling with alcoholism who pretends to be a model citizen. There are the parents whose children are using drugs and making bad choices. One family sits in the pew stone-faced, still grieving over their son who was killed in a car accident.

If we look at our own web of connections, all of us should know people who are in pain. Maybe it's a physical disease or mental illness; maybe it's a relationship breakdown or a financial crisis; maybe it's losing a job or a loved one. There is the ache of the human heart, the loneliness of so many.

And when we ask why God made a world with so much suffering, we are never satisfied with the answer – as if there is an answer. What did we do to deserve this? Why does God allow it? Doesn't God care about us?

These questions were asked of Jesus two thousand years ago.

Pilate had killed some Galileans who happened to be innocent of any crime. Why did they die? Were they greater sinners than other people? Or take the case of the eighteen people who died when a tower collapsed and fell on them. Were they the worst sinners in Jerusalem that God singled them out for death? Did they really get what they deserved?

In both cases Jesus denies there is any connection between tragedy and sin. The Galileans were not the worst sinners in Galilee; those killed by the falling tower were not the worst sinners in Jerusalem. So, to the question of whether tragedy or suffering is punishment from God for sin, our Gospel today suggests not.

So, why do tragic things happen in this life? After all, couldn't God have made a better world than one with so much suffering and pain? Philosophers and theologians throughout history have been unable to reconcile a loving God with a suffering world. Many noble attempts have been made – one thinks of C.S. Lewis's *The Problem of Pain*, for example. When his wife died, though, he did not find much comfort in his own book. Rational explanation could not comfort his aching heart.

In the face of some unexplained suffering or calamity, we ask, "Why?" Job asked that question when he lost his health, wealth and children. St. Paul asked that question when he was afflicted with a physical infirmity, he does not say what it was. Voltaire asked that question when he got news of the Lisbon earthquake of November 1, 1755 when thousands of believers worshipping in their churches on All Saints Day were killed. How, Voltaire demanded, could a loving God allow so much suffering?

When we look to Jesus, he doesn't answer the "Why" question. He just assumes that tragedy and suffering are part of the human condition. Bad things happen all the time, whether they are tornadoes or earthquakes or hurricanes, or people getting cancer, or dying of heart disease, or mass-murderers killing innocents on the streets of Paris or in a public school in the United States. Bad things happen because this is the way the world is. And this should not surprise us.

A novel I return to frequently is Thornton Wilder's, *The Bridge of San Luis Rey*. The story takes place in a little village in South America. Each day the villagers must cross a bridge to go to work in the fields. One day, without warning, the bridge snapped. Six persons fell to their deaths. There was a Franciscan friar in the village who decides to investigate the lives of these six people to determine if they deserved to die. The friar studied every aspect of their lives for six years, and in his book came to this conclusion: that those six people were no worse or better than anyone in the village.

The friar's book finds a place at a convent of nuns who care for the deaf, the mentally ill and the dying. The novel ends with the Abbess declaring: "There is a land of the living and a land of the dead and the bridge is love, the only survival, the only meaning."[1]

"Love, the only survival, the only meaning" – that is the key to responding to tragedy and suffering in our world and with ourselves. Tragedy happens. That's the way life is. So, the question is not why bad things happen to good people, but how do we respond to the pain and suffering of the people around us?

Jesus tells us to expect tragedy and suffering as part of our human existence. Life is a "vale of tears" as Roman Catholics put it. In this world, there are heartaches and heartbreaks a plenty. We will never fully know why there is suffering, but we can combat it. In other words, suffering should make us want to do good, the pain of others should bring forth compassion in us, and the tragedies of life should motivate us to trust God, even in the face of things we cannot understand, much less justify. I don't know any other way to deal with suffering except to let it bring out the best in us rather than the worst.

The French writer Albert Camus wrote a story called *The Plague*. The setting is Oran in Algeria, a city suffering from a plague in which residents are dying in great numbers. The novel focuses on how different people in the city respond to the pestilence.

Dr. Bernard Rieux is an atheist, but he believes the plague must be fought, even if it is a losing battle. "For the moment I know this: there are sick people and they need curing." That is all that matters to Dr. Rieux – heal the sick, relieve suffering. That is what it means to be a human being.

Then there is Jean Tarrou. He is an idealist who wants to live for a cause greater than him, and maybe even become a saint, though he, too, does not believe in God. He organizes teams of volunteers to fight the plague, calls people to take responsibility for what is happening to their city, and in the end becomes one of the plague's last victims.

Raymond Rambert is a journalist who tries to escape the city to be with his girlfriend in Paris, but at the last minute decides to stay and fight the plague. He comes to realize that the plague is everyone's business, and he cannot walk away from it and live with himself.

None of these three characters are religious people, yet they all recognize that to be a human being they must fight the forces of disease and suffering that threaten our humanity. They know what must be done. Fighting the plague is their mission because to do anything else is to be less than human.

In Camus's world, death ultimately wins, if not today, then tomorrow, or at the end of history. In the end, all things end in death, no matter how much we protest to the contrary or seek to build a culture of life. However, Christians know that death has been defeated. Even if it continues to have short term victories, death has lost the war. Christians believe in a God who enters the suffering of his people, who is human in every way that we are – in our heartbreak, pain and sorrow. This God is with us now in all who fight suffering and sickness and death. "Where is God in time of plague?" Christians answer, "Look to the ones with outstretched arms and helping hands who come to be among us, to heal us, comfort us, and to save us. God is in them and with them, living and dying for us."

My Uncle Nick was a Veteran of World War II who fought in North Africa. During one brutal barrage of tank fire, my uncle saw several of his comrades die before himself being wounded and shell shocked. He was sent back to the United States for treatment, though I do not think he ever fully recovered from the horror of battle. He rarely talked about his time in North Africa, but he did wonder why he was spared while some of his fellow soldiers got blown to pieces. He could never answer that question, but he did not stop there. He became an active member of the Disabled American Veterans, and at the end of his life was elected Commander of his Post. While he never could answer the "Why?" question, my uncle committed his life to helping other veterans heal and recover from their wounds. He did not speculate but he served.

Suffering happens. It is not for us to ask, "Why" – Why do bad things happen in our world? – but "How?" – How can I relieve the suffering of others? Or to put it another way – How can I be an agent of healing in a hurting world?

When natural disasters happen – tornadoes, earthquakes, fires and hurricanes – relief efforts by total strangers willing to help people who are suffering allow us to see God amidst the tragedy. People who care for people, doctors and nurses who volunteer, rescue workers digging people out of rubble, firefighters battling blazes, the Red Cross and the Salvation Army providing food and water, and in so many other ways we witness the light and love of God to a hurting world.

Yes, I know… life does not always go according to our plans. Sometimes things happen which we do not expect or understand. We get tired and weary, barely holding on, hanging on, for another week or another month. There is pain in the people around us and within our own selves. Sometimes we just don't know if we can cope anymore. However, in the power of God, we can rise above our pain and face the future with faith, hope and love, because Christ has defeated death once and for all. In him the light of God sustains us through the darkness.

Several years ago, I got a call that a young woman confined to a wheelchair and unable to care for herself had finally died after contracting pneumonia. The parents deeply loved their daughter. They did everything they could to save her life, even as the doctors tried to prepare the couple for her death. When she died, they were heartbroken.

I was called to the hospital to be with the family and recite the prayers for the dead over their daughter's body. After anointing her body with oil, I commended her soul to God:

> *Depart, O Christian soul, out of the world;*
> *In the Name of God the Father Almighty who created you;*
> *In the Name of Jesus Christ who redeemed you;*
> *In the Name of the Holy Spirit who sanctifies you.*
> *May your rest be this day in peace,*
> *and your dwelling in the Paradise of God.*[2]

After concluding the prayers and giving both father and mother a big hug, the father, with tears in his eyes, said to me, "She is now singing and dancing with the angels of God."

There are no easy answers to life's heartbreaks except to believe that God is good even when things go bad. This life is not the end but the beginning of new life with God. So, hang in there and keep the faith. Don't stop loving. Don't stop caring. Don't stop showing compassion and kindness and mercy. Don't close your heart to tragedy but open it wide to the people in need. No matter how many towers fall, or tornadoes hit, or terrorists strike, or hurtful things happen in your life, God will prevail against all the heartbreaks and heartaches in our lives and in our world.

March 3, 2013
St. James Westminster Church, London, ON

SALVATION IN NO ONE ELSE

ACTS 4:5-12

Jesus says: "I am the way, and the truth, and the life. No one comes to the Father except through me" (Jn. 14:6, NRSV). Those words seem plain enough, and yet we may wonder if people who are not Christians can be saved. Can a person go to heaven without explicitly believing in Christ as Savior and Lord? The question has profound implications for Christology (who is Jesus and what did he accomplish?) and for evangelism (sharing the Gospel with non-Christians). Often Christians are presented with two extremes: exclusivism which denies salvation to anyone who has not made an explicit faith commitment to Jesus, and pluralism which affirms that Christianity is just one of many ways to God. Is there a third option that affirms Jesus as the only way to God but includes people who have not made an explicit faith commitment? This sermon explores that question.

Back in 1955, sociologist Will Herberg wrote an important book titled *Protestant-Catholic-Jew.* Herberg argued that when people in the United States are asked who they are, their first response is instinctively to say, "I am an American." Then they would add, "I am a Protestant," or "I am a Catholic," or "I am a Jew." About

96 percent of Americans back in 1955 associated themselves with one or another of these groups. Even if they were not explicitly religious, they identified as Protestant, Catholic or Jew.

Today, in 2018, it is hard for any of us to think of our nation as religiously homogeneous. We live in a multi-faith America, and most of us probably know at least one person who is neither Christian nor Jew. Perhaps you know someone who is Muslim or Hindu or Buddhist. Perhaps you know people who were raised Christian but would no longer classify themselves as Christian – after all, the fastest growing group in the United States are people without any religion. Or you may know people who are attracted to native spirituality, holistic healing practices, ethical humanism, earth spirituality, or even atheism or agnosticism. The truth is: Americans are all over the place in their religious beliefs.

While there are about 2.3 billion Christians in the world – the largest of any of the world's religions – there also are about 4.8 billion people who are not Christian. So, what happens to these non-Christians when they die? Do they go to heaven? Are they saved? Do they enjoy eternal life with God? Or do they cease to exist, or even go to hell?

In our text from the Book of Acts, Peter and John are brought before the Jewish Council of Elders and questioned about a healing of a crippled man that took place at the temple gate. "By what power or what name did you do this?" (Acts 4:7, NRSV) they are asked. Peter replies "that this man is standing before you in good health by the name of Jesus Christ of Nazareth... There is salvation in no one else, for there is no other name under heaven given among mortals by whom we must be saved" (Acts 4:10,12, NRSV).

Notice that last line: "There is salvation in no one else, for there is no other name under heaven given among mortals by whom we must be saved" (Acts 4:12, NRSV). That statement may make you feel uneasy. After all, we like our non-Christian friends and we may even have non-Christian relatives and family members. But because they are not Christian, does that mean they are not saved? By that I mean, do non-Christians have any chance of enjoying eternal life with God?

The church has not been of one mind on the issue of salvation, but I think there are two extremes we need to avoid: exclusivism and pluralism.

Exclusivism claims non-Christians cannot be saved because they have not explicitly confessed Jesus Christ as Lord and Savior. If we take this approach, we would be condemning most people who have ever lived on the planet. Why, after all, would a supposedly loving God create people who are destined to suffer for all eternity in hell or even be annihilated? The very idea seems abhorrent and deeply inconsistent with the Christian claim that God is love.

We also need to avoid the other extreme, which is called **pluralism**: that all religions lead equally to God and that Christianity is in no way superior or uniquely true. This is a popular view today, but we find it even in the ancient world. The fourth century rhetorician Symmachus maintained in his debate with St. Ambrose: "It is impossible that so great a mystery should be approached by one road only."

Pluralism is more attractive than exclusivism because it is so reasonable and respectful of differences. Think, for example, of the world's religions as different routes to a mountain summit. Imagine a group of mountain-climbers intent on reaching the summit. There are many routes to the summit, some of them tougher than others, but all of them will get the climbers to the top. For some theologians, that's the way to view the world's religions. Every religion has its own route to God, but in the end they all lead to the summit.

I remember in divinity school, the professor of mission saying to us that the different religions in the world could be equated to different kinds of restaurants. You might enjoy Chinese, or Greek, or Italian or Mexican food. We all have our own taste and preference. In the same way, the professor said, there are different religions for people of different preferences with none better than any other.

On the surface, this point of view seems to make sense. It avoids religious conflict because there is no need to engage in evangelism. To convert a Hindu to Christianity, for example, would be like converting someone who prefers Indian food to Italian food. There would be no point in converting anyone because religion is a matter of taste and preference. Whatever works for you, is fine – different strokes for different folks, as they say.

Pluralism appeals to modern sensibilities because it stresses fairness, equality, personal choice and avoids religious conflict and conversions.

However, pluralism has its problems. There are simply too many verses in Scripture to ignore the claims about Jesus as God's supreme and sufficient revelation. More than that, the pluralist approach insults the major religions by claiming that they are basically teaching the same thing. It disregards what the major religions teach.

Now certainly there are common ethical strands in all the great religions of the world – some variable of the Golden Rule, for example. However, there also are significant differences that cannot be easily reconciled. The Christian belief in one personal God, for instance, cannot be reconciled with Buddhism and Hinduism. The Christian view that God is a God of grace and mercy who can be reached through faith alone is foreign to the Allah of Islam. The Christian claim on the deity of Jesus is rejected by Judaism and other religions, as is the idea of God as Trinity.

Christianity stands or falls by the claim that there really are three persons in one God and that the second of them, the eternal Son of God, became incarnate in Jesus Christ. Of course, there are elements of truth and goodness in other religions, as St. Augustine acknowledged, but Christianity claims that God's revelation in Jesus is the fullness of truth for all people everywhere.

Moreover, Christianity, as we know it, would collapse if Christian churches ever accepted pluralism. One of the reasons early Islam so easily converted the Christians in North Africa and the Middle East was that the churches there were so influenced by Arianism and other heresies that they had no strong incarnational-redemptive Christology. If Christianity is just one way among many, then why not accept Islam? If Jesus is not the supreme and sufficient way to God, then why not accept some other way that seems equally plausible? It made sense for Christians in North Africa and the Middle East to abandon Jesus for Mohammed, just as it makes sense to many mainline Protestants today to put Christianity on a level footing with every other religion.

The result of pluralism is that twenty-first century mainline Protestantism continues to decline, ignores and even rejects evangelism, and adopts what can only be termed a "live and let live" philosophy in which it really doesn't matter what you believe. No wonder mainline Protestantism is in decline as members seek out a stronger belief system in other churches or give up on Christianity entirely.

The early Christians saw a savior risen from the dead, heard a message that said he was the only way to God, and read scriptures that teach truths out of step with culture, and that's why they attracted so many seekers.

So, in the end, pluralism like exclusivism fails. Exclusivism would condemn the vast majority of people that have ever lived on earth, including our non-Christian friends and family members, while pluralism would relegate all religions to a level playing field in which different people search for God in different ways, thus abandoning the supreme and sufficient revelation of God in Jesus.

However, there is another approach called **inclusivism**. This approach accepts Jesus as the only way to God, who embraces and accepts all people of good will, even if their own understanding of God is flawed, or even if they do not believe in God. In this inclusive approach, non-Christians may indeed be saved, but they are saved through Jesus whose love is always more ready to embrace than condemn.

The most notable proponent of this view is the late German Jesuit theologian Karl Rahner who proposed the idea of the "Anonymous Christian" – people of any faith or no faith who lead lives of integrity, act according to conscience, and show mercy, compassion and justice in the world. These people may, without realizing it, live the way of Christ without explicitly believing in Christ. They reflect Christ in their lives even if they don't profess Christ on their lips.

Perhaps you know such people. I know lawyers, for example, who are dedicated to social justice but who are not Christians. They are committed to rectifying wrongs and making the world a better place, and I thank God for them. There are doctors, who volunteer to serve in developing countries among the poorest people on earth, and some of them are not Christians. There are humanitarians, social workers and caregivers, all doing works of mercy and showing love, yet without any explicit belief in Christ. Who would deny that these people are following the way of Jesus even if they have yet to believe in him? These are Karl Rahner's "Anonymous Christians" – people who live the way of Christ without explicitly believing in Christ.

If we take this inclusivist approach to salvation, then our text from Acts takes on new meaning: Jesus is God's attempt to reach out to humanity and embrace all people everywhere. Here is why we say, "there is no salvation in no one else, for there is no other name under heaven given among mortals by whom we must be saved" (Acts 4:12, NRSV). Jesus is God's inclusive love in action – a love that that never stops loving, a love that loves sinners and saints and everyone in between, a love that loves the unlovable, a love that never gives up loving us even when we give up on loving him, a love that even on the cross cries out, "Father, forgive them, for they do not know what they are doing" (Lk. 23:34, NRSV). In his life, death and resurrection, Jesus shows us God's heart with outstretched arms ready to embrace and accept everyone.

A book I first read in high school and has stayed with me over the years is A.J. Cronin's *The Keys of the Kingdom*. It was made into a movie starring Gregory Peck back in 1944. The book is about a Scottish priest named Francis Chisolm who is sent to the China mission in Pai Tan. There he struggles against all sorts of difficulties, including poverty, civil war, and plague. He is assisted by his friend Dr. Willie Tulloch who is an atheist with a generous heart. Willie gives the mission medical supplies and is on the frontline combating the plague. His efforts save the lives of many people, but tragically, he is the last to perish from the disease.

Father Chisolm believes his dear friend Willie Tulloch was a good-hearted man who is now in heaven with the God he could not believe in on earth. One of the nuns at the mission is appalled that any atheist could possibly be in heaven. Father Chisolm responds that Willie could not believe in a God he never knew, but that God judges us by how we live and die, and that Willie lived and died fighting the pain and suffering of other men.

Dear people, anyone saved is saved through Jesus. That is not an exclusive but inclusive statement. Jesus embraces everyone, even people who do not know him, or those who, for whatever reason, find it difficult to believe in him. Even if people do not believe in God off the top of their heads, they still may manifest God from the depths of their lives. They may bear witness to the love, compassion, and mercy of God in a world too resistant to forgive and too eager to condemn. Willie Tulloch is a character from a novel but there are many like him. I would never want to think any such people are not saved.

Yes, Jesus is the only name by which we are saved. All roads lead to Jesus. Whoever we are and wherever we are on our journey of faith, Jesus is always there to love and accept us, just as we are.

April 22, 2018
Church of the Nativity, Scottsdale, AZ

THE CASE FOR RELIGION

MATTHEW 22:34-40

The First Letter of John declares: "Beloved, since God loved us so much, we also ought to love one another. ...Those who say, 'I love God,' and hate their brothers or sisters, are liars; for those who do not love a brother or sister whom they have seen, cannot love God whom they have not seen" (1 Jn. 4:11,20, NRSV). Not everyone shares this view. Some people in the name of religion hate other people, and even kill them. Not all religion is healthy for you. Since September 11, 2001, religion has been under attack by the New Atheists and hardened secularists. Would a world without religion be a better, more enlightened world, free from prejudice, more tolerant and humane? There is little evidence for such a claim. It can even be argued that any humanism apart from God is an inhuman humanism. Despite religion's failures and travesties, this lecture argues that a good case can be made that Christianity is the best way to bring about a civilization of love.

In January 2006, the noted biologist and atheist Richard Dawkins presented a two-part documentary on British television called *Root of all Evil?* In newspaper advertisements for the program, there was a picture of the Manhattan skyline with the caption "Imagine a world without religion." What was the connection? The twin towers of the World Trade Center were conspicuously present.[1]

You do not have to be an atheist to agree with Dawkins that there has been and continues to be a great deal of unhealthy religion throughout history and up to the present day. Many evil things happen in the name of faith. There is a mean streak in religion that can be very destructive in the time it takes to say a prayer.

"We have enough religion to make us hate, but not enough to make us love one another," said Jonathan Swift. My college philosophy professor Dr. William Marra, a devout Catholic, had to admit, "Religion breeds madness." The French thinker Blaise Pascal wrote, "Men never do evil so completely and cheerfully as when they do it from religious convictions." Nobel Prize winner Steven Weinberg put the case against religion succinctly when he observed, "With or without religion, good people can behave well, and bad people can do evil. But for good people to do evil – that takes religion."[2]

In the first Munck Debate held on January 8, 2011 in Toronto, Canada, former British Prime Minister and convert to the Roman Catholic Church Tony Blair squared off against noted atheist and writer Christopher Hitchens. The resolution for debate was: "Religion is a force for good in the world."

Blair, as expected, pointed out all the good things religion does in the world: feeding the hungry, sheltering the homeless, works of mercy that cause more light to shine in the darkness. Hitchens countered that religion does those good things to remedy for all the bad things caused by its teachings. For example, the Roman Catholic Church does a significant amount of relief work in Africa, but that same church declares it a mortal sin for anyone to use a condom to protect against AIDS. In other words, the doctrines of religion cause pious people to do unhealthy, even deadly things.

As an example of religious fanaticism, Hitchens cited Catholic convert Cardinal John Henry Newman who wrote that the church: "holds that it were better for sun and moon to drop from heaven, for the earth to fail, and for all the many millions who are upon it to die of starvation in extremest agony, so far as temporal afflictions goes, than that one soul, I will not say, should be lost, but should commit one single venial sin, should tell one willful untruth, though it harmed no one..."[3]

As an example of religious fanaticism, I am not sure many of us would disagree with Hitchens' characterization of Newman's passage. Yes, Christians believe that any sin, no matter how slight, is an offense against God, unacceptable and intolerable, but if the alternative were untold suffering and pain in the world, would not the commission of one venial sin be a better, more reasonable option?

I am not going to answer that question, though I think Newman is making a valid but difficult point. However, I want to agree with Hitchens that not all religion is good for you. We have this fact on no less an authority than Jesus himself, who lived in an even more religious environment than ours. Jesus regularly lambasted the sickness and prejudices of the religion around him and insisted that the whole basis of religion was found in just two commandments – to love God and to love people.

There is plenty of bad religion. I have had to minister to people who have been broken and battered by it. I don't just mean Islamic suicide bombers or the violence between Hindus and Muslims in India, Al Qaida beheading Christians in North Africa, or even the sexual abuse scandals that have shaken the Roman Catholic Church. For most human beings, these are obvious acts of evil, but there are more subtle and insidious examples that do enormous damage to people.

I remember once speaking with a woman who was in utter fear of going to hell because her church taught that she had to speak in tongues to prove she was fully baptized in the Spirit. Since she could not speak in tongues, she felt anxious about her salvation and wondered why she was not "Spirit-filled" like her friends at church. She sat in my office in tears wondering if she would go to hell.

On another occasion, I was asked to visit a young Roman Catholic couple whose newborn infant died in the hospital. When it seemed clear that the infant was struggling for its life, the couple asked their priest to come to the hospital and baptize the baby. The priest refused, claiming that baptism outside of church was only permitted in the most extraordinary of circumstances, and the possibility of the baby's death was not a sufficient reason.

When the baby died unbaptized, the couple went into a panic because they believed – and the Roman Catholic Church taught at the time – that a deceased unbaptized baby did not go to heaven but to limbo. I had to assure the couple that their baby was in heaven. Limbo was a theological fiction concocted by theologians to deal with sinless but unbaptized infants.

Today, the Roman Catholic Church no longer believes in limbo. It was dropped from the Catholic Catechism. That, however, was no comfort to the couple, who at the time suffered terribly not only in the death of their child but in believing that their baby was not in heaven.

So, I agree with Christopher Hitchens that there has been (and is) a lot of bad religion in the world. Think of the Inquisition, or the brutal execution of Christians by Christians during the time of the sixteenth century Reformation, or the seventeenth century Thirty Years War between Catholics and Protestants, or the strange doctrines and teachings of some Christian churches today. As a priest, I can list many things that are sick and unhealthy about organized religion.

None of this should surprise us, especially if we believe, as

I do, in Original Sin – that human beings are fallen creatures prone to evil and error who don't always get it right. In fact, human beings sometimes do the worst of things out of the best of intentions. That is true not only of Christians and people of any religion. It is also true of people of no religion. Sin or evil is an empirical fact; everyone is infected by it. Alexandre Solzhenitsyn was quite correct that the line between good and evil runs through every human heart. So, it doesn't surprise me that people who are religious, including Christians, do bad things and believe bad teaching.

That said, I continue to believe there is a lot of healthy religion. In fact, the history of Western civilization is the embedding of the Judeo-Christian ethic in the social and moral fabric of nations. Think, for example, how much more civilized, just and compassionate we are today than in the ancient world. Practices the ancient world readily accepted are completely unacceptable to us today.

Almost all Western nations influenced by the Judeo-Christian ethic, and even many American states, have now abolished the death penalty. Even when the death penalty is used, it is only for murder in the most egregious circumstances. That was not the case in the ancient world which used the death penalty to punish a multitude of crimes.

Or take the idea of a social safety net that ensures every person has a basic level of subsistence and care. We think it intolerable that people should starve, sleep on the streets or even go without adequate medical care, but these were all accepted as normal in the ancient world.

The ancient world had vices as we do today. It had prostitution, gambling and drugs, tribal rivalries and blood sports fought even to the death. We might think that human beings today are not that different from our forebears.

But take another look. Look at the churches and their acts of compassion and mercy, or the day care centers, public libraries, hospitals and health care centers, hospices for the dying and shelters for the homeless, transient centers and institutions for the disabled, soup kitchens and women's shelters, colleges and universities, and free public education. In our law courts, people who are poor are treated the same as people who are wealthy – at least theoretically, if not always in fact. Social justice and advocacy programs support the weak and the marginalized and every developed country has a social safety net to support the poor and disadvantaged. Even in sports, though some of them are quite violent, none of them are to the death.

The ancient world had none of this, but gradually, incrementally, unsteadily but surely, they have all taken root in nations that have been influenced by the Judeo-Christian ethic. I challenge you to go to any atheistic nation in the world – North Korea, China, Cuba, or whatever – and find the level of ministry to the intellectual, social, physical and spiritual needs of people that you will find in those countries influenced by the Judeo-Christian ethic. Nor will you find the upholding of human rights, civil liberties, the rule of law and the dignity of the human person.

Search out the histories of the great universities, hospitals, and social service organizations and you will find, more often than not, that they were founded by Christians who had a deep commitment to Jesus Christ and his message of love for God, love for people, and reaching out to those in need.

I would argue to Christopher Hitchens, Richard Dawkins and all the others who attack religion that a world without Christ would not have as much love as there is now. It would be a world without hope and without a future, without a purpose for existence. Human rights and civil liberties only have a solid foundation when a society affirms that all human beings deserve equal treatment under the law because they are created equal by God. Dostoyevsky was right when he wrote that if God does not exist, then everything is permitted. That, of course, means either chaos or totalitarianism.

Look at every society throughout history that claimed to be atheistic and you will not find one that was humane – not the Soviet Union or Communist Eastern Europe or Communist China or Pol Pot's Cambodia or Castro's Cuba. Where do you go to find a humane, compassionate atheistic society that upholds human rights and the dignity of the human person? Nowhere.

I would further argue that the Christian Church, with all its faults, is the one community that cares about people, their spiritual welfare to be sure, but also their physical and social lives. On the whole, it has done greater good than any other organization in the world.

That is why I need to belong to a church. I need to be in a place that keeps my heart caring and feeling full of compassion. I need to be able to reach out to others without undue self-concern. Without that ability to care, I am an incomplete, truncated and unfulfilled human being. The church challenges me, as no other institution does, to feel some of the great pain in the world – not to simply think about the suffering of others but to respond to it – to feel with others their pain and their joy, their shame and their longings, their degradation and their grandeur, their terror and their courage. I believe that to feel deeply is to be in touch with the heart of God.

In my time as a priest, I have served many parishes. In all of them there has been a desire to serve the poor, to care for those who cannot care for themselves, and to be advocates for justice and peace. In the churches I have served, every one of them has cared deeply about mission and outreach, giving considerable sums of money and other assistance to people and causes beyond the church. In one church I served, parishioners donated the money to build a school in India. In another church, they built a social service center that included housing, food and counseling for people on the streets. In still another church, they welcomed a special needs preschool to their campus at no cost. In most of my churches, I, as Rector, had a discretionary fund to be used primarily for people seeking church assistance for rent, medical expenses or food.

People donated gladly because they had a heart for the poor and the less fortunate. They took seriously the command of Jesus to love others as he loves us. "Truly I tell you, just as you did it to one of the least of these who are members of my family, you did it to me" (Mt. 25:40, NRSV). Of the thousands of church members I have served over the years, the vast majority of them took to heart those words of Jesus.

When our focus is on God, it inevitably leads to a concern for our fellow human beings, thinking not just of ourselves but of others, caring for people in need, sharing our resources generously, and helping others, and especially the weakest, the most helpless, and the most vulnerable among us.

This is the strongest case for religion, or at least Christianity. Religion at its best makes us more generous human beings who desire to make this world a better place for everyone. This is where religion crosses the line from being personal and becomes a corporate matter, where my salvation becomes involved with yours, and our salvation becomes involved with the salvation of everybody.

Actual monetary giving verifies the generosity of religious people. Religious people are much more likely to donate to charitable causes – including secular causes – and they give much more than non-religious people by a significant amount. People who attend religious services regularly give significantly more money than those who never attend religious services. They also give their time, being far more likely to volunteer.

Giving of our time, talent and treasure are fundamental to the Christian life – and not just Christians helping Christians but sharing their resource with any in need. Jesus never let religion become a purely private matter. You cannot read the Gospels of Matthew and Luke without realizing how much Jesus emphasized good works – "For I was hungry and you gave me food, I was thirsty and you gave me something to drink, I was a stranger and you welcomed me, I was naked and you gave me clothing, I was sick and you took care of me, I was in prison and you visited me" (Mt 25:35-36, NRSV). Similarly, Luke's Gospel has several parables on mercy and compassion – the Good Samaritan (Lk. 10:25-37) and Lazarus at the gate (Lk. 16:19-31).

"You shall love your neighbor as yourself" Jesus says (Mk. 12:31, NRSV). This is not an option for Christians. It is a command. This is what Christians do – they love others, reach out to the hurting, relieve suffering, and make the world a better place by their being in it. The only true spiritual life is one that is shared.

I can testify that my Christian faith makes me a more generous, joyful, self-giving person, more caring and compassionate than I might otherwise be if I were not a Christian. Following Jesus means following the way of love for others, being concerned about the needs of the world, caring for the planet, and living a responsible life. I doubt I would do any of these things, at least not as passionately and wholeheartedly, were I not a Christian or did not believe in God. What I do know is that God gives the strength, power and grace to live as a follower of Jesus and to bring a little more light into this sometimes-dark world.

At the core of the Christian life is the belief that God loves everyone everywhere without exception. In the end, what matters is not how we think about God but the way we love God, and we love God by loving people. This is a cardinal axiom of the Christian faith.

Leo Tolstoy tells a beautiful story in his tale, *Where Love Is, God Is*. A dream alerts Martin the cobbler that Jesus will visit him before the next day is out. In the course of the day Martin encounters and aids people in need, but at the end of the day Martin goes to bed bitterly disappointed that Jesus never came to his door. In a second dream, Jesus appears to Martin and explains that each time Martin welcomed a needy person into his shop, he had welcomed Jesus himself.

That, I believe, is what Christians seek to do – welcome the stranger as we would welcome Jesus himself. We care for the hungry, the homeless, and people in need of assistance, whether financial or spiritual, as if we were responding to Jesus at our door. It is no accident that in addition to having the traditional seven spiritual works of mercy, the church also has the seven corporal works of mercy: To feed the hungry; to give drink to the thirsty; to clothe the naked; to shelter the homeless; to visit the sick; to visit the imprisoned; and to bury the dead. These practices are as much a part of our faith as receiving Holy Communion or confessing our sins. They are integral to the Christian way of life.

So, yes, not all religion is healthy for you, but in this less than perfect world Christianity is the best option – not because the church doesn't make mistakes or get it wrong at times, or even contributes unwittingly to hurt and pain in the world. I acknowledge all that. In the end, however, being a follower of Jesus is the best way to bring about a "civilization of love" where the dignity of the human person is affirmed, valued and upheld.

October 26, 2014, Revised April 2020
St. John's Anglican Church, Elora, ON

PART THREE

FANNING THE FIRE: THE SPIRITUAL JOURNEY

Episcopal scholar Diana Butler Bass has claimed we are living "the Fourth Great Awakening in American religion." That may seem odd since Christianity, and especially North American mainline Protestant churches, are in steep decline. Dr. Bass knows this full well. In her book *Christianity After Religion*, she acknowledges: "The old religious world is failing, but the Spirit is stirring anew."

If we accept, as I do, that there is a Fourth Great Awakening happening now, then preachers will want to make spirituality a major theme in their preaching. Spirituality is a notoriously nebulous term, difficult to define, with multiple meanings. My approach throughout these sermons is to follow Archbishop William Temple in his book *Nature, Man and God*, and define spirituality as our relationship with God, the world, and other human beings. Spirituality is not simply what we do with our solitude, as Alfred North Whitehead categorized religion, but involves awe, wonder and mystery at the created life around us and within us.

At the heart of spirituality is an openness to God and other people. This implies a certain insecurity and vulnerability because we let down our defenses and we make ourselves available to others in a way that may go against our self-interest.

These sermons are designed to promote an open spirituality: drawing people to God, but also helping them find their purpose in life and living for something greater than themselves. While life can be difficult for the best of us, a spirituality grounded in Jesus Christ assures us that in the midst of winter, spring is coming; in the midst of pain, love is going to triumph; in the midst of dying, we are moving toward eternal life.

Spirituality 101 describes spirituality as our connection with God, nature and other human beings. Spirituality is being aware of the moment, a kind of mindfulness, but seeing God in all things and all things in God. It is experiencing the divine in the human, the heavenly in the earthly, and appreciating the mystery and majesty of life. At the heart of the universe is not a black hole that drains the life from us, but holy love that embraces and caresses our existence.

The Mysterious Miraculous God begins by admitting that not all spiritual experience is comforting, as philosopher A.J. Ayer discovered. And yet, almost all human beings will claim some kind of spiritual experience, even if they are not believers in God. How do we interpret our spiritual experiences, make sense of them, and respond to them?

The Mystery of Unanswered Prayer is relevant to anyone who has made a request to God which seemed not to be answered. Even devout Christians may lose faith when their prayers seem to go unanswered. And yet, as the sermon points out, God does answer every prayer, but not always in the way we would want.

The Human Paradox is an Ash Wednesday sermon which explores our mortality. Someday we are going to die, and our body will turn to ashes. This is not a depressing fact for Christians since we believe that death is not the end of life, but the beginning of new life. We are indeed dust and ashes but also precious children of God.

A Tale of Two Characters is a Maundy Thursday sermon comparing Judas and Peter. Judas betrayed Jesus, while Peter denied him. And yet, Peter became a saint while Judas committed suicide. What made the difference?

Earth Spirituality is a Harvest Thanksgiving sermon preached in London, Ontario. Canada is a nation rich in natural resources, but the use of those resources, and how they affect the environment is a hotly debated issue, especially in light of the carbon emissions from the Alberta oils sands. Rather than offer any solution to what is a highly complex topic, this sermon provides an earth spirituality or a theological understanding of the environment.

My Jesus Moment deals with a near-death experience that unexpectedly occurred right after the Christmas holidays. After the specialist reviewed my test results, he came into the office and said, "You had a Jesus moment." In other words, I almost died. From that experience I came to realize that there comes a grace-filled moment when we confront the reason we are on this earth and the time we have left to make the most of our lives.

Reaching Your Full Potential is on how we can be everything that God calls us to be. Often our own inadequacies hold us back from achieving our full potential. We get plagued by self-doubt and focus on what we can't do. Instead, we need to focus on who we are – a child of God who has a purpose for living by making a positive difference in the world.

Get Out of the Boat is on conquering our fear and being willing to do what we think we can't if we believe God is calling us to do it. Often it is not a lack of ability that holds us back from achieving our potential, but a lack of faith.

Choosing Who You Become is on the choices we make and how

they affect our character. We all want to be persons of integrity, living as authentic human beings, true to ourselves and our God. Are our beliefs and behavior in sync? Do we practice what we profess? This sermon challenges listeners to consider whether their lifestyle reflects their life. Are they being true to themselves by the choices they make on a daily basis?

SPIRITUALITY 101

2 PETER 1:16-18; MATTHEW 17:1-9

You don't have to be a Christian to experience the mystery and majesty of life, or even sense a divine presence on earth. "The world is filled with the grandeur of God," wrote the priest-poet Gerald Manley Hopkins. The experience of mystery, wonder and awe is the foundation of the spiritual life. Without one's heart being touched by the wonder of life and the mystery of love it is impossible to believe in God. In some sense, every believer in God is a mystic. The French philosopher Gabriel Marcel put it succinctly when he noted that life is a mystery to be lived, not a problem to be solved.

As a priest, one of the things that has amazed me is how many people will claim they have had some kind of spiritual experience – and not just Christians or churchgoers but people who would not classify themselves as religious. There are these unexpected, grace-filled moments in our lives that cannot be rationally explained but are real, nonetheless. There is an increasing yearning today to find inner peace and contentment, and to experience a greater harmony with the world around us. In our better moments, we know that there is more going on in the world, more going on in us, than science or technology has been able to grasp.

Perhaps this is one of the reasons why you are here this morning. You have some inarticulate, nevertheless real desire to connect with a wider spiritual universe. You yearn to establish a felt relationship with the deepest meaning and powers governing life. You probably would not say it that way, but you would say, "Yes, I want to know more. My life isn't some psychological problem to be solved; it's a mystery to be enjoyed." It's as if there really is someone, something out there, or in here, trying to get through to you.

With all the people today who claim to be "spiritual but not religious," church remains one place where we have the courage to explore the mystery, to venture forth into that too little discussed territory called the transcendent or divine – what Christians call God.

If you ever have had some kind of mystical or spiritual experience, the Christian tradition is here to affirm you in your spiritual journey. Mystical experience is at the very heart of our faith. Think about it. What is it that most of us want from church? Why do we come to this place week after week and go through this strange ritual we call Eucharist? The answer, I think, is quite basic: we come to experience the blessing of something greater than us that not only demands the best from us but brings out the best in us. For the truth is, unless we human beings serve something greater than ourselves, we will inevitably become something less than ourselves. Worship of the holy God is the most human thing we can do.

Biblical religion is decidedly experiential. People in the Bible do not just think about God; they experience God. Look at today's Gospel. Jesus and three of his disciples go up on a mountain and the disciples awaken to see Jesus arraigned in a dazzling white garment. They hear a voice from heaven: "This is my beloved Son, the Beloved; with him I am well pleased; listen to him!" (Mt. 17:5, NRSV). Later, in his letter, Peter writes with deep feeling about this experience: "For we did not follow cleverly devised myths when we made known to you the power and coming of our Lord Jesus Christ, but we had been eyewitnesses of his majesty. For he received honor and glory from God the Father when the voice was conveyed to him by the Majestic Glory, saying, 'This is my Son, my Beloved, with whom I am well pleased.' We ourselves heard this voice from heaven, while we were with him on the holy mountain" (2 Pet. 1:16-18, NRSV).

Something very strange happened on the Mount of the Transfiguration – something outside ordinary experience. Peter, James and John saw in Jesus a reflection of God like they had not seen in anyone else. It was blasphemous for any good Jew to refer to a human being as God. And yet, here on the mountain Jesus is revealed as the Son of God – beyond all the conventional categories of the Jewish understanding of God.

A sixteen-year-old Jewish schoolboy studying at Rugby, was in his room one afternoon when he claimed to see a figure in white who called him to be his follower. The boy believed this figure was Jesus. He knew nothing about Jesus. He was raised a good Jew, but he knew the figure was Jesus. The experience filled him with an overpowering joy, and he found that he had become a Christian as a result of a totally unexpected spiritual experience. That experience would control his whole life, recounted Hugh Montefiore, one of the most scholarly and well-respected bishops of the Church of England in the twentieth century.[1]

Many of us may not have had that kind of dramatic experience, but all of us have our stories to share about those moments – unexpected, grace-filled moments – when some divine power, some holy presence – call it God if you will – burst into our lives in some amazing way. Reflect on your life and you will probably remember moments that were out of the ordinary, moments that were deeply spiritual, even mystical, where you were transported outside the realm of rational experience.

As an eleven-year-old boy, I was with a group of classmates and teachers who climbed a mountain in upstate New York at Harriman State Park. On the way to the summit, we stopped along this mountain creek churning down. Around us were the black-green trees and the soft black-green moss on the rocks and banks. Out of the small brilliant blue patches of sky above came these shafts of white light which turned the splashing waters into showers of diamonds. It was an almost mystical experience, and I thought to myself that in a place like this, it's easy to believe in God.

While in university in New York, a friend of mine invited me to attend Corpus Christi Roman Catholic Church for Easter High Mass. Corpus Christi is the church where Thomas Merton worshipped until he entered Gethsemane Abbey to become a monk. That Easter Sunday the choir sang a Palestrina Mass. As the polyphony of sounds intertwined with each other, built and rebuilt, it took my breath away. I felt as if my heart, lungs and stomach had come into the physical grip of God. The Easter message was mine! God really did raise Jesus from the dead! God did that. God tore that rock away from the tomb and called forth Jesus of Nazareth and set him on high. I knew that. It really happened!

This past summer, Heather, Allison and I visited Jackson Hole, Wyoming where we got to see the Grand Tetons. Seeing these snow-capped mountains took my breath away, and I thought for sure this was a glimpse of heaven. Then I thought, "Gary, you haven't seen anything yet!"

If we take the time to really see our world and look around us, we may begin to see glimpses of God right before us. These are the "big picture" moments, the rich intervals of stillness and of calm, the times of knowing that the Lord is God, of sensing the Holy Spirit at work in your heart.

Two years before I came to St. Bartholomew's, my sister-in-law Jane discovered that she had a particularly aggressive form of breast cancer. Jane was a very tender person: incredibly sweet but not particularly courageous. The news that she had cancer frightened her terribly. The first course of treatment was a radical mastectomy. She hesitated but finally decided to go through with the surgery. A few days after the surgery she said to Heather, "I never knew I had such strength. God is working in my life, I know it."

Despite the best efforts of the doctors, Jane fought a losing battle with the cancer, which eventually spread into her liver and lungs. The doctors told her, "Jane, we're not talking cure anymore." And yet, as Jane told us the news, there was a calm trust in God we had never sensed in her before. Where does a person gain that inner peace? Well, Jane had a loving family, supportive friends, and most of all, a deep faith in Christ. Even amid terminal cancer, one can be transfigured.

I have been in the ministry almost twenty-two years, and in that time, I have seen just about everything that can happen to a human being. I have also seen with my own eyes the transforming power of Jesus Christ to bring peace to the dying, hope to the despondent, courage to the weak and direction to the aimless. I have seen lives that I thought were spiritually dead rebound with new life. I have seen people whom I would have dismissed as hopeless turn their lives around because they found a reason for living that transcended their petty selves. It is grace, amazing grace. I have known such grace, and you have, too.

Soon we will leave this church to re-enter an often busy, hectic, anxious world where life can be difficult for the best of us. We leave with the same problems we came with today. But as we leave, we have been to the mountaintop. We have seen our Lord transfigured before us. In ordinary bread and wine, the extraordinary presence of God comes to us in Eucharist. We receive God's blessing. We feel God's touch. We experience God's peace. We know we are God's beloved children. Of this we are certain: God's love will never fail us, not now, not ever.

February 6, 2005
St. Bartholomew's, Poway, CA

THE MYSTERIOUS
MIRACULOUS GOD

MARK 9:2-9

Spiritual experience or an encounter with the supernatural is more common than we may think. When we pause and reflect on our lives, we probably have had some kind of spiritual experience. While not all spiritual experiences lead to belief in God, they can be the basis for re-evaluating our life, values and priorities. For Christians, spirituality moves beyond the nebulous with its focus on Jesus. In Jesus, the transcendence and immanence of God are united. As Bishop John Robinson put it: "Jesus is the human face of God."

Have you ever had an encounter with God, or an experience with the supernatural? Remarkably, even in this secular age of ours, many people say they have had a spiritual or even mystical experience that defies rational explanation.

Take, A.J. Ayer, for example. He was one of the most militant – and brilliant – British atheists of the twentieth century, an Oxford philosopher, and a leader in the school of logical positivism which claimed that anything that could not be logically proved or empirically verified was rubbish.

In 1988, A. J. Ayer fell seriously ill, had to be taken to the hospital where his heart stopped for four minutes, and it seemed as if he had died. Thanks to the work of his doctors, his heart began to beat again, and he made a remarkable recovery.

By his own account, Professor Ayer claimed to have had a death experience – not a near death experience but an experience of being dead. In fact, his first words uttered to a friend at his bedside upon his awakening were, "Did you know that I was dead?" He then recounted what he had experienced when his heart stopped.

He said, "I was confronted by a red light, exceedingly bright, and very painful even when I turned away from it. I was aware that this light was responsible for the government of the universe. Among its ministers were two creatures who had been put in charge of space." Ayer went on to describe the two creatures and his attempt to communicate with them but to no avail. He became desperate when they ignored him. Then, suddenly, his experience ended.[1]

A.J. Ayer, the logical positivist, the Oxford professor who would, at one time, have dismissed anyone saying such outlandish things, came to believe that "there is rather strong evidence that death does not put an end to consciousness." He was not prepared to believe in God, but he was now open to the notion that our personal identity survives us when the body dies. How and in what manner he was not sure, but he could no longer dismiss the possibility.

In 1989, less than one year after his death experience, A.J. Ayer died. In many ways he reflects the secular but spiritual mindset that refuses to believe we cease to exist upon our death, though at the same time being reluctant to believe in a personal God who makes eternal life possible.

What fascinates me about A.J. Ayer is that although he

never considered becoming a Christian or joining any church, at least towards the end of life he became increasingly open to the supernatural – to exploring a dimension of being beyond logic and empirical fact.

We hear talk these days about the decline of institutional religion, how churches are losing members and how the nation itself is less religious today than it was twenty-five years ago, with belief in God in decline. People will often say they are "spiritual but not religious" or even "secular but spiritual" meaning organized religion is no longer an option.

That may be true, but the reality is that people today are perhaps more spiritual than they have ever been in the history of our country. Think how "mindfulness" is now being widely encouraged among professionals in business, medicine and law. Think how many people now practice Yoga, Tai Chi, or Zen meditation. Think of all the television programs and movies that have supernatural or spiritual themes. In our postmodern world, logic has given way to intuition, thinking to feeling, rationalism to mystery.

Amid what might be termed a spiritual revival, the church can reach seekers and even hardened secular-minded people, not by stressing dogma but by offering them an experience of God. That experience might come through worship, or fellowship, or service to the poor, but I think our focus should be Jesus. He is at the heart of our life as Christians and without him there is no faith.

Think about it. A young man whose father is a carpenter grows up working in his father's shop. He has some kind of religious experience in the desert, then submits to baptism by an itinerant preacher by the name of John. He hears a voice from heaven and then begins preaching, teaching and healing the people in the countryside. He gathers a group of disciples around him but also attracts other followers, including women. He does this for about three years. Then he is arrested, tried, convicted and sentenced to death. He is executed along with two common thieves. He is then buried in a borrowed tomb.

That should be the end of the story. And yet, here we are today in church celebrating his life, death and resurrection, believing that he lives like no other person who has ever lived on earth, and joining about 2.3 billion other Christians around the world who call this Jesus Lord and Savior, and in some sense even God.

What is it about Jesus that so captivates us, enraptures us, draws to him, even when we may resist following him?

When I served a parish in Lancaster County, Pennsylvania, there was a young woman who would come to worship with us, always sitting in the last pew. Karen was a seeker, someone who had not made a firm commitment to any particular faith or church, but she was drawn to the Episcopal Church by the Eucharist. One Sunday I spoke to her after the service. "So what brings you to St. Thomas?" I asked her.

"A feeling," she said. "A feeling of being drawn toward something, someone, a feeling of which I wasn't really aware until last Sunday. It was after communion when everyone was standing as usual and singing, 'He is Lord. He is Lord. He is risen from the dead, and he is Lord.' I just got taken up."

"Taken up?" I asked.

"Yes. Like taken away. Like I lost consciousness, or maybe gained consciousness. It was if I were alone, standing in the church. Just me, bathed in this soft, warm wonderful light. When I came to, we finished singing, and I was genuinely surprised to see people standing there with me, in the church. And I had to sit down to regain my composure. And I smiled because I knew that I believed in Jesus."

What would you say about such an experience? Was it an over-active imagination or an authentic mystical experience? All

I know is that from that moment on, Karen could not imagine life without Jesus. Jesus had touched her life in some special way, and she became a committed Christian, eventually finding her way to a Mennonite church.

I suspect that most of us are here in this church because Jesus has in some way touched our lives. We are here, not because religiosity has gotten the best of us, but because Jesus somehow draws us to him, into his life, death and resurrection, into the mystery of the God-made-man or God incarnate.

The truth is, we are all created to be mystics in some sense. We can't manipulate those moments or force them upon us, but they come as gift in the most unexpected ways. With Jesus there are visions, there are wonderful, mystical, sometimes baffling, maybe even frightening moments when he gives us the gift of sight, when the veil separating us from God is pulled back, even if briefly, and we see as we have never seen before.

I was an eleven-year old boy in a Catholic military school – my first year away from home and having a miserable time of it. There was strict discipline, lots of marching, and endless routine. Except when we had free time (which was not much), the cadets were always in uniform with shirts and ties. One cold November afternoon while on the marching field, I somehow lost my tie. I don't know what happened or how I lost it, but at dinner that evening, I showed up without wearing a tie. As soon as I sat down at the dinner table, a nun came up to me and asked, "Where is your tie?" I said I lost it. "What," the nun said, "there will be no dinner for you until you find that tie. If you don't find it, God help you."

So, off I went into the darkness of that marching field (there were no lights, and this was mid-November) looking for a black tie. I walked around the marching field several times and couldn't find anything. In fact, I couldn't even see the ground because it was so dark. I was afraid, terrified about what would happen if

I came back without my tie. I was also feeling helpless, at my wits' end because despite my best efforts, I could not find the tie anywhere.

Feeling a mixture of panic and despair I began walking back to the dining hall to face the wrath of the nun. I started to cry, and then I stopped for a moment and prayed, "Jesus, help me find my tie. If you are there, if you really are God, please let me find my tie."

Then, as I continued walking to the dining hall in the pitch black of a mid-November night, I tripped on a rock and fell to the ground. And my hand landed right on my tie.

Now what do you think? Was it a miracle or an accident, an answer to prayer or a random occurrence? I know what I believe. From that moment on, I have never doubted the existence of God and I have never wavered in my faith in Jesus. In fact, that incident, I am certain, played a large part in my desire to become a priest. God was all too real for me ever to ignore him in my life.

I wish A.J. Ayer had known the Jesus I experienced on that cold, dark mid-November night. Ayer's encounter with that red light was dark and foreboding, but Jesus fills us with his light and love, prodding us to draw near to him who has drawn near to us.

Hear the good news, dear people: Whoever you are and wherever you are on your journey of faith, Jesus loves you always and forever.

February 11, 2018
Church of the Nativity, Scottsdale, AZ

THE MYSTERY OF
UNANSWERED PRAYER

2 CORINTHIANS 12:2-10

*St. Paul tells us that God is our "Abba" or "Father" (Rom 8:15,
NRSV). However, what are we to think when the Father does
not answer our prayer the way we requested? The key is not to
become angry or bitter but to open ourselves to the will of God
whose ways are not our ways. God never promises to spare us
from hardships, difficulties or trials. There is heartache and
heartbreak a plenty in this world, as any human being knows.
The key is to believe that even when things go bad, God is good.
St. Paul says: "My grace is sufficient for you, for power is made
perfect in weakness" (2 Cor. 12:9, NRSV).*

Months before we tried to have children, Heather and I prayed
every night for a healthy, normal child. Then came the news.
Heather was pregnant. It was Gospel to our ears. For the next
eight months we continued to pray that our baby – boy or girl,
it did not matter – would be born healthy and normal. We had
no reason to expect otherwise. After all, we were good people,
religious people, doing the Lord's work, even at personal sacrifice

on our part. We trusted that God would hear our prayer, and not only hear but answer.

It was not to be. Within an hour of her birth, the doctor told us that Allison had Down syndrome. We were stunned. What had gone wrong? We prayed that God would give us a healthy, normal baby, and we did not get one. Why?

The days after Allison's birth were not easy. What was especially difficult was when the doctor told us that from the moment of conception Allison was destined to have Down syndrome by virtue of an extra chromosome in her genetic make-up. For almost nine months, we had been praying for an outcome that already had been biologically determined otherwise.

So, what was the point of our prayers? Were we simply engaging in self-delusion or wishful thinking? Our prayers seemed to be futile – a kind of cruel hoax by a God who did not care about us.

Although we loved Allison as soon as she came into our world, we found ourselves struggling with the meaning of prayer. Some of our Christian friends told us that we should have been more specific in our prayers. Tell God precisely what you want done. After all, they said, doesn't Jesus tell us to pray for specific things? "Ask, and it will be given you; search, and you will find; knock, and the door will be opened for you" (Mt. 7:7, NRSV). We are to pray for our material needs – "Give us this day our daily bread" (Mt. 6:11, NRSV) – and our spiritual well-being – "Stay awake and pray that you may not come into the time of trial" (Mt. 26:41, NRSV). We are "to pray always and not to lose heart" (Luke. 18:1, NRSV). Jesus flatly says: "So I tell you, whatever you ask for in prayer, believe that you have received it, and it will be yours" (Mk. 11:24, NRSV). Does this mean that every unanswered prayer indicates a lack of faith?

This was the dilemma confronting the friends of David Watson, the English priest and evangelist. Watson had long been involved in the healing ministry, but at the age of fifty he was diagnosed with pancreatic cancer. He, along with family and friends, prayed for a miracle. Prominent pastors flew from California to London to pray and lay hands on Watson. English bishops visited Watson, prayed for him; gave him communion, anointed him with oil, laid hands on him – all seemingly to no avail. Watson died at about the time the doctors predicted. Healing never occurred. Why, his friends asked, didn't God heal him? There certainly was no lack of faith.

As I reflected on David Watson's death, I came to understand what happened to him was not the exception but the norm. Healings, even miracles happen, but they are not as common as we would like to believe. Many of us may wonder where was God when we prayed for healing for ourselves or a loved one, and the healing did not occur? Does God hear our prayers? If God does hear, then why doesn't God answer? What good are our prayers, anyway?

C.S. Lewis told the story of a woman whose thighbone was eaten through with cancer. It took three people to move her into bed. The doctors predicted a few months of life; the nurses, who knew better, a few weeks. A priest came to her bedside, laid hands on her and prayed. A year later the patient was walking and the man who took the last X-ray photos was saying, "it's a miracle."

On the other hand, this same C.S. Lewis experienced severe depression when his beloved wife Joy died of cancer. His prayers for her recovery were not answered. She died as the doctors predicted. Why had God not answered his prayers? In his journal, later published in a book titled *A Grief Observed*, Lewis called God a "Cosmic Sadist" for not healing his wife.

Truthfully, healings may be less common than we want to believe. I know a priest who confessed that he does not pray specifically for the healing of persons who are seriously ill. He prays for relief of pain, strength to bear suffering, guidance for doctors, or support for loved ones, but not for outright healing. "I have prayed for the healing of too many who have died," he said to me.

So, how do we deal with the reality that not all our prayers are answered? Perhaps we have to expand our view of prayer. After all, the essence of prayer is request, and a request may or may not be granted. True prayer is never a matter of manipulating God to do something that God would not otherwise do.

That said, I believe God hears every prayer, whether we see "results" or not. Moreover, I believe that God answers every prayer, though not always in the way we want or expect.

My understanding of prayer has evolved over the years and is now rooted in three principles which help me grapple with the mystery of unanswered prayer.

First, prayer requires the faith to let God be God. St Paul tells us, "For now we see in a mirror, dimly" (1 Cor. 13:12, NRSV). In this life, at least, faith substitutes for sight.

Years ago, Anglican priest J.B. Phillips wrote a little book entitled *Your God Is Too Small!* That is often the case when we pray. We feel sure the more we believe, the more God will do as we ask. But that's not prayer! That is magic. We should not place our preconceived plans before God and expect God to rubber stamp them. In prayer we do not lay our demands before God. We do not negotiate or bargain with God. Instead, we open ourselves to the mystery of God's will for our lives.

One of the most common tendencies among some Christians today is to trivialize prayer by asking not for God's will to be done, but for our own ego preferences to be satisfied. God becomes the agent of the American dream: the guarantor of the good life – a sort of divine insurance policy against anything bad happening to us. The result is that many of us, unwittingly, have bought into the "health and wealth Gospel" in which we give God our prayers and God gives us prosperity; we give God homage and God gives us health; we give God praise and God gives us success. However, if the health and wealth Gospel were true, then Jesus would never have been crucified.

You don't think of the sports section of a newspaper as having anything to do with prayer, but there was an interesting article in the *San Diego Union Tribune* last year. The New York Yankees were playing the Red Sox in the play-offs at Boston. On Sunday morning, Joe Torre, the manager of the Yankees, did what he always does on Sunday, he attended Mass at a local Roman Catholic church. After the Mass, Joe went to a side altar to light a candle and say a prayer – something he frequently does. A die-hard Boston Red Sox fan recognized Joe and said, "I hope you're not praying for those Yankees to beat us in the game today." Joe looked at the man and replied that he never prayed about winning baseball games. There were too many more important things to pray for.

Joe Torre refused to trivialize prayer. After all, if he prayed that the Yankees should win the game, then he would also be praying that the Red Sox should lose. But does God really take sides in baseball? In any case, the real question is not whether God is on our side, but whether we are on God's side.

Abraham Lincoln understood that even where seemingly clear-cut issues are at stake, we need to be incredibly careful about assuming which side God is on. During the Civil War Lincoln wrote these words in his diary: "I have been driven many times to my knees by the overwhelming conviction that I had nowhere else to go. My own wisdom and that all about me seemed insufficient for the day."

We have only one God, and our task is to discern his will and follow it. Of course, we can still pray to God with our requests, but we must always let God be God. Keep in mind that Jesus, who in the Garden of Gethsemane began his prayer with a request – "Abba, Father, for you all things are possible; remove this cup from me" – but ended in an act of faithful submission, "yet, not what I want, but what you want" (Mk. 14:36, NRSV). Jesus let God be God. So should we.

This leads to the second principle. In prayer we must never forget that God's ways are not our ways. The prophet Isaiah reminds us: "For my thoughts are not your thoughts, nor are your ways my ways, says the Lord. For as the heavens are higher than the earth, so are my ways higher than your ways, and my thoughts than your thoughts" (Isa. 55:8-9, NRSV).

Severe suffering may tempt us to doubt God or even deny God's existence. Job was tempted to curse God, but he refused. Still, Job could not reconcile God's goodness with his suffering. The marvel of the story is that when Job is finally vindicated, God does not tell him why his prayers were not answered. God makes no apologies. God simply reminds Job that the majesty of the Creator surpasses the comprehension of the creature. And then, God concludes, "Shall a faultfinder contend with the Almighty? Anyone who argues with God must respond" (Job 40:2, NRSV). Of course, Job cannot.

"Why God, have you allowed this suffering to come upon me?" We ask that question when we cannot fathom the rhyme or reason for God's ways. It is then that we may begin to second guess God, wonder whether God is really God, or if God exists at all! After all, if God cares about us, then why doesn't God respond to all the pain and suffering and injustice in this world?

There is a mystery here – a mystery which must be lived rather than understood. Prayer as both the Hebrew Scriptures and the New Testament understand it always begins in a spirit of humility: the acknowledgement that we are not God, and therefore cannot presume to tell God what to do or when to do it. True prayer requires humility. That we know in part; but God knows in whole; that there is more to life than we can possibly know, and more to the universe than we can possibly grasp. So, there are times in our lives when we must live with the mystery rather than demand answers. Yes, we can and should make our requests boldly to God, but we must never presume to demand that God give us what we want when we want it. That, in fact, is what it means to live by faith

In prayer we need to let God be God – for God's ways are not our ways. These two principles are supported by a third: "All things work together for good for those who love God" (Rom. 8:28, NRSV).

As a priest I know full well that many people suffer terribly with all kinds of burdens too heavy to bear. Some people never move beyond their pain. Their stories are heartbreaking as they ask, "Why has God allowed this to happen?" I cannot answer that question. Nobody can. Suffering, like prayer, is a mystery.

In our lesson from First Corinthians, St. Paul says that three times he prayed that a certain affliction would be taken from him. It was not. Instead, he received the assurance, "My grace is sufficient for you, for power is made perfect in weakness" (2 Cor. 12:9, NRSV).

Sometimes, in fact, it is precisely when we are weak and most vulnerable that the power of God is made manifest in our lives. Franklin Roosevelt was a much more compassionate and caring human being – traits that would make him a great President – after his bout with polio. Candace Lightner founded MADD – Mothers Against Drunk Drivers – after her thirteen-year-old daughter, Cari, was killed by a drunk driver. And although the British evangelist David Watson died at the peak of his ministry at the age of fifty-one, his journal during the battle with cancer,

Fear No Evil, is one of the most inspiring and honest books of a Christian dealing with a terminal illness that has ever been written. Countless people suffering from cancer have taken comfort in Watson's words.

There are no answers on why God does not answer our prayers the way we would hope. In the end, we simply must trust that God is good even when things go bad. "For God so loved the world that he gave his only Son," (Jn. 3:16, NRSV) means that God loves us even in the most difficult moments of our lives. God doesn't give up on us. Neither should we give up on ourselves.

When our daughter Allison was born, she had to remain in the hospital after Heather was discharged. Allison, like so many Down syndrome newborn infants, was diagnosed with a hole in her heart, and doctors wanted her to remain in the hospital pending any surgery. Going home without our newborn baby was agony for both Heather and me. The car was all set up with a baby seat, but there was no baby to bring home. Both of us were in tears as we began the drive home.

Finally, I said to Heather, let's go to our favorite state park and try to recoup. So, we traveled about an hour and parked near a waterfall. We sat down on the grass just looking at the waterfall, hearing the birds chirp, and enjoying the fall colors on the trees. We sat silently, quietly, not saying a word to one another.

Then, all of a sudden, I felt an overwhelming peace that everything would be all right. I was not to worry, because Allison would be well, and not only well but a blessing to us and to those around her. I turned to Heather and told her about what I had experienced. I was sure it was from God, who, despite our difficult situation, was with us still.

And you know something? It did turn out all right. Allison was released from the hospital the next day without any need for surgery. She has grown into a beautiful young woman who gives her parents immense joy and blesses those around her. We did not know it then, but God gave us a great gift in giving us Allison, and to this day we continue to marvel at God's mysterious and grace-filled ways.

Today, twenty-six years after the birth of our daughter Allison, Heather and I cannot imagine life without her. She has brightened our lives immeasurably and shown me as a priest what it means to love unconditionally with a simple child-like trust. There have been difficult times, to be sure, but we would never want to undue Allison's birth. What seemed like an enormous burden at the time has turned into a great blessing.

So, does God answer prayer? Of course! Does God answer our prayers always in the way we would like? Of course not! God, who is our Father in heaven, like any loving parent, may respond to our requests with a variety of answers: yes, no, not now, or give us something entirely different. And sometimes, like a parent, God weeps over what happens to his children. So, we need to hang in there when our prayers are not answered as we want. After all, prayer is not magic. It is communion with the God who loves us, and who never stops loving us. Prayer is the confidence that God always comes through, even in ways we cannot comprehend. Prayer is trusting that no matter how bad things get, God is with us every step of the way.

The mystery of unanswered prayer will remain a mystery. None of us will ever know for sure why things happen as they do. We may never know God's way, but we can be certain of God's love. That love never ends, even as it may lead us along roads we may not have chosen to travel.

No one has put this better than an anonymous soldier during the Civil War who wrote these words:

I asked God for strength that I might achieve,
I was made weak, that I might learn humbly to obey.
I asked for health, that I might do greater things,
I was given infirmity, that I might do better things.
I asked for riches, that I might be happy,
I was given poverty, that I might be wise.
I asked for power, that I might have the praise of men,
I was given weakness, that I might feel the need of God.
I asked for all things, that I might enjoy life,
I was given life, that I might enjoy all things.
Almost despite myself, my unspoken prayers were answered.[1]

July 8, 2012
St. James Westminster Church, London, ON

THE HUMAN PARADOX

MATTHEW 6:1-6, 16-21

Human beings require a balance of ego and humility – to know that we are created in the image of God but are dust and ashes. It is difficult for any human being to avoid the sin of pride but also to recognize that we are precious children of God. The key to any successful leader is to recognize that the world does not revolve around "me" alone, but we must have a fierce determination to build a better world in whatever capacity we find ourselves. St. Hilary of Poitiers prayed: "Although I am dust and ashes, Lord, I am tied to you by bonds of love."

It is not very often that political gatherings offer moments of illumination, but that occurred at the New Hampshire Town Hall Meeting in February 2016. Hillary Clinton and Bernie Sanders, both candidates for the Democratic nomination for President, answered questions from people in the audience. One question was from Rabbi Jonathan Spira-Savett. In my judgment, he asked the best question ever posed to a candidate running for political office. The question was this: "Rabbi Simcha Bunim taught that every person has to have two pockets, and in each pocket, they have to carry a different note. And the note in one pocket says the universe was created for me. And in the other pocket the note says I am just dust and ashes."

Rabbi Jonathan then asked Mrs. Clinton: "I want you to take a moment and think about what you would tell us about your two pockets. How do you cultivate the ego, the ego we all know you must have – a person must have to be the leader of the free world – and also the humility to recognize that we know that you can't be expected to be wise about all things that the president has to be responsible for?"[1]

Apply and adapt that question to yourself. How would you answer it? "The universe was created for me" and "I am but dust and ashes." This is a question about ego and humility, about maintaining our humanity and respecting the humanity of those around us. It is a question that asks us to hold in balance the paradox that we are created in the image of God, but also, we are dust and ashes.

Maintaining this balance is difficult, especially for those in positions of leadership, whether as bishop of a diocese, or rector of a parish, or the head of a department, or the Prime Minister of Canada, or the President of the United States. It is the paradox of the human condition: we are dust and ashes but made in God's image.

One of the most important pastoral tasks for me as a priest is to help people deal with their own inadequacy. I have met people who not only feel inadequate but worthless. They do not feel attractive enough or intelligent enough or as fortunate as others. The success they dreamed of obtaining has not happened. As they grow older, the childhood dreams of being someone important begin to vanish, and they become angry, bitter, and resentful. They may even begin to feel increasingly uptight or junky.

However, there is good news for their lives and ours: God made us, and God doesn't make junk. We are created in the image of God. We are molded in the likeness of our Maker. Like God we can reason and think, we have a mind, a memory and a will. God even gave us dominion over the earth – not to savage the planet but to care for it. God was pleased when God created human beings and said that "it was very good" (Gen. 1:31. NRSV). God made nothing more special or more beautiful than us. Made in the image of God, we control much of our destiny.

Yes, God made each of us, and God doesn't make junk. We produce the junk in our lives when we let sin get the best of us. We try to attain unattainable goals and then labor under feelings of failure, or we get our priorities all mixed-up. It is then we walk life's way apart from God.

That's why knowing that the "universe was created for me" needs to be balanced by the realization that "I am but dust and ashes." I realize that none of us like to be reminded that we are "poor frail flesh" who someday will die. We are not immortal. We are not infallible with all the answers to all the questions that challenge us in life. We are imperfect, flawed human beings, every one of us. The traditional Lenten disciplines, especially fasting and self-denial, are designed to remind us of the fragile character of our existence.

In the end, nothing can save us from death. Only God can save us, and that God does by the power of Christ who on Good Friday and Easter morning snatches us from the jaws of death and carries us with him to the paradise of God. And so, the church's burial office prays:

> "You only are immortal, the creator and maker of all; and we are mortal, formed of the earth, and to earth shall we return. For so did you ordain when you created me, saying, 'You are dust, and to dust you shall return.' All of us go down to the dust;

151

yet even at the grave we make our song: 'Alleluia, alleluia, alleluia.'"[2]

The old Papal Coronation Mass, following the election the previous day, saw the new Pope carried on a special chair or *sedia* through St. Peter's Basilica. It was a grand ceremony reflecting the pomp and ceremony of the Roman Catholic Church. However, before the new pope could take his seat on the throne of St. Peter, and the tiara placed on his head, a cardinal would take a bundle of flax, and igniting it on a gilded staff, held it before the pontiff until it was burnt into ashes. The Master of Ceremonies would then say three times in a solemn voice: *Pater Sancte, sic transit gloria mundi* – "Holy Father, the glory of the world passes away." Here was a vivid reminder of the transiency and emptiness of all human praise.

While I was in divinity school, I had the privilege of meeting the Archbishop of York, Stuart Blanche. It was just at the time when Robert Runcie was appointed Archbishop of Canterbury. Someone asked Archbishop Blanche if he were not disappointed that he failed to ascend to the See of Canterbury as his predecessor Archbishop Coggan had done. I shall never forget his reply: "When you get to be my age," he said, "ascending the church ladder has little importance compared to preparing for one's death and knowing one is saved by Jesus."

Archbishop Blanche knew full well the issues we find so pressing in life will seem petty at the point of death. Not money or power or praise; not intelligence or education or good taste or lifestyle; only Christ matters.

As Christians we know that death will not have the last word in our lives. Yes, our physical bodies will turn to dust, but our spiritual bodies – the essence of who we are – will live with God forever. We can live freely, faithfully and fully in this life knowing that the best is yet to come. We can give more, love more, and care more, because with God our work is not in vain. We can do our duty in whatever capacity we find ourselves, take responsibility for our lives, be good stewards of the planet, and do our part to alleviate human misery and leave this world a better place because we have lived in it.

When I served in Lancaster, Pennsylvania, one of my dearest friends was the Senior Minister of the neighboring Presbyterian Church. Bob Williamson was an outstanding pastor and preacher, a man of deep faith who dearly loved the Lord. A short while after his retirement, Bob was diagnosed with terminal cancer. It was totally unexpected – a shock to those of us who loved this man.

As Bob's health declined, his wife Beulah arranged for Bob's friends to have one last visit with him. As I knocked on the door to say farewell, I was feeling sick to my stomach, anxious and fearful. I did not know what to expect or how I would react when I saw him. Beulah opened the door and led me to Bob who was sitting on a sofa. When Bob saw me, he smiled and said just three words: "God is good." For the rest of our time together, we talked about the blessings of life and ministry, and how we were both so fortunate to be pastors. Bob looked back on his life with profound gratitude, no bitterness or anger. He had taught his people how to live well, and now he was showing them how to die well. As I left his house, I thought how odd that Bob had ministered to me more than I had ministered to him. He was God's pastor to the end.

I hope that when I die, I am like Bob Williamson, a faithful Christian and pastor. I hope that from life to death, I will never waver from God, never falter in my mission, never stray from the faith.

Ash Wednesday reminds us that our bodies will turn to dust and ashes, but the essence of who we are will be with the Lord in heaven. God may not spare us from suffering, but God will see us through it.

Hold on to your faith. Be vigilant, be courageous and trust God. Remember you are dust and to dust you shall return, even as you are made in God's image, called into God's family and declared Christ's own forever.

February 10, 2016
St. James Westminster Church, London, ON

A TALE OF TWO CHARACTERS

LUKE 22:14-30

Judas and Peter both fell from grace: one died in despair; the other became a saint. Why the difference between these two men? Both were called and mentored by Jesus. Both walked with Jesus throughout his ministry. When they fell from grace, it was not that one was forgiven and one was not. It had more to do with their response to the forgiveness that Jesus offered – one was able to accept it while the other despaired of ever obtaining it. God's forgiveness is always greater than our sin. No matter our sin, we must never despair, but neither should we presume that we will never fall on the day of trial. As St. Augustine put it: Two thieves were crucified with Christ. One was saved, do not despair; one was not, do not presume.

The Last Supper is a sign of contradiction. Picture the scene. Jesus and his disciples are gathered in an upper room in what would be their last meal together. On the surface, things seem peaceful enough. There is friendship. There is fellowship. There is a common person and a common purpose that holds this group together. On the surface, at least, the Last Supper is a picture of community at its best.

Beneath the surface, the forces of darkness are at work. Beneath the friendship and fellowship there is bickering and petty jealousy. Beneath a common purpose there is disillusionment with the "cause." Beneath a common person there is misunderstanding of his mission.

The Last Supper began the longest and most emotional night in the life of Jesus – a night that was marred by betrayal and denial by the very ones who broke bread together.

And here lies a story: the tale of two characters, Judas and Peter. Both were weak men. One betrayed his Lord; the other denied him. One hanged himself and was buried in potter's field. The other became the leader of the early church and a martyr for his Lord. One was a tragic figure. The other rose from tragedy to triumph. Why this difference? Let us examine this tale of two characters.

Judas was an educated man from the city unlike the other disciples who were mostly fishermen from the country. He had a broad outlook on life. He was sophisticated. He had good taste. He knew the value of a dollar, which is why he, rather than Matthew, became treasurer for the disciples. Judas saw himself as an asset to Jesus, someone who was better than the others. This may well have made him a loner, someone who did not share deeply with the others and kept his doubts and discomfort to himself.

Why then, did Judas betray Jesus? One theory holds that Judas was a zealot who longed for the overthrow of the Roman occupation of Israel. Judas probably saw Jesus as a political Messiah. He harbored hopes that Jesus would lead his fellow Jews in armed revolt against the Roman tyranny – much as Judas Maccabeus did against the Syrians one hundred and eighty years before. But when Jesus rejected all attempts by the people to make him king, a disgusted and disillusioned Judas betrayed him, perhaps to force his hand into taking decisive political action.

Another theory holds that Judas might have grown disillusioned with Jesus, seeing him as a leader who put his person above the cause. The Gospel of Mark records how a woman anointed Jesus with a costly perfume. Judas became indignant. He argued that the money could be better spent helping the poor. It is at this point, so the Gospel records, that Judas went to the priests to betray Jesus.

Despite his unfavorable image in the Gospels, Judas manages to gain our sympathy. In some ways, he is a thoroughly modern anti-hero. The musical *Jesus Christ Superstar*, for example, portrays Judas as the conscience Jesus rejected – the dedicated, selfless revolutionary completely committed to the cause – in some sense, the true martyr of the passion narrative.

I remember an old Jesuit at Georgetown University remarking that if Judas were alive today, he would be calling on the churches to sell their buildings and works of art to give the money to the poor, forgetting that the beauty of holiness contributes mightily to a holy world. Judas lacked any sense of transcendence. Temporal and earthly minded, politically pragmatic and functional in his use of money, Judas yearned more for utopia than the kingdom of God. He cared more for satisfying the needs of the body than fulfilling the needs of the soul.

And that was Judas's downfall. He saw things from below rather than from above. When the full force of his betrayal became evident, he focused on his own sin rather than on God's love. No doubt he experienced remorse, but not forgiveness. Confronted with the dastardly deed he had done, Judas could only cry out in consternation to a God, he believed, had condemned him. No one can live for long in the dark shadows of despair without ending life. Is it any wonder, then, that Judas, in the depths of depression, hanged himself? Remorse without forgiveness leads to despair, and despair leads to death.

The real tragedy of Judas is not in betraying Jesus, but in being unable to accept the gift of forgiveness. When Judas kissed Jesus in the Garden of Gethsemane, their eyes must have focused on each other. Jesus still must have loved him, but Judas was unable to accept that love. All he could see was his own sin. Judas despaired. It was a short step from despair to death.

Could Judas have been forgiven? Perhaps that is the wrong question – for Judas had already been forgiven, if he could have only realized it. Jesus, who said we are to forgive our enemy not seven times, but seventy times seven, surely must have forgiven his friend Judas. If Judas had only realized that, though weak and frail as he was, Jesus still loved him. If that love had seeped into his life, Judas would have realized he was a forgiven sinner now called to forgive himself.

Could there have been a St. Judas? Absolutely – if only Judas had accepted that God's love is greater than his sin.

Compare Judas with Peter. Judas is calm, deliberate and reflective. Peter is impulsive, impetuous and a bundle of contradictions – someone who confesses Jesus as the Messiah only to turn around and tell him what to do! Like Judas, Peter might have been a political zealot, or he would not have drawn his sword in the Garden of Gethsemane. Whatever the case, Peter clearly did not understand Jesus until after the resurrection.

At the Last Supper Peter boldly announced that he would never disown or abandon his Lord. It is a self-confident statement, to say the least. Here is presumption – to believe that when we are faced with temptation we will never fall. Impulsive Peter spoke too quickly, and we know what happened. While Jesus was being interrogated by the Sanhedrin, three times Peter in the courtyard denied he was a disciple of Jesus – denied he even knew Jesus. He cursed and swore and protested: "I do not know or understand what you are talking about" (Mk. 14:68, NRSV). This was denial as serious as Judas' betrayal. Luke records what happened at the break of dawn: "The Lord turned and looked at Peter. Then Peter remembered the word of the Lord, how he had said to him, 'Before the cock crows today, you will deny me three times.' And he went out and wept bitterly" (Lk. 22:61-62, NRSV).

John's Gospel tells us that when Judas betrayed Jesus, he went into the "night" (Jn. 13:30, NRSV). When Peter denied Jesus, he "wept bitterly" (Lk. 22:62, NRSV). Judas went into the night where there is remorse without forgiveness. Peter wept bitterly because even in remorse, he knew he was loved. Judas went into the night burdened by guilt and overcome with despair. Peter wept bitterly convicted of sin but knowing he was forgiven.

When Jesus looked at Peter, he did not have to speak to him. His face told it all. It was one silent stare. It's as if he had said to Peter that despite his denial, he was still loved, forgiven and his friend.

Peter wept bitterly. His were not tears of despair, but tears of knowing that he was loved. Peter accepted the forgiveness of Jesus, which is why he is St. Peter. Later on, as an apostle mature in the Lord, he would write from the full force of his convictions that "love covers a multitude of sins" (1 Pet. 4:8, NRSV). Peter knew that to be true – because love covered his sins.

The tradition has it that Peter was in Rome during Nero's persecution. Fleeing for his life, he was on the Appian Way when he encountered Jesus. "Where are you going, Lord?" he asked – *Quo Vadis, Domini?* And Jesus replied, "I am going to Rome to be crucified again." Hearing that, Peter returned to Rome where he was arrested and sentenced to be crucified. When the sentence was pronounced, Peter cried out that he was unworthy to die like his Lord. The Romans obliged and crucified him upside down.

Even with his denial of Jesus, Peter never turned away from his Lord. After the resurrection, he would live for Jesus and even die for Jesus. His love for Jesus was even unto death because he knew that Jesus loved him. Judas knew no such love. He could not believe that Christ's love was greater than his sin, that Christ's pardon was more powerful than his faults, and that God's amazing grace was greater than his guilt. He could have been a saint, but he ended up hanging on a tree.

It was the French writer Gustave Thibon who said that the one great tragedy in life is not to be a saint. The tragedy of Judas teaches us that remorse without forgiveness leads to despair, and despair leads to death. The triumph of Peter is that his presumption he would not sin did not lead to despair when he did sin. Whether we become like Judas or Peter depends on how much we accept this truth: God's forgiveness is greater than our sin.

If we have any doubt about it, then ponder this: we gather on this Maundy Thursday as the church. It is Christ's church. He bought it with his blood. When the cock crows, it crows not for Judas the traitor, but for Peter the apostle. When we hear the crowing, we weep; we do not despair.

Judas went into the night, but Peter wept bitterly. Dear people: let us walk in the light of love rather than in the darkness of despair. Sinners though we are, we are forgiven sinners called into companionship with Jesus. That makes all the difference.

April 17, 2014
St. James Westminster Church, London, ON

EARTH SPIRITUALITY

ISAIAH 5: 1-7; MATTHEW 21:33-46

Earth spirituality affirms the mystery and wonder of creation. To diminish any part of the planet is to diminish ourselves. We are not the owners of the planet but its stewards or caretakers, responsible not just for ourselves but for future generations. All life on earth is interdependent. How we live affects the life of us all. There are no loners or solitary individuals. We live in a web of connections where all of us must take responsibility for one another and for our planet. Rachel Carson put it this way: "The more clearly we can focus our attention on the wonders and realities of the universe about us, the less we shall have for destruction."

Back in 1982, when I was a divinity student at Trinity College, University of Toronto, I had a conversation with the then Provost of the college, Dr. Kenneth Hare. He was a distinguished Canadian climatologist, and not a person to exaggerate. He always chose his words carefully. I asked him about climate change and whether it was a matter to be taken seriously. He looked at me and said, "I believe climate change is the defining issue of our time. How the world responds to climate change will determine a great deal about the state of humanity and the condition of the planet."

Today, no one would deny that the earth's temperatures are getting slightly warmer with rising ocean levels, glacial melts, intensified storms and more frequent droughts, which often affect the most vulnerable and poorest communities. Climate change is resulting in massive population shifts, famines, natural disasters, civil unrest, and refugees fleeing their homelands. Whether climate change is part of the natural evolution of the planet or the man-made result of carbon emissions, the fact is the planet is getting warmer.

The issue is not whether climate change is happening but how do we respond to it. We might begin with a healthy dose of realism. Despite demands to the contrary, we can't fully prevent climate change. Since the beginning of life on earth, climate change has been happening. There have been extremely cold periods – the Ice Age, for example – and there have been relatively hot periods such as during the age of the dinosaurs. The beautiful Arizona and Southern California deserts were once part of a great ocean, and the magnificent boulders, mountains and rock formations were on the ocean floor. Climate change is an ongoing reality and not a recent event. It is part of the evolution of our planet.

That said, it also is true that since the industrial era human beings have affected the climate by carbon emissions in the atmosphere. As a result, temperatures are rising. No one is quite sure what impact that will have on the overall climate, but we do know that ocean temperatures have been warming steadily since 1970, and for the past twenty-five years or so, they have been warming twice as fast. This will have a major impact on coastal communities around the world, and especially fisheries. So, reducing carbon emissions seems to be not only desirable but necessary if we can stem the tide of ocean warming. After all, who could possibly be against clean water, fresh air, and a green, flourishing planet with lush vegetation? Isn't that the vision God has for our planet? In the very first chapter of the Book of Genesis we read: "God saw everything that he had made, and indeed, it was very good" (Gen. 1:31, NRSV).

The symbol for God's abundance in the Hebrew Scriptures is the vineyard. Think of an oasis in the middle of the desert. That is how the ancient Hebrews thought of a vineyard. It was a thing of beauty, an image of life. The vineyard represented abundance. It was a reminder to the Hebrews that God cared for his people, that he provided for them, and that he loved them.

In our lesson from the prophet Isaiah, we have a parable about a vineyard. Ancient Israel was a promised land flowing with milk and honey. It had many vineyards. But it did not stay that way. Bad farming practices managed to deplete the soil and turn fertile fields into dry, desolate wastes. The great forests of Lebanon and Hermon were eventually destroyed, and the soil eroded.

By Isaiah's time, the land that once flowed with milk and honey was becoming barren of much of its vegetation. The result: flood shortages became common. Hoarding, even stealing became accepted practice. Draught became an increasing threat. The vineyard was turning into a wasteland. The prophets were quick to explain Israel's ecological crisis as a broken relationship with God resulting in a broken relationship with the land.

In Isaiah's parable (Isa. 5:1-7), the vineyard is a symbol of Israel itself which has declared its independence from God and rejected God's ownership. Because the people of Israel have severed their dependence on the Creator, they lost their interdependence with creation. Their sense of proportion was gone. They worked nature to excess; they did not recognize their limits; they wasted their resources. In their attempt to dominate the earth, they abandoned being stewards of the land.

In Isaiah 24 we read about what happens when human beings usurp the Creator by seeking to dominate the creation: "Now the

Lord is about to lay waste the earth and make it desolate, and he will twist its surface and scatter its inhabitants. ...The earth shall be laid waste and utterly despoiled; for the Lord has spoken this word. The earth dries up and withers, the world languishes and withers, the heavens languish together with the earth. The earth lies polluted under its inhabitants, for they have transgressed laws, violated the statutes, broken the everlasting covenant" (Isa. 24:1,3-5, NRSV).

In our Gospel, Jesus changes the details of Isaiah's parable, but his point is the same. The vineyard is God's exclusive and rightful possession, but the ownership of the vineyard is in dispute. The tenants of the land attempt to overthrow the owner's claims and keep the vineyard for themselves. So, the question is: Whose vineyard is this, anyway? Who owns the land? Who calls the shots around here? Who sets the priorities? Who makes the decisions – the owner or the tenants?

All too often we forget who owns the land. We confuse our stewardship with God's ownership. When that happens, an ecological crisis is bound to occur as wants outpace needs. Enough becomes excess. Abundance becomes avarice. Ours becomes mine. The delicate balance of life is ignored. In this crisis, it is not just a matter of technology gone rampant. It is a matter of the heart gone wrong.

Sin scars the earth. That is the message of the very first book of the Bible. After the Fall of Adam, the Lord says to him: "Cursed is the ground because of you..." (Gen. 3:17, NRSV). Because we have lost our peace with God, we have lost our peace with nature. Because our hearts are in disarray, so is the earth. Only God can restore our harmony with the earth. In other words, it is only when we are in a right relationship with God that we can be in a right relationship with the earth.

This is the Christian contribution to the environmental debate.

Christians know – because the Bible tells us – that the root cause of our ecological crisis is sin: the tendency in human beings to want to usurp the Creator – to be gods of creation rather than stewards. In the poet Swinburne's words, we boast a new hymn of praise: "Glory to man in the highest / for he is the glory of things." The age-old temptation of the serpent in the Garden haunts us still – the promise that "you will be like God" (Gen. 3:5, NRSV). Isn't that what causes us to despoil the earth – our desire to dominate and exploit it?

However, our attempt to play God on earth is bound to end with the same results that cursed the people of Israel during the time of Isaiah. Enough becomes excess. The demand for profit becomes an excuse for pollution. The earth is exploited. The environment damaged. Precious resources wasted. God's ownership of the earth is ignored. The paradox of all this, the more we seek to control – to consume and possess – the more the earth goes array. An ecological crisis is bound to occur anytime wants outpace needs. That, the Bible tells us, is sin.

The Bible also tells us that peace with the earth is possible when human beings find peace with God. For when God's peace enters our hearts, we form new values and develop a new set of priorities. We begin to see the world through a new set of eyes.

Life, we come to realize, is to be managed, not manipulated; used, not abused; cared for, not exploited. Paul tells us in Romans that redemption in Jesus Christ includes the liberation of the earth itself. "For the creation waits with eager longing for the revealing of the children of God; for the creation was subjected to futility, not of its own will but by the will of the one who subjected it, in hope that creation itself will be set free from its bondage to decay and will obtain the freedom of the glory of the children of God" (Rom. 8:19-21, NRSV).

If the theological and scientific case for the care of the planet is so strong, why is there continued resistance by some of us? Perhaps we fear that in caring for the planet we will cease to care for people – that our jobs and livelihood will suffer. There is some truth to this fear. I have noticed that debates on the environment often are presented as an either/or choice – care for the environment or care of people – as if we must sacrifice people to save the planet. That is a false choice. We can do both, and one without the other is simply not a viable option. And yet, I do think that meeting human needs without a larger caring for the earth is ultimately impossible. You cannot have healthy people on a sick planet.

God has given us the freedom to be responsible stewards of the earth. We can make choices that our life-giving or death-dealing. We can choose our future on this planet. We can treat the earth as God's vineyard or a human wasteland.

Do you recall the Golden Rule that Jesus gave us? He said, "In everything do to others as you would have them do to you" (Mt. 7:12, NRSV). Perhaps we ought to apply this rule to the earth, as something worthy of our deepest love and attention. Treat the environment the way you would want the environment to treat you. After all, we have only one planet. If we do not work to ensure its survival, we will all know the true meaning of homelessness.

As Christians we ought to be able to agree on a fundamental theological principle: Because God created the natural world, it is wrong to abuse it. And therefore, we should uphold the integrity of creation, that all things on this earth are interdependent and that what happens to one affect us all. To diminish any part of this planet is to diminish ourselves. It is to violate our role as stewards of the earth rather than owners.

Now, more than ever, we in the church are called to the pastoral care of the earth. Christians understand pastoral care in terms of persons, but we need to expand our thinking to include the planet. We are to treat nature tenderly, respectfully and responsibly. We are to affirm the integrity of creation – the web of interactions – that make up the earth, that all things on this earth are interdependent, and that what happens to one part, say the Amazon, affects us all. A constant theme in Rachel Carson's writings is the interdependence of all living things – we are all connected in one great ecosystem.

Speaking of Rachel Carson, her book *The Silent Spring* is one of the most influential books ever written on the environment. Back in the early 1960s, Carson was battling cancer and she felt an urgent need to complete the book before her death. She ran into enormous opposition from chemical and other companies who did not want her book published. However, she managed to publish it, and it changed the entire environmental debate in the United States. Under President Richard Nixon the Environmental Protection Agency was created to ensure a clean and safe environment.

Today there are two different ways of handling climate change. The first is what might be termed a model of scarcity. The world is like a pie in which there are only so many pieces to go around. Human beings are demanding more pieces of the pie than are possible to eat. There is simply not enough to go around, and therefore we must live with restraint, regulation and restriction. Government will redistribute the resources and determine who gets what. We all must lower our standards of living, our expectations for a better life, pay more for almost everything and learn to live with less. This is the price for the survival of the planet – the move away from consumption to conservation.

A second option is a model of abundance: there is always enough and more thanks to innovation, new technologies, government economic incentives and free markets. This is an optimism scenario in which the world enjoys a greener and cleaner economy of sustained economic growth and prosperity. This approach gives us every reason to be hopeful about the planet's future without sacrificing economic growth.

It is not for me to say which approach would be most effective in addressing climate change. It may well be a combination of both. The world is at a crossroads and must decide, but inaction is not an option. Which approach do we think will best save the planet: a radical restructuring of the economy, extensive government regulation and a reduced standard of living, or technological and scientific innovation encouraged by government incentives and free markets?

As we think about climate change and our response to it, let me offer two points for consideration.

First, we need to resist framing climate change in apocalyptic terms. The world is not going to end in twelve years or twenty years or fifty years as some politicians and activists claim. There always have been people throughout history who have forecast a dire and apocalyptic future for the planet. Thomas Hobbes, the seventeen century English philosopher, in his book *Leviathan* pictured a grim, depressing future. He argued that only an all-powerful State could prevent human beings from falling into a condition described as "solitary, poore, nasty, brutish, and short." In 1798, Thomas Malthus argued that there was a tendency in nature for the population to outstrip all means of subsistence. His was a vision of a dying, starving planet in chaos. Then there was the forecast of the Club of Rome in 1971 of a planet overrun by starvation and disease. None of these apocalyptic scenarios happened, and today there is a lower percentage of the world's population in poverty than at any time in human history. The world is getting better, not worse. True, we have a long way to go, but we have come a long way.

All this pertains to our environmental challenges. Thirty years ago there were predictions of a "nuclear winter" which was subsequently replaced by "global warming." Today the catchword is "climate change." Yes, the climate is changing, but there is no need for panic. We are far from a Doomsday future. In fact, the best is yet to come if we manage climate change properly. The Bahamas, for example, was devastated by a recent hurricane. Almost all the homes on some islands were destroyed. However, those homes can be rebuilt to withstand even a Category 4 or 5 hurricane – we have the technology.

Christians need to resist apocalypticism which is a bad attitude resulting in panic, fear, hysteria and scarcity. Moreover, it is counterproductive to progress and contrary to scripture.

Second, we must never forget that the care of the earth is dear to God's heart. It should be dear to ours as well. Just read Genesis 1 and 2 or Psalm 8 to be reminded that God created us to be stewards of the planet. We are here to tend the earth, not to exploit it. We are responsible for the health of the environment: for the air we breathe and the water we drink, for the well-being of the animals, trees, plants and vegetation. This is our home. Future generations are depending on us to be good tenants of this earth, but always to remember that God is the owner.

My daughter, and your children and grandchildren, trust us to leave them a world where the sky is wide open and filled with the breath of life; where the waters are clear and clean; where the fields and forests remain havens for hectic lives. Of course, the kind of world we leave them is up to us. Will it be a vineyard or a wasteland? The choice is ours.

October 2015, revised September 27, 2019
St. James Westminster Church, London, ON

MY JESUS MOMENT

PSALM 90; MARK 9:30-37

We have a limited time on this earth. The Bible says our days are numbered. Some of us will live longer than others, but all of us will die. How are we making the most of the one and only life God has given us? Often it takes some kind of crisis in our lives for us to deal with the issue — perhaps an illness, or an accident, or the death of a loved one, the end of a marriage, or the loss of a job. We come to a moment when we rethink our lives, why we are on this earth, and what we want to accomplish before we die. The time to live life to the full is now. Mitch Albion, the author of Tuesdays with Morrie, put it like this: "Mortality means you don't have forever to work things out. You can live your life unexamined but then on the last day you're going to think: 'I've left things a little late.'"

Have you ever had a Jesus moment? That is what a doctor said to me about my time in the emergency room several years ago. He looked at the test results and said, "You know, Father, you could have died. Consider that a Jesus Moment. Take what I am saying to you seriously. Focus on your health and be well."

I do not know if the doctor was a Christian, but I am amazed he used the term "Jesus Moment" to describe my condition.

It all started very unexpectedly one early January day. I was at my physician's office complaining of chest and back pain. Suddenly I became nauseous, sweaty, and white as a ghost. It was serious enough for the doctor to call the ambulance which raced me to the hospital. Frankly, as the ambulance was speeding to the hospital, I thought I was going to die, but thankfully, I recovered sufficiently to be discharged late that evening. Today, several years later, I am in good health, but my Jesus Moment has stayed with me.

As a priest, I accept that at some point in my life I am going to die. Life on this earth does not last forever. We get sick or old, we start to fail physically or even mentally, and eventually we die. As Ash Wednesday reminds us, we are mortal and to dust we shall return. Some of us may act like we will live forever, but we will not. We may even think of ourselves as indispensable, but as Charles De Gaulle famously observed: "The graveyards are filled with indispensable men."

One of my favorite verses of scripture, one that I find myself pondering more frequently as I get older, is Psalm 90:12 in the Book of Common Prayer translation: "So teach us to number our days, that we may apply our hearts to wisdom."[1] If you were to do that – number your days – you would come up with a number somewhere around 31,025. That is assuming you reach 85 years of age which a healthy American with good medical care should expect to live – 31,025 days. That is a long life, but then there are those unexpected Jesus Moments that could threaten you at any time.

My Jesus Moment – a blessing in hindsight – prompted me to rethink my priorities in life, my reason for being, my purpose for existence, and how I want to live the remainder of my life. Sometimes it takes a Jesus Moment to make busy people slow down and heed the advice of Jonathan Swift: "May you live every day of your life."

Jesus lived about 12,045 days on this earth, or roughly 33 years, yet he lived a full life in a short time. From age twelve, he demonstrated that he knew his life's purpose: to do the will of God. Even when God's will for him was painful, even when his friends abandoned him at his hour of greatest need, he still lived only to fulfill God's will for his life.

A card I received from a friend read: "God's will – nothing more, nothing less, nothing else." That could easily have been the motto of Jesus – to do God's will without question or reserve. The philosopher Soren Kierkegaard said that purity of heart is to will one thing, and in that sense Jesus was completely focused on doing his Father's will: teaching about the kingdom of God, preparing his disciples for their ministry when he was departed from them, and saving humanity from the sin which they could not save themselves.

Jesus had a laser-like focus on his purpose because he was thinking with the mind of God. Throughout the Gospels, we read of Jesus spending time in prayer. Through prayer, he filled his mind with the thoughts of God, he filled his heart with the will of God, he filled his mouth with the words of God, and he pointed his feet in the ways of God, even when that way led to death on a cross.

In our Gospel passage today, Jesus is almost at the end of his journey on earth. He has been with his disciples for about three years, and yet they seemed not to have any idea about his mission or approaching death. They may have still thought he was the Messiah in a Maccabean sense – a conqueror who would bring about a radically new kingdom by force. They could not imagine a Messiah dying on a cross and being vanquished by his enemies. Nor could they comprehend how resurrection connected to the mission of Jesus.

Jesus tells them once again: "The Son of Man is to be betrayed into human hands; and they will kill him, and three days after being killed, he will rise again.' But they did not understand what he was saying and were afraid to ask him" (Mk. 9:31-32, NRSV). Then, with just a short while remaining before his death, he says to them, "Whoever wants to be first must be last of all and servant of all" (Mk. 9:35, NRSV).

He was telling his disciples that there is more to life than being number one. He was trying to help them put things into perspective and gain a sense of balance about what it means to live as a human being fully alive to God and one another.

Eugene O'Kelly was the CEO of KPMG, one of the largest accounting firms in the United States. In May 2005, O'Kelly learned that he had inoperable, incurable brain cancer, and was told he would die in six months or less. In fact, he died on September 10, 2005. But before he died, he wrote a book, which was published posthumously, about his reflections on his life and pending death. The book is titled: *Chasing Daylight: How My Forthcoming Death Transformed My Life*. It is a book about how a successful man learns to redefine success in the last months of his life.

O'Kelly's illness prompted him to re-examine his priorities and values, look at his life/work balance and focus on living in the moment rather than some indefinite point in the future. He drew a map of relationships in his life as a series of concentric circles – his wife was at the center, then his children, on through family and close friends, and finally close business associates. He realized that he had spent far too much time in the outer circles and not enough on the inner ones. His lifestyle had not been in sync with his priorities. He had given too much attention to the outer circles and not enough to the inner circles, to his wife and daughter.

It would be a helpful exercise for all of us to take a sheet of paper and draw five circles – one for your spouse, your children, extended family, close friends and business or other associates.

How much time do you commit to each circle? Does the time you spend in each circle reflect your priorities and values? In other words, is your life consistent with the beliefs, values and priorities you profess? If the answer is yes, you are living an authentic life. If the answer is no, then why not do something about it while you still have the opportunity? No one need live a life that does not reflect who they are.

Life is too short not to live it well. We have only one life to live, so why not live it as authentically as possible, being true to yourself and your deepest values. After all, what's the point of living a life that does not reflect who you are, or what you believe, or what you think important? None of us on our deathbed wants to look back on our life and regret all the missed opportunities for a deeper, meaningful life. What's the point of having it all if we die feeling a failure?

When I lead stewardship workshops, I invite participants to do a spiritual check-up on their lives. I give each person two sheets of paper. On one sheet, I ask them to write the answers to three questions: Who am I? What values do I hold? What is important to me? On the second sheet, I ask them to answer two more questions: How do I live? For what purposes do I use my time, talent and money?

Then I ask them to set both sheets of paper side by side. Would they recognize these as descriptions of the same person? Or, to put it another way, is "Who am I?" in sync with "How I live?" If we are true to ourselves, then "How I live" should be a mirror of "Who am I." That, I think, is the key to an authentic life: being true to who you are by how you live your life.

A corporate executive shared with me his rule of operating a business. He said that he would do nothing privately that he would not be willing to share publicly. In other words, his private life was a mirror of his public life. In that way, he maintained his integrity.

He never had to worry about saying something in public that was not true. His public and private lives were in sync.

Sadly, some people climb the ladder of success leaning against the wrong wall. By the time they get to the top, they realize it is not what they expected. I remember a law student telling me that his goal in life was to make seven figures. The law itself was simply a means to make money. He did become a successful lawyer, but happiness eluded him, and he wonders now whether there is something more in life that he may have missed.

Instead of valuing fame, fortune and position, how about we focus on other measurements for our lives, such as the individuals I have been able to help to become better people. I think what matters, and what gives our lives meaning, are the lives we touch, the kindnesses we show, the generosity we demonstrate, the compassion we offer one another, and the changed lives that result when we help others know God.

Someone has said that we should imagine what people say about us at our funeral. Many of the things we think important may not be mentioned, but the little things – like our caring, our compassion, and our concern for others – will surely be mentioned.

The point in life is to love – to give love, to share love, to be loved and to love others. The more loving we are, the more caring we are, the more we share ourselves with those in need, the brighter, better place our world becomes.

Sometimes it is children who teach us the most important lessons of life. Thanks to my daughter Allison I have learned so much, not only about Down syndrome, but about what it means to be a loving human being. You will notice that almost always Allison has a smile on her face. She loves life, but she is the most non-competitive person in the world. Winning does not matter to her. Loving is what matters, and that is something she knows how to share generously with others. In her own way, she is making this world a brighter, better place.

My Jesus Moment taught me that we have only so many days on this earth. I hope I get to 31,025 days, but if not, I want to live whatever time I have on this earth well. I want to be the servant that Jesus expects all his disciples to be. In fact, when I retired from parish ministry after my Jesus Moment, I took as my motto, "Following Jesus, serving others." Whether as a lawyer or a priest, I have tried to be true to that calling and live as if each day matters – because it does.

The question for us is: How will we make the most of the time we have left? Time is running out. Use your days wisely. Do the best you can with the gifts God has given you. Realize your full potential. Strive to make the most of yourself. There is nothing wrong with any of that, but keep in mind Eugene O'Kelly's five circles and ask, "Am I spending my time on what matters most to me?"

September 23, 2018
Church of the Nativity, Scottsdale, AZ

REACHING YOUR
FULL POTENTIAL

MARK 8:31-38

You achieve your potential when you give yourself to a cause worthy of your commitment that makes the world a better place by your living in it. Human beings need to live for something greater than themselves to find themselves. If we focus on ourselves, we will never know contentment or experience happiness. The miser is always miserable. The ones who give themselves to a higher purpose and make a better world are the happiest people. Blessing comes by being a blessing to others. In the end, if God is at the heart of our life, everything else will fall into place. The Jesuit philosopher Bernard Lonergan put it like this: "So, being in love with God is the basic fulfillment of our conscious intentionality. ...That fulfillment bears fruit in a love of one's neighbor that strives mightily to bring about the kingdom of God on this earth."

Ignatius Loyola is the sixteenth century founder of the Society of Jesus, better known as the Jesuits. As a student at the University of Paris, Ignatius met an academically gifted and ambitious young man by the name of Francis Xavier. Ignatius tried to persuade

Francis to join him in a new religious order, but Francis balked. Ignatius tried again, and Francis again turned him down. The pattern repeated itself several times, until finally Ignatius posed a question to Francis that Jesus poses in today's Gospel: "For what will it profit them to gain the whole world and forfeit their life?" (MK. 8:36, NRSV). Faced with the gravity of that question, Francis abandoned his carefully laid out plans and joined Ignatius in what would become the most powerful and influential religious order in the Roman Catholic Church.

Eventually Francis would travel to the Far East, sharing the Christian faith in India and Japan, before dying off the coast of China. Church historians count him as one of the greatest missionaries of all time.

Today I want to examine our Gospel text that so profoundly changed Francis Xavier and has the power to change us as well. If we can find the humility and courage to hear and accept what this text tells us, we may grow spiritually in ways we can scarcely now imagine.

The first thing our Gospel tells us is that only if we are willing to lose our lives will we be able to save them. The only way to gain your life is to let go of it. The only way to save yourself is to give yourself to something greater than you.

This seemingly goes against the view that you need to be assertive, aggressive and even relentless in achieving your goals. Take all you can, be all you can, grab what you can, hold on to what you have, and success will come your way. How can we possibly reconcile this philosophy with the teaching of Jesus that I will lose my life if I try to save it?

Perhaps Jesus is challenging us to live for something greater than ourselves. That may mean taking risks, stepping out of our comfort zone, and opening ourselves to what God may be calling us to do. The paradox here is that if we are willing to look beyond ourselves, we may find ourselves. When we reach out to others, we may secure ourselves. When we let go of our tightly drawn plans, we may find new opportunities, new possibilities and new horizons for our lives that we couldn't otherwise imagine.

A parishioner of mine in a previous church went for his annual physical, and the tests showed he might have an aggressive type of cancer. The doctor would have to do more tests to confirm the results. In the meantime the man waited in dread that he might not have long to live. A month later, he was notified that the initial diagnosis was wrong and that the new test results showed he did not have cancer. The man described it as the closest thing to resurrection. The experience gave him a whole new perspective on life. He said, "I began to see the beauty of God's creation in a way I had never seen it before. I began noticing things that before I would have ignored. I had a heightened sense of the life around me. With the prospect of my death, I began to make the most of every moment."

Then this parishioner said to me, "Why is it that when we think we're dying, we only then begin to live?" In hindsight, this man recognized he had been given a great gift in coming to terms with the true meaning of life.

If you live your life responsibly and faithfully and joyfully in a way that helps other people as well as yourself, if you enjoy your life, savor it and celebrate it as a gift from God, then you are going to end up discovering that your life was rich and full whether you always realized it or not.

A Disney film released last week is *McFarland*. It hasn't gotten much notoriety, but it's an impressive film for the whole family. The film is a true story about a high school football coach who failed at almost every job he had until the only job left was to coach a track team in McFarland, California – a poor, predominantly Hispanic town in the Central Valley fruit belt. You go to McFarland because you need a job, not because you want to be there. That's the coach's attitude until he and his family get to know the residents, appreciate Mexican American culture, and eat Mexican food. The coach begins to love his students. He genuinely cares about them. He doesn't just want them to win races but to be the first in their families to go to college.

When his team wins the state track championship, the coach is offered a lucrative job at one of the top high schools in one of the wealthiest communities in the state. He turns it down to stay at McFarland where he would lead the team to nine state championships until his retirement. Only as the coach gave himself to others did he find himself, and in finding himself he fulfilled his true potential as a teacher and mentor of young people.

That's the key to a successful, fulfilled and rewarding life: let God lead you in doing your best, wherever you are and whatever the challenges that confront you.

The second thing our Gospel tells us is that at the end of our life, we don't want to look back and wonder if we have wasted all the opportunities God has given us to live a meaningful and purposeful life. Life is all too short for the best of us. We had better make the most of time we have on this earth. The worst thing for any of us is die with lots of regrets... the "What ifs" of life... what if I had taken that risk, or taken that job, or pursed that career... you can name your own "What if?" Wouldn't it be a tragedy to look back and regret that we had our mission and failed to accomplish it, that we were given our calling and failed to pursue it. We did not make of this one life all that we could have made of it. If we lack passion, or enthusiasm, or dedication, then we are not going to realize our potential as God intends, and that will be a tragedy.

When I lived in New York, I attended the actors' church, the Church of the Transfiguration, affectionately known as "the little church around the corner." I got to know several aspiring actors who wanted to work in the theater. Trying to get an acting job in the theater is tough, especially in New York. You audition, and maybe if you are lucky, you will get a call to come back for a second audition, and then if you are luckier still, you might actually get a small part in a play that may or may not have a long run. Then you start all over again. So how do these aspiring actors cope with a life like that?

One these young actors told me that you have to live with passion. You must live with intensity. You've got to be resilient, hold nothing back and really want to be an actor, giving it all you've got and more. That's the difference between those who succeed and those who don't.

When you look at your life, what do you see? Are you living and even sacrificing for something greater than yourself? How much of your time, energy and money are you investing in yourself and your family and how much in efforts of one sort or another to better the lives of people who are less fortunate? Would it not be awful to think you are gaining the whole world and end up discovering that you lost so much of what makes for real life?

I began this sermon with a story about Francis Xavier. Let me end with another remarkable figure. Harvard Business School professor Clayton Christensen is one the leading scholars on innovation in the world today. He is a hard-nosed numbers cruncher, deeply analytical, not someone we would consider introspective. And yet, in 2012 he wrote a best-selling book titled *How Will You Measure Your Life?* In an interview on measuring success, Christensen shared these reflections: "Four years ago, I had a heart attack. Then I was discovered to have advanced cancer that put me into chemotherapy. About two years ago, I had a stroke. I had to learn how to speak again one word at a time."

What do you do when you are a Harvard business professor,

a "take control" kind of guy, an extrovert who takes initiative and relies on his own abilities to achieve his goals, and then you find yourself helpless, relying on others, starting over to relearn the most basic function of living? If you are Clayton Christensen, you rethink your life, examine what is really important, and set a new course for the time remaining on this earth. Professor Christensen went on to say:

> The more I focused on the problems in my life, the more miserable I was. And then somehow, I realized focusing on myself and my problems was not making me happier. I started to say, 'Every day of my life I need to find somebody else who I could help to become a better person and a happier person.' Once I started to reorient my life in this direction, the happiness returned. *** The most important piece of planning is, 'How are we still going to orient our lives on helping other people become better people?'"[1]

Like Clayton Christensen, our Gospel today calls us to self-examination. It reminds us that we are, day by day, making our lives what they ultimately will be. We reach our potential by sharing our life with others. Fulfillment, satisfaction and genuine happiness come to us as we move away from selfishness toward selflessness. A strange paradox, at least in the eyes of the world, but true, nonetheless.

March 1, 2015
St. James Westminster Church, London, ON

GET OUT OF THE BOAT

MATTHEW 14:22-33

We never know what we can do until we try to do it. So often fear paralyzes us into inaction. Jesus wants us to get out of our boat, step out of our comfort zone and trust God to uphold us in new adventures. This does not mean being reckless or irresponsible. Christians are followers of Jesus, not Don Quixote. When we find ourselves in an unsatisfactory situation, we need not whine and complain but do nothing to improve ourselves. Instead we can practice "holy discontentment" and step out of our boat. St. Basil of Caesarea prayed: "Steer the ship of my life, Lord, to your quiet harbor, where I can be safe from the storms of life and conflict. Show me the course I should take. …And give me the strength and courage to choose the right course, even when the sea is rough and the waves are high, knowing that through enduring hardship and danger in your name we shall find comfort and peace."

Many items pass my desk including a church bulletin announcement that read: "The sermon this morning: 'Jesus Walks on the Water.' The sermon tonight: 'Searching for Jesus.'"

Would you agree with me that walking on water is not something that most of us think possible? And yet, there are some people who have such charisma or such a record of accomplishment that we might think, if they had to, they could find a way to walk on water. Think of Richard Branson, Elon Musk or some of the entrepreneurs in Silicon Valley, for example. There always seem to be people who are willing to try the impossible. They may succeed or they may fail, but they try. They do not sit back on their laurels and let a challenge go to waste. They move out of their comfort zone, think beyond the box, and go, as Stark Trek put it, "where no one has gone before."

Jesus must have been that kind of person. In our Gospel today, we see an extraordinary human being who had a dramatic impact on the lives of those around him.

Consider the setting. The disciples are out in a fishing boat. A storm suddenly comes upon them, and they begin to panic. They are frightened, even terrified. With the pounding rain, ferocious winds and crashing waves against the small boat, the disciples must have felt completely helpless. It is at this moment of utter desperation that Jesus comes to the disciples. What is more, he comes to us as well in those moments when our fears threaten to overwhelm us.

Fear is a terrible thing, isn't it? Fear can literally paralyze us. It can demoralize us. It can wear us down. It can drain the energy right out of us. It saps us of our hope and happiness, and even our ability to live.

Do you know the biggest barrier to success for most people? It is the fear to get out of the boat – to move beyond our comfort zone, to let go of the familiar, to take a risk and move into a new horizon. We are not happy with our lives. We are dissatisfied with our work. We are discouraged and disillusioned that life seems to be passing us by. And what action do we take? Nothing!

Most of us are afraid to get out of the boat. We are afraid to start that new business we have been dreaming about for years.

We are afraid to change jobs or careers even though we feel totally unfulfilled. We are afraid to follow that dream of returning to school and learning new skills. Afraid to apply to the college we really want to attend. Afraid to stand up for some cause we really believe in. Afraid to say, "I love you."

I know at least two people who live in New York who will never visit me in Arizona because they are afraid of flying – and driving long distances is out of the question. Fear can prevent us from living a satisfying and fulfilling life.

But fear can be even more insidious.

I remember a woman who told me she was scared to death to tell her friends about her health problems because she was afraid that they would no longer accept her. I asked how she could believe such a thing, and her answer startled me. She said, "In my circle of friends, you have to be perfect. Once you have any serious problems, you will no longer get invited. People will no longer call, and you will be dropped from the social roll."

We all have our fears, don't we? Maybe it is fear of being socially rejected, or fear of losing our money, or fear of immigrants, or fear of people who are different from us, or fear of loneliness, or fear of dying too soon or living too long – you name it, and we fear it. Fear is pervasive in our society and it is reinforced in the media. Think of all the television commercials to sell us gold or silver to hedge against the financial Armageddon allegedly coming our way. We Americans are becoming a fearful people.

The Gospel assures us that Jesus comes to us when our hearts are troubled and we feel most helpless. Jesus comes across our troubled waters and says to us, "Don't be afraid. It is I." And he beckons us to leave the security of the boat and walk on water. What powerful imagery! What would it mean for you to get out of your boat? It means different things to different people.

I know a woman who was a paralegal for the first part of her life. She never felt she was smart enough or good enough to be a lawyer. But after a family crisis, when her children were of age, she applied to law school, got admitted to Columbia University Law School, and after graduation was offered a job at one of the leading Wall Street law firms in the country. She got out of the boat and walked on water.

Or think of J.K. Rowling. She was a woman on welfare living a survival existence. But she got this out-of-the-box idea about transforming an English prep school into a school for wizards, and the result was the Harry Potter novels. J.K. Rowling refused to let her fear of inadequacy and lack of self-worth prevent her writing novels. It was her dream, and yes, it could have been a colossal failure and a waste of time, but she knew that unless she tried, she would never succeed.

And then, there is Ben Stein. He writes an occasional financial column for *The New York Times,* appears on cable news channels, has acted in several movies, and even produced his own. He is a comedian who can be very funny, but he is also a savvy investor who has accumulated a great deal of money over the years.

Ben Stein did not start out that way. In fact, as he tells it, he started out as a struggling lawyer working for the federal government in one of the most seedy areas of Washington. He had no money. He could barely pay his monthly credit cards. He could go at most two weeks without being paid.

One steamy August morning Ben Stein walked down the green linoleum hallway to his cubby hole for an office which was so shallow that he did not have room for a chair in front of the desk. No one in the office seemed to care about that very much, or for that matter about anything else, so why should he care? But he did. At that moment, he resolved that life did not have to be that way. It could be better.[1]

Ben Stein could have stayed a civil servant for his entire

career, gotten by without taking any risks, and lived a thoroughly mediocre life. Instead, he decided to launch out into the deep, to risk and try some new things, to move beyond the safe and secure because only with that inner freedom was there the possibility of finding happiness and achieving a meaningful life.

Yes, there are times when you must step out of the boat. You cannot let your fears, failures, sense of inadequacy or circumstances hold you back from fulfilling your God-given calling. People will keep telling you that what you want to do is impossible, impractical or just not feasible, so don't bother. Still, you have this passion in your heart, this desire to make a difference, this belief that God is calling you to move beyond your comfort zone into a new horizon. So, you trust God, take that leap of faith, and get out of the boat. God who gives you the call will also give you the grace. God will help you become what God calls you to be.

Of course, there is no one way for everyone. God's call can sometimes shout at us in moments of crisis, or it can whisper in times of solitude. Often God speaks in times of quiet reflection when we dare to ask ourselves: What are the passions of my heart that reflect the gifts of my life?"

When I counsel young people about discerning the right direction for their lives, I say to them, "Find that point of intersection of what you do well and what you really like to do. Then make sure that work is meaningful and has a beneficial impact on others." That, I tell them, is probably their calling in life.

We all have a calling, a reason for being, at any age and at any stage of our life. Don't let fear hold you back. Get out of the boat and walk on water, whatever that might mean for you: finding a second career in retirement, or doing the work you always wanted to do but circumstances did not allow it. Perhaps it is writing or painting or some kind of artwork. Or, it may be going back to school, or taking courses in a particular subject area, or resolving to make your marriage work, or spending more time with your children and grandchildren, or becoming more involved in a church ministry, or volunteering in the community, or starting some new ministry, or being an advocate for peace and justice issues, or just doing the right thing, regardless of the cost. All I am saying is, do not let fear keep you in the boat. Embrace what God is calling you to do.

It all comes down to faith, doesn't it? Are you willing to commit to a new way of living, a new way of thinking, a new way of being the person God is calling you to be? Will you go for it or will you go home and pout at how bad life is treating you?

For many years before, and even during, my law practice in New York City, I felt this strange call to be a priest. And yet, as I became more proficient in my work, I also became increasingly reluctant to abandon law to go to divinity school. Many of my lawyer friends said I was foolish even to consider such an option. However, like Francis Thompson's description in the "Hound of Heaven," the call simply would not go away.

Finally, I had a candid discussion with my spiritual director, a wise Holy Cross monk. He said to me, "Why don't you just accept God's call, go to divinity school and become a priest?" I said to him: "I am afraid to let go of what I have achieved, and anyway I don't feel fully committed." He then looked at me intently and said: "Face your fear but go to divinity school, and then you'll feel committed."

Well, I ended up getting a leave of absence from my law firm, went to divinity school in Canada, got ordained in the Diocese of Quebec, and served five small churches along the Gaspe Coast. People on the coast were amazed that a New York lawyer would want to serve in such an isolated and poor part of Canada, but I found the people to be some of the kindest and most authentic human beings I have ever known. They ministered to me as much as I ministered to them. I certainly do not regret being there, but it would never have happened without the faith to get out of the boat, believing that God would uphold me with everlasting arms.

Whatever fear is holding you back from the abundant life promised us by God, Jesus can help you overcome it. Jesus loves people who dream great dreams, who still believe that all things are possible to those who believe in him, who are willing to step out in faith and trust him. Focus on Jesus, get out of your boat, and then leave the rest to God. With God all things are possible, even to walk on water.

August 13, 2017
Church of the Advent, Sun City West, AZ

CHOOSING WHO YOU BECOME

MATTHEW 21:23-32

Along life's way we make countless choices each day. Some of those choices are inconsequential, for example, whether we eat vanilla or chocolate ice cream. Other choices, however, have profound implications on ourselves and others. They build and strengthen our character or they weaken and deform it. Life's choices are ours to make – to choose the good over the bad, or the bad over the good. In the end, we become who we are by the choices we make. Our lives are not destined by fate but by our own free will. If we don't like who we are now, there is still time to change. Nothing holds us back but ourselves. Ralph Waldo Emerson advised: "The only person you are destined to become is the person you decide to be."

A dear friend of mine is Ted Schneider, who is the retired Lutheran Bishop of the Washington D.C. metropolitan area. Before becoming bishop, Ted and his wife lived in Lancaster, Pennsylvania where he was a parish pastor. Throughout their married lives they had never owned their own home. The couple had always lived in a parsonage. However, the position of Bishop of Washington did not come with a parsonage, and so for the first time in their married lives they sought to buy a home. Washington housing prices were high and Ted's salary was not extravagant.

After an exhausting search, Ted and his wife found what they thought was the perfect house in northern Virginia. The next step was to qualify for a mortgage. As part of the process, the bank asked them to supply a budget of their income and expenses. The mortgage officer in examining the budget noticed that their charitable contributions were unusually high. Ted had tithed his salary – 10 percent – from his earliest days as a pastor. The banker could not believe how much money Ted and his wife were giving to charity. He looked up at the couple and said to them: "You know, if you were to cut this figure in half, I could qualify you for this mortgage." Without a second thought, Ted replied: "Everything in our budget is negotiable except that figure. We tithe because that's who we are. We can't cut our giving without compromising our deepest values."[1]

At that moment Ted and his wife had to make a choice on whether to compromise on what they held inviolate. They passed the test.

The choices we make shape our lives. Often our choices impact on the happiness and well-being of our family and friends. They can help or hurt ourselves and other people. They can impact our community, our church and even our world. Choices matter.

Today's Gospel is one of the shorter parables, just a few lines. It begins with the question: "What do you think? A man had two sons..." (Mt. 21:28, NRSV). One son always said yes to his father. In fact, whenever the father was around, he was always careful to say what the father wanted to hear. He was a textbook case of a passive-aggressive personality. He said yes, but never did anything. The other son was more overtly rebellious. He would raise questions, and once in a while he would say "no," but ended up doing the right thing. Jesus asks: "Which of the two did the will of his father?" (Mt. 21:31, NRSV).

Jesus is saying we make choices that are either consistent or inconsistent with our deepest values and beliefs. We choose and make decisions that are either life-affirming or life-denying. In school we choose to learn or not to learn. We meander through an ever-changing collection of relationships. We pick friends and discard them. We make alliances and then break them. In our morality it is the same thing. We choose to tell the truth or tell lies; to be honest or dishonest; to be generous or stingy; to show compassion to hurting people or ignore those people; to think of others or think only of ourselves.

Through the choices we make in life, we become the persons we are today. In other words, goodness is not a matter of birthright or genetics or race or class. Nor is the lack of goodness. Instead, the outcome of our moral life is a series of choices – little choices – day by day decisions that we make. What shall I wear today? How shall I relate to her? What is my responsibility for him? How shall I operate my business? How should I treat my employees? How should I use my money?

Occasionally there are defining moments in our lives when we make big decisions that clearly have enormous impact on our character. We choose to steal or we choose be honest. We choose to be faithful to our spouse or we choose to cheat. We choose to squander our possessions or to give generously to worthy causes. We choose to get involved with improper or even illegal business practices or to maintain our honesty and integrity.

There are defining moments that have the power to affect us for the rest of our lives. However, the truth is, most of our lives are caught up in little choices. The choices we don't think much about.

No better novel illustrates this point than Oscar Wilde's *The Picture of Dorian Gray.* His portrait was that of a handsome young man, but slowly by his hurtful, spiteful conduct, his insensitive and cruel actions to people who were closest to him, the portrait transforms into a hideous creature that he could barely look upon. Dorian Gray became what he detested by his own behavior. It didn't happen immediately, but over a period of time in which a man of enormous potential transformed into a truly awful human being.

Every time you make a choice in life, every time you choose one thing over another, do one good deed or one bad deed, a central part of you changes into something a little different from what it was before. It may not be noticeable at first, and it may take years to show itself, but over time by the choices you make, your personality, your character, your inner self changes into something bright and beautiful or dark and deadly.

I remember a play that begins with an old, miserly, mean-spirited man who is on his deathbed. That's the first scene of the play. With every scene, the play takes a step backward in this man's life. We see him as the owner of a company, treating his employees harshly and pushing them beyond their limits. We see him alienated from his wife and children by his indifference and cruelty. We see him as a young, energetic man beginning his career, ambitious and determined to make a success of himself. We see him in college working hard to excel at his subjects. The final scene is of a young man making the commencement address at his high school. He says to the class: "We must hold to our ideals and make a better world."

That is the way it is with many of us. We begin life with high ideals, noble purposes and the best of intentions. Who in youth doesn't want to make a better world? But something happens to us along the way, and step by step, choice by choice, we lose our moral compass and become the person we never thought possible.

Every choice we make has some kind of moral undertone.

Through those choices you begin to turn yourself into a particular kind of human being. What you are today is built upon all the little choices that you have made along the way.

Now here is the good news: you can change who you are by changing the choices you make. Maybe you are not happy with the choices you have made in life. You have made some bad choices along the way. You may think there is an inevitable direction to your life. Perhaps you are even fatalistic that there is nothing you can do to turn your life around, but that is not so. The point of the story is to give you time to make some other choices, and to bend your life again toward God and the things of God while you still have the opportunity.

All of us will make choices to say yes or no when God calls us to do something. We would do well to ask ourselves some questions: Are we living our lives in accord with our deepest held values and beliefs? Do we base our decisions on principle or expediency? Are we compromising our integrity to achieve success? Remember it's the little choices that count. As a Chinese proverb says, "It is better to light one candle than to curse the darkness."

When I was rector in San Diego, I learned of a man who was searching for a deeper meaning in his life, something more sustaining than cars and boats and golf. So, he got into his car and headed for Mexico. He crossed the border and found a woman cooking tamales over a burning fire for a bunch of ragged kids playing in the dirt. She had found them living in junk cars and eating garbage. So, she took them in and started an orphanage of sorts. The man decided then and there to take up an offering for her, an offering which over the years has helped build dormitories, a soup kitchen, a clinic and who knows what else

This man never considered himself a social activist, but he was determined that no child should have to eat garbage, or drink contaminated water, or play in filthy conditions. When he was asked how he managed to give so much of his life to the orphanage, he said that when he took early retirement, he made a decision to leave this world a better place by his being here. That led to one choice after another, and eventually to the orphanage.

That man made a series of choices in life. He was wealthy enough to take it easy, relax and have fun: play golf, go to the beach, and enjoy his country club. But he decided that life was more than any of those things, and that the way for him to save his life was to share it with others. That choice impacted not only him but the children of a poor town south of the border.

So, what are you waiting for? When God calls you to do something, do it. Don't just "talk the talk" but walk it. Do the right thing, even if it's inconvenient and moves you out of your comfort zone. Let your light shine and let your life go.

September 28, 2014
St. James Westminster Church, London, Ontario

PART FOUR

THE WORLD ON FIRE: CONTEMPORARY ISSUES

Philosopher Michael Novak has argued that democratic capitalism requires a three-legged stool: political liberty, economic freedom and moral responsibility. Remove any one of those legs and the system collapses. All three are essential for a vibrant, prosperous democracy.

The church, and particularly preachers, have a duty to address topics involving moral responsibility, whether they be corporate excess, racism and other forms of discrimination, civility in our political discourse, violence, terrorism, school shootings and economic disparity. While there will be voices that oppose the church addressing political, social and economic issues, Christianity is not an esoteric, pie-in-the-sky religion. In the first chapter of John's Gospel we read: "And the Word became flesh and lived among us" (Jn. 1:14, NRSV). This is the God who enters our world and experiences all the joys and pains of being human. As a result, we make a profound mistake if we divorce the spiritual from the temporal in our preaching.

The German Lutheran pastor Dietrich Bonhoeffer in his *Letters and Papers from Prison* coined the phrase "religion-less Christianity" in which he called the church to a "this-worldliness" mindset – a church that is not so focused on "religious" matters that it neglects the pains, problems and suffering in the world. In preparing sermons, preachers should be mindful of Bonhoeffer's challenge to embrace the world and not simply deal with purely religious matters. They should be familiar with current events as much as they know the Bible. This does not mean preaching on a news story each week, but preachers may want to address particularly important news stories that resonate with parishioners. The task is not to solve the problem or even offer a solution, but to understand an issue from the standpoint of Christian faith.

Cross-Centered Living was an Independence Day sermon preached in 2019 but it just as easily could be a Canada Day sermon. Both the United States and Canada enjoy economic prosperity and political freedom, abundant natural resources and diverse, multicultural populations. However, secularism is making it more difficult to be a faithful Christian in both countries. How can Christians be faithful citizens but maintain their spiritual integrity?

The Moment to Decide was inspired by the fall of Joe Paterno – one of the most beloved and successful college football coaches of all time. Paterno was forced to resign as Coach of Penn State football after reports that his assistant Jerry Sandusky had sexually abused numerous young boys over the years. When Paterno was informed of the allegations, why didn't he act more decisively, call the police, insist that university officials investigate the matter, or do something that would have shown he cared?

The Promise of Peace in a Less Than Perfect World was prompted by a series of school and church shootings which are becoming an all-too-common occurrence. It is not for the preacher to propose gun reform laws, but rather to explore the issue from a Gospel perspective on how God's presence is with us even in the midst of violence and chaos.

When the World Falls Apart is a sermon preached in London, Ontario in response to the 2015 Paris massacre. Paris, the City of Light, became a center of darkness when terrorists struck unexpectedly and killed over one hundred people. Canadians have a special bond to France as one of the two founding nations of the country. My goal was not to give any political response to the massacre but to address the reality of evil, our duty to oppose it, and not despair.

Race in America is a sermon on racism in the United States, beginning with two stories from my time in Lancaster, Pennsylvania. Racism is a challenging issue, because it is not just about black and white, but about differing perspectives and experiences that can make it difficult for people of good will to understand one another. Racial reconciliation is a painful but necessary process.

The Hard Truth declares that God cares about our economics as much as our soul. Too often we divide life into separate categories, with believing having very little to do with behaving. According to the prophet Amos, God has a much more wholistic view of our lives where belief and behavior are in sync with one another. We cannot separate how we worship on Sunday from what we do the other days of the week.

God's New Economy is on the growing gap between rich and poor in the United States. America's suburbs are some of the most prosperous in the world, while the inner cities are some of the most violent. How can we bridge the gap between two very different worlds and create a more just and equitable social order? The sermon addresses the issue in light of the Gospel of Lazarus and the rich man.

The Myth of More addresses what it means to live a contented and fulfilled life. One option is to pursue "more" of everything, as if at the end of life "the one with the most toys wins." Another option is to give ourselves to some higher cause, some noble purpose that brings out the best from us. Abundant life is always received by sharing it with others.

How Can I Live in a World Like This? is a question we ask when none of the choices before us is perfect. We live in an imperfect, flawed and fallible world where we often have to choose and make decisions, with none being perfect. We take the world as it is, and not as we would have it. In the midst of an imperfect world, we are called to love. How we put love into practice will be a judgment call on our part. And yet, love we must.

Christian Civility in a Coarse Culture deals with civility in our politics. How can we rise above an increasingly vitriolic and acerbic political divide? Is there a way for people to come together, accept their differences, and live, argue and debate in an atmosphere of mutual respect? How can Christians promote a civil culture? This sermon points a way forward.

CROSS-CENTERED LIVING

GALATIANS 6:14-16

This Independence Day sermon reminds us that truth is not always popular, nor is being a Christian easy. Christians need the courage to stand against culture rather than always go along with it. We need to be clear on the essentials of our faith, the beliefs and values which we cannot compromise, regardless of the consequences. We also need to acknowledge that we are different from everyone else. We are disciples of Jesus and follow a way of life not popular with power brokers and media moguls. St. Paul says: "May I never boast of anything except the cross of our Lord Jesus Christ" (Gal. 6:14, NRSV).

Independence Day is a time for Americans to come together as one people. With all the political divisions in our country right now, we Americans have far more that unites us than divides us. As I often say, if you were born in America, or if you are an American citizen or resident, then you won the world's lottery. Of the over seven billion people on the planet, you and I are blessed to be Americans.

And yet, would you agree with me that being a Christian in America today is not easy? Secularism is now dominant in American culture, along with multiculturalism and religious pluralism. The

Judeo-Christian ethic, once the mainstay of America, is beginning to wane. This is to be expected given the demographic diversity in our country, but it has made being a Christian more difficult. There is now a greater dichotomy between being a Christian and being in the world.

When I was a Roman Catholic teenager growing up in Brooklyn, New York, there was a controversy about a certain movie and whether Catholics should be permitted to see it. In those days there was a "Legion of Decency" that would rate movies as to their moral and spiritual content. I thought the idea of rating movies was offensive to people who had their own minds to make judgments about what to see or not see. I told my priest that everyone should be able to see whatever movie they wanted. He simply looked at me and said, "You're a Catholic. You are not like everyone else."

Sadly, I think many Catholics have lost that sense of being different and held to a higher standard of living than non-Catholics. And yet, it is important for all of us who call ourselves Christians to recognize that what is lawful for everyone else is not necessarily permissible for us. That the ways of Jesus and the ways of the world, even the world of mainstream America, are not identical. That possessing a worldview or a code of moral behavior that prevails in secular circles is no assurance of goodness and virtue. Jesus makes some special demands on us that occasionally require us to be out of step with the culture. It is only when we recognize we are different from the world that we have a chance of being strong enough to obey the teachings of Jesus in those areas of living that really do make a difference in our lives.

In our New Testament lesson today, St. Paul says, "May I never boast of anything except the cross of our Lord Jesus Christ, by which the world has been crucified to me, and I to the world"

(Gal. 6:14, NRSV). Let me give you some background on how St. Paul could make such a statement.

There was a time in his ministry when he struggled with how to tell people about Jesus. Once he found himself in the great city of Athens. In the city which gave the world Socrates, Plato and Aristotle, Paul was brought to Mars Hill and invited to speak about his faith to the learned and the wise. The speech is recorded in the Book of Acts 17:16-31, and by all accounts it was brilliant. Paul flattered his audience. He paid tribute to their culture. He quoted their poets. He appealed to their reason. He followed the rules of rhetoric. It was a magnificent speech, but it was a miserable failure. Upon hearing Paul, some scoffed. Others shrugged their shoulders in bewilderment. At Athens, at least, Paul's Gospel had been tried and found wanting.

What went wrong? Traveling the long road from Athens to Corinth, Paul must have asked that question a thousand times. Why was his message so lacking in power?

As he approached Corinth, came the answer. At Athens he had praised the culture. He had quoted the poets. He had followed the rules of rhetoric. He had appealed to reason. Why, he even mentioned the resurrection. However, he failed to mention the cross. When he arrived in Corinth, there was a new power in his preaching. Listen to his words: "For the message about the cross is foolishness to those who are perishing, but to us who are being saved it is the power of God" (1 Cor. 1:18, NRSV).

For St. Paul, the power of the Gospel is found at the foot of the cross. This is what he says in his letter to the Galatians: "May I never boast of anything except the cross of our Lord Jesus Christ..." (Gal. 6:14, NRSV).

Here is where Paul found all the power he needed, to be all that God called him to be – at the cross of Jesus Christ. Paul understood that when you accept Jesus as Savior, you also accept his cross, and with it a resolve to be different from the world. The world's values and Christian values are not always the same, and sometimes they are in conflict.

Think, for example, of a recent federal prosecution here in Arizona of a man whose only crime was to offer food and water to migrants crossing the border illegally. His faith compelled him to feed the hungry and give drink to the thirsty, to welcome the stranger and help those in distress, but the government said he could not do those things. What do you do when the government says one thing, but Jesus says something quite different?

Then there are doctors, and I know several, who are under enormous pressure to perform abortions when their faith and their conscience tell them that it would be wrong to do so.

If you have read Martha Beck's book *Expecting Adam*, you know the pressure to have an abortion if you are a graduate student in an elite university. How could you possibly have a child if you are serious about getting your doctorate? Martha Beck recounts one of the most distinguished professors at Harvard being shocked when he heard the news that she planned to give birth to a Down syndrome baby. When her husband, a fellow graduate student, told the news to the professor, he said to "have it taken care of as soon as possible." But her husband mustered the courage to tell his professor, "It's not only Martha... I mean it is her choice to make, but I agree with her. I want the baby, too."[1]

Martha Beck and her husband were not pro-life Christians. Martha was, in fact, pro-choice, but her choice was the life of her baby. She and her husband made their decision, convinced it was the right one for them.

You can think of your own scenario, I am sure. Increasingly, Christians have to stand against culture, swim upstream, and live according to a different set of values. Will Willimon and Stanley Hauerwas wrote a book several years ago titled, *Resident*

Aliens. Some mainline Christians did not like the book because it challenged them to stand out in society, to recognize that Christians in life and viewpoint are somewhat different from those around them. Christians are pilgrims, alien citizens who hold to certain values and stand for certain beliefs that challenge the dominant secular culture around them.

In a certain sense, Christian values make no sense to the world. After all, we Christians live in what Donald Kraybill has termed, an upside-down kingdom. The world values self-assertion, self-esteem, even self-aggrandizement. Look at the radio and cable news commentators. They are not at all hesitant at telling us that they are right and everyone else is wrong. Or look at groups that pressure universities to prevent certain speakers from coming on campus, as if they have the whole truth and nothing but the truth. Follow their ideology and way of thinking or face their wrath and suffer the consequences.

We all need to step back and admit that none of us know it all. We all are flawed, fallible human beings, prone to mistakes, and with faulty judgments. I like the way Supreme Court Justice Oliver Wendell Holmes put it in a letter to the philosopher William James. He wrote: "The great act of faith is when a man decides he is not God."

The greatness of God and the insignificance of self is a strange idea to the world. So is the notion of sacrifice, the willingness to live for a greater good, even at the cost of our own self-interest. We see this virtue in the military academies, at West Point, for example, where the motto is "Honor, Duty and Country." And yet, how many politicians mention sacrifice when they promise entitlements but fail to mention the taxes needed to pay for them?

Some of us are old enough to remember President John F. Kennedy's inaugural address in which he said: "Ask not what your country can do for you; ask what you can do for your country."

Back in 1961, those words were well received. I am not sure they could be spoken by any politician today. Some commentators think we are now living in an age of entitlement. We expect to receive benefits from government with someone else footing the bill. The idea of "giving back" for living in the greatest country in the world doesn't resonate with us as it did for our forebears. Even some churches have shunned the notion, treating worshipers as consumers rather than raising them as disciples of Jesus.

Being a Christian is not easy. Discipleship has its cost. We Christians are being called to love, serve, and even sacrifice for things that matter. We live in the world but we are not of it. We are flexible, tolerant people but we do not compromise what is essential to being a Christian. On some things we draw a line, take a stand and say no. It seems that wherever we are and in whatever we do, we are being challenged to stay true to our faith and values. You may be on a university campus, or working in the corporate world, or teaching at a public school, or being a nurse or doctor at a hospital. Whatever your circumstances, to take up your cross and follow Jesus is a challenge for us all.

A politician I admired was the late Governor Robert Casey of Pennsylvania. He was in many ways a typical Democratic politician except that he was a devout Catholic and staunchly pro-life in opposing abortion. This did not make him popular with his own party. When he asked to speak at the 1996 Democratic National Convention, he was refused. This, despite the fact, that he had won re-election in the Commonwealth of Pennsylvania by one of the largest margins in state history. However, as Bob Casey discovered, in his party it was impossible for a pro-life Christian to have any prominent role or influence. Being marginalized was the price he paid for being pro-life.

What happened to Bob Casey pales in comparison to what happened to Thomas More. He was the Lord Chancellor of

England who resigned his position because he could not accept that King Henry VIII rather than the Pope was the head of the Church in England. More's resignation did not satisfy the king who had him stand trial for treason.

In Robert Bolt's play, *A Man for All Seasons*, Richard Rich, who once sought a job from More, gives perjured testimony against him at trial. As Rich is leaving the witness stand, More notices a Chain of Office around his neck. He is told that Sir Richard has been appointed the Attorney General of Wales. More looks at Richard and says, "Why, Richard, it profits a man nothing to give his soul for the whole world... But for Wales!"[2]

More was convicted and sentenced to death. As he stands on the scaffold about to be beheaded, he is given an opportunity to say his last words. The king has commanded him to be brief. More simply says: "I die the King's good servant, but God's first."[3]

In his death as in his life, Thomas More could say along with St. Paul: "May I never boast of anything except the cross of our Lord Jesus Christ" (Gal. 6:14, NRSV). He had the courage, as we all should, to suffer the contempt of the world in faithfulness to the God who loved him and gave himself for him, Jesus Christ. He died in the faith in which he was raised and would not betray that faith for any worldly gain or honor, even to save his life.

We Americans can take a lesson from Thomas More. We should love our country, but God first.[4]

July 7, 2019
Church of the Advent, Sun City West, AZ

THE MOMENT TO DECIDE

MARK 1:9-15

We make decisions all the time, but some decisions are more important than others They have a lasting impact on ourselves and those around us. The key to a right decision is to rise above our apathy, indifference and fears, and instead seek to discern and follow God's will, doing what we believe to be right, and trusting God with the outcome. Sometimes a right decision will not be in our self-interest. The important thing is that we believe it to be God's will, regardless of the cost to us. St. Josemaria Escriva de Balaguer, the founder of Opus Dei, prayed: "Come, O holy Spirit! Enlighten my understanding in order to know your commands, strengthen my heart against the snares of the enemy; enkindle my will. I have heard your voice and I do not want to harden my heart and resist saying, 'Later... tomorrow.' Nunc coepi! Right now! Lest there be no tomorrow for me"[1]

Joe Paterno sat in his office back in 2002 and was doing what he did so well – focusing on football. He was the Head Coach of one of the great football powerhouses in the United States – the Nittany Lions of Penn State University. Every home game that the Nittany Lions played was packed to capacity – over 107,000 fans per game. Compare that to the Toronto Maple Leafs who also play to a sellout crowd of 19,300.

Football at Penn State was not just a game; it was big business. In 2010 the football team generated revenue of more than $106 million and a profit of over $18 million. Joe Paterno personally raised millions of dollars for the university. He was the most influential and admired person on campus.

Unlike many football coaches, Joe Paterno valued education, insisted his athletes maintain their grades, and had a special love for ancient Greek and Latin literature. When the university was about to cut the graduate classics department, Paterno raised the money to maintain the faculty. No wonder the library was named after him. Why, there was even a statue of him, and he wasn't dead yet!

Joe Paterno was a living legend, but every legend has a shadow side. One day, as he sat in his office, a shaken graduate assistant told him that he saw former assistant coach Jerry Sandusky engaging in improper conduct with a young boy in a locker room shower. The allegation, if true, was an awful crime. At that moment, Joe Paterno had to decide what he would do. He could call police. Or he could confront Jerry Sandusky personally. However, he did neither of those things. Instead, he followed procedures, informed his superiors about the allegation, and then returned to the business of football. After all, he had so many important duties and so many people counting on him.

Should Joe Paterno have done more? After all, people looked up to him. If anyone could have pursued the case, it was the coach. He had enormous personal authority. He also knew that Jerry Sandusky ran a charity for underprivileged children and that he was around young boys all the time. But he did nothing, except to inform his superiors. As it turned out, the university's only response was to forbid Sandusky from bringing young boys on campus. The police were never notified of the allegations.

In 2011 Jerry Sandusky was finally arrested for sexual assault with countless young boys over a fifteen-year period. Joe Paterno, the most winning coach in the history of U.S. college football was fired by university trustees for his failure to act.

No one denies Coach Paterno's character, faith or decency. He should have retired in a blaze of glory for all his accomplishments in over fifty years at Penn State. Instead, he was forced to leave in disgrace, an eighty-five-year-old man who could not be bothered taking the keys to the office away from an alleged sexual predator.

Just weeks before his death from lung cancer on January 22, 2012, Paterno admitted to a reporter: "With the benefit of hindsight, I wish I had done more."

Tragic, isn't it, that one incident should tarnish the legacy of one of the greatest football coaches of all time? For Joe Paterno there was a moment of decision. He had to make a choice – and his choice was found wanting.

One of the poems I remember from high school was James Russell Lowell's "Once to Every Man and Nation." The poem was set to music and became a popular hymn which is found in *Common Praise*. Lowell wrote the poem in response to the reluctance of many Northerners in the ante-bellum United States to confront their Southern brothers and sisters over the issue of slavery. Northerners, especially in New England, did not like slavery but neither were they prepared to fight over it. "Keep the peace at any price" was the attitude of many. Lowell disagreed. And so, he wrote:

> Once to every man and nation
> comes the moment to decide,
> in the strife of truth with falsehood,

for the good or evil side:
some great cause, God's new Messiah,
offering each the bloom or blight;
and the choice goes by forever
'twixt that darkness and that light.

Jesus had those moments of decision. In the wilderness he had to decide whether to affirm his call as God's chosen one, the Messiah of Israel. Throughout his ministry he had to decide what kind of Messiah he would be: a bread king, who gives people what they want or a Suffering Servant who gives his life as a ransom for many. On that dark night before he died, in the Garden of Gethsemane where his sweat was as thick as drops of blood, he had to decide whether to submit to his Father's will and embrace the cross or abandon his ministry and save his life.

Yes, Jesus had his moments of decision, and so do we. There comes a moment when we have to decide one way or another – to choose action or inaction, to raise our voice or to remain silent, to take a stand on principle or to go along with the herd, to do what is right or to do what is expedient, to act for the common good or to act in our own self-interest.

Abraham Lincoln had to make the decision whether to issue the Emancipation Proclamation during the Civil War. You may recall that the Civil War was originally fought not to end slavery but to save the Union. Lincoln, however, struggled with the issue of slavery, personally opposed it, and finally made the decision to issue his proclamation, despite opposition from almost all Democrats and even some members of his own party. It was his moment of decision. It was time to end slavery and there could be no more hesitation about the issue.

When Dietrich Bonhoeffer came to the United States in 1939, he, too, had to make a major decision. His friends in Germany pleaded with him to stay in the United States until Hitler and the Nazis were out of power. His friends in the United States echoed those sentiments and begged Bonhoeffer to stay in America where he could teach at the prestigious Union Theological Seminary in New York. However, Bonhoeffer became convinced that if he were not with the German people in their suffering, he would have no right to guide and pastor them after the war. And so, to Germany he returned where he would be imprisoned and eventually executed just a few weeks before the end of the war.

Sometimes we have to stand up and make decisions which are not in our self-interest. We may have to challenge authority when the safe course is to remain silent. Or we may need to confront injustice when it would be safer for us to go along with the crowd. Isn't that the lesson of the Nuremburg trials after World War II when Nazi leaders were tried for war crimes? We must take responsibility for our actions. We cannot give the excuse that we were acting under orders or that there was nothing we could do. There is always something we can do. We have the power of choice, the freedom to act one way or another.

Yes, we may end up being a martyr like Dietrich Bonhoeffer. Or we may have to forfeit a political career. Think of Bishop Dennis Drainville who, at one time, was a member of the Ontario Provincial Parliament. When the NDP government moved to legalize gambling and insisted on a party-line vote to pass the legislation, Dennis said that his conscience would not allow him to vote for gambling and instead resigned from Parliament. That is a Canadian profile in courage.

> *By the light of burning martyrs,*
> *Christ thy bleeding feet we track,*
> *toiling up new Calvaries ever*
> *with the cross that turns not back.*

New occasions teach new duties;
time make ancient good uncouth;
they must upward still and onward
who would keep abreast of truth.

If there is one movie that you need to rent and see this Lenten season, it is the French film with English subtitles, *Of Gods and Men*. The film is a dramatic interpretation of a true-life story.

In March 1996, seven monks from a Cistercian monastery in Algeria were kidnapped by Muslim radicals opposed to the country's government. Two months later, their severed heads were found. Their bodies were never recovered. A state funeral for the monks in Algiers drew a crowd of 100,000.

The film examines the monks' lives as they attended to the Muslim villagers around them and watched Algeria descend into violence from 1993 until their kidnapping. It shows the monks living their vows of poverty, chastity and obedience, running a medical clinic for the poor and growing their own food as the violence engulfs the countryside. The monastery is a house of peace where Muslim villagers and French Christians share a long history and mutual regard. Yet war encroaches on that house as fundamentalist Muslim rebels become more antagonistic to the monastery and government officials become more suspicious of the monks' willingness to treat everyone in need of medical care. Both sides are heavily armed; both sides are given to brutality, and these monks are caught squarely in the middle.

Finally, the monks get word that both the Vatican and the French government want them to leave Algeria. It is at this point that a decision must be made – to abandon the monastery and leave the villagers to the ensuing chaos, or to remain and face the imminent threat of death. As they gather to discuss the matter, the monks remember their vows. What kind of poverty is it if you leave and the people you are connected to must stay?

The monks choose to remain at the monastery and face death rather than flee. And, of course, death is inevitable. The monks know that, yet they make their decision as persons of faith, even amidst their own doubts and fears. As he casts his vote to stay, one of the monks – who stayed through the terrors of the Nazis and the war of Algerian liberation says in a soft whisper: "I am a free man."

Yes, we are free to choose and make decisions. We can choose life. We can choose love. We can choose to live by faith rather than be ruled by fear. Some things are more important than our comfort or safety, our self-interest or well-being, or even football and hockey. Sometimes we must stand up and be counted. Do the right thing, say the right word, act in the right way, and let the consequences fall where they may. In the end, whether we succeed or fail, we are in the hands of Almighty God, always and forever.

So, take courage and heed the words of the poet:

> *Though the cause of evil prosper,*
> *yet 'tis truth alone is strong;*
> *though her portion be the scaffold,*
> *and upon the throne be wrong,*
> *yet that scaffold sways the future,*
> *and, behind the dim unknown,*
> *standeth God within the shadow,*
> *keeping watch above his own.*[2]

February 26, 2012
St. James Westminster Church, London, ON

THE PROMISE OF PEACE IN A LESS THAN PERFECT WORLD

JOHN 14:23-29

Nothing frightens parents more than the school shootings routinely reported on the news. No place seems to be safe anymore, not a school or even a church. In this dreadful environment, Christ gives us the inner peace to deal with whatever comes our way. When present circumstances threaten to engulf us, we need to keep in mind that God's peace is an objective reality for all who trust Jesus. In him our future is secure. Therefore, no matter the trials and troubles that may come our way, we hold fast to the words of Jesus: "Peace I leave with you; my peace I give to you. I do not give to you as the world gives. Do not let your hearts be troubled, and do not let them be afraid" (Jn. 14:27, NRSV).

"We moved to Newtown to escape this kind of violence." That is what one parent said after the shooting death in Newtown, Connecticut that killed twenty-six people, including twenty children. Another parent said, "Where do we have to go and what do we have to do to keep our children safe? I just don't know the answer to that."

Not even private religious schools are any guarantee against violence. In March 2012, a Spanish teacher fired earlier in the day killed the headmaster of the Episcopal School of Jacksonville, Florida and then killed himself. That same year there were the murders of church workers at an Episcopal church in Ellicott City, Maryland. Not even churches are safe from violence these days.

A few years ago, there was a Canadian Broadcasting Corporation report on a special community meeting between police officials and parents in Abbottsford, British Columbia. The subject was predators, psychopaths and drug pushers – how to recognize them, what to do about them, and how to protect your children from them. Not a pleasant topic, to be sure, but a symptom of the kind of world we now live in.

All parents worry about their children. We try to protect them from all sorts of dangers and bad choices, and at times it seems like a losing battle. We parents love our children, but we also are afraid for them, and rightly so. There are so many dangers lurking in our world.

I make no apologies for being a protective parent regarding my daughter Allison. After all, she has Down syndrome and will need assistance throughout her life. She has an independent spirit and wants to be self-reliant, but she will always require help. Heather and I pray for Allison every day, and we are doing our best to plan for her future, especially when we are no longer around to care for her.

And yet, there is no guarantee that we can perfectly protect Allison from the dangers that threaten. This became clear to me after an incident occurred when we lived in New Jersey. Allison was blessed to attend an outstanding school for special needs children, but every day she had to travel in a van for forty-five minutes each way along a busy highway. In the winter months, that highway could be treacherous. One icy, cold winter day, there was an accident that forced the van off the road. The passengers were stranded for more than an hour. Thank God no one was hurt, but what if in that accident Allison was injured or even killed? It then dawned on me that there is no full-proof insurance policy against the troubles and tragedies of life. No matter how hard we try, we cannot protect our children from every danger that may threaten them.

So, what can we give our children that is of lasting value? I suggest that the one thing we can give them is inner peace. Isn't that what we mean when we say, "All I want for my children is that they should be happy?" What we want for our children is what Jesus wanted for his disciples – inner peace, inner strength, inner confidence that will allow them to stand tall in the time of testing; that will strengthen and sustain them throughout their days

"Peace I leave with you," Jesus says, "my peace I give to you. I do not give to you as the world gives. Do not let your hearts be troubled, and do not let them be afraid" (Jn. 14:27, NRSV).

On the night before he died, Jesus gave all who believe in him a promise of peace. It comes not a moment too soon. Peace is something we all want, isn't it? Certainly, we want world peace, but we also desire inner peace – the peace that helps us cope with anxiety, worry and fear. Perhaps that is why we come to church. We search for something to help us sleep better at night, and for something to get us through the day. We want something that will help us face life's challenges with courage, conviction and integrity.

When we were on vacation in Florida recently, Heather was at the pool of our hotel speaking with a couple from Boston. Naturally, she asked how they were coping considering the Marathon bombings. "We are going to be fine," said the woman. "Everything will be okay. We're strong and we can get through this."

"But" Heather asked, "what about all those who were injured – those who lost limbs, who have shrapnel embedded in their bodies and are facing a long, difficult recovery?" The woman did not want to go there. The heartbreak was just too great for her to face that reality. She kept repeating, "We're going to be all right. We'll be fine. We'll get through it."

I like that woman's spunk, but positive thinking is simply not enough to get us through the tough times of life. It will not fill the vacuum in our souls when life's tragedies start to drain us.

In a world filled with reasons for worry, we need something tougher than positive thinking or "name it and claim it" theology. Yes, Jesus promises us peace, but he also tells us to expect trials and tribulations. The question is, "Where is the peace of God when the world around us is in turmoil?"

When I practiced law in New York City, I was mugged on the subway. I was coming home from work after a late night at the office. As I was about to put my token into the turnstile, two men grabbed me, threw me against the wall, pulled out a knife, pointed it to my belly and took my wallet. That experience changed my life. Never again did I ride the subway alone at night. I always had my law firm pay for a cab. More important, I kept thinking to myself, "What if there wasn't enough money in my wallet and the robbers decided to kill me?" On that dark Tuesday night on May 20, 1980, where was the peace of God for Gary Nicolosi?

As I shared the story of my mugging with my law colleagues, the most common response was, "Somebody was sure watching out for you." More specifically, the response sometimes implied, sometimes stated, was that God was watching out for me because I was not physically harmed. At first, that was comforting, but later it made me wonder what those people would have said about God if one of the robbers had killed me. Where is the peace of God when you are the victim of a crime?

I suppose you could name your own scenario... the school children in Newtown, Connecticut, the victims of the Boston

Marathon bombings, the skyrocketing number of shootings in Chicago and the murders in Detroit, soldiers killed by roadside bombs in Afghanistan, the thousands upon thousands of people killed in natural disasters – earthquakes, hurricanes, tornadoes, floods and tsunamis... the accidents on the 401 and other heavily traveled highways... Just this past week, five people were killed in a roadside accident in Surrey, British Columbia. Like it or not, these things happen, and they are more common than we like to imagine.

So where is the peace of God when life goes terribly wrong?

"Peace I leave with you; my peace I give to you. I do not give to you as the world gives. Do not let your hearts be troubled, and do not let them be afraid" (Jn. 14:27, NRSV).

After the 9/11 attack, members of my church, like all Americans, were deeply upset by the massive loss of lives, in New York City, Washington and Shanksville, Pennsylvania. One woman came to my office in tears. She had not been able to sleep for two nights since the attack. She just kept thinking of the devastation and loss of life at the World Trade Center. She had been an investment banker in New York before retiring to San Diego. She knew the Twin Towers all too well. Many times she had eaten at Windows on the World and rode the elevator to the top floors for meetings. She kept thinking to herself that had the attack happened two or three years before, she probably would have been in one of those buildings. Then she said to me, "I don't know if I can believe in God anymore."

The following week this woman came to see me again. She told me that her faith had been restored. I asked her what had changed. She said it was a picture in the newspaper. The picture was of two beams from one of the collapsed buildings that had formed a cross on top of a pile of debris. In her mind, there was no denying that God was present in that place of ruin.

Those beams forming a cross are today at the National September 11 Memorial and Museum. That cross reminds us that even amid the most awful moments of life, God is there for us. God weeps with us, knows our pain and heartbreak, but gives us the strength and courage to face the future with faith, not to lose hope, or let despair have the word in our lives. As St. Paul puts it, in Christ "we are more than conquerors through him who loved us" (Rom. 8:37, NRSV).

Keep that in mind next time some bombshell drops in your own life – as you cope with sickness or the loss of a loved one, as you are numbed by suffering or wonder if the world will ever rebound from tragedy, as you struggle with doubt or feelings of despair, or whatever life throws at you. Never forget there is a God who took on all the evil powers of this world and won – a God who conquered death itself, and therefore can conquer whatever difficulties may come your way.

That is why we have peace even when the world around us is in chaos. It is not a "feel good" peace or a "wishful thinking" peace. It is an objective peace that does not depend on feelings or even circumstances. It is a peace the world cannot give or take away, because it is God's gift to every believer in Jesus.

Are you worried or afraid? Are you troubled or distressed? Is your heart breaking from some tragic loss, or is the pain so great that it hurts too much to cry? Then claim the promise of Jesus for your life. He is our perfect peace in this less than perfect world.

"Peace I leave with you; my peace I give to you. I do not give to you as the world gives. Do not let your hearts be troubled, and do not let them be afraid" (Jn. 14:27, NRSV).

May 5, 2013
St. James Westminster Church, London, ON

WHEN THE WORLD FALLS APART

MARK 13:1-8

This sermon was preached the Sunday after the November 13, 2015 Paris terrorist attack in which 130 people were killed, with over 350 injured. In the face of such callous indifference to innocent human life, it is easy for the best of us to despair. Christians face the evil in the world with hopeful realism. Unlike optimism which views history as a straight line of inevitable progress, hope faces the reality of evil with the confidence that Christ has won the victory. There is no straight line of inevitable progress, but Christians do not lose hope. We focus on the triumph of Christ amid life's tragedies. In the end, God wins. St. Teresa of Avila prayed: "Let nothing disturb you. Let nothing frighten you. All things pass. God does not change. Patience achieves everything. Whoever has God lacks nothing. God alone suffices."[1]

Today's sermon is not the one I prepared to preach. My original sermon was titled, "When the Church Falls Apart." But the recent terrorist attack in Paris compelled me to change the sermon to, "When the World Falls Apart." It seems that way, doesn't it? This past week we have been bombarded with terrorist attacks on an airplane and on the ground – in Egypt, Lebanon, Paris – suicide bombings, massacres of innocent people, and calculated violence designed to do the most injury and instill the most fear. If you are like me, you feel sickened by these events; find it difficult to watch news reports or to read the horrific stories of such devastation and carnage.

What makes the Friday terrorist attack even more painful is that it happened in Paris – the city of light and love. The victims were mainly young people enjoying a night out with their friends, having a meal at a restaurant, a drink at a bar, or enjoying a rock concert. None of those who were at these places expected to die that night. No one thought their lives were in danger. I am sure many of these young adults felt they had a marvelous future ahead of them, plans, opportunities and dreams to be realized. No one thought they would die or come close to dying on a Friday fun-filled night. It was Paris, after all, where life is to be celebrated and savored.

My heart goes out to the French people, as I know yours does too. France is one of the founding nations of Canada. Canadians have a special relationship with France, and when the French people suffer, we suffer. Today we are all French.

All of us, whoever we are and wherever we live, if we believe in civility, decency and the sanctity of life, then we probably feel angry, anxious and fearful about what is occurring in our world today. What we need is a good dose of hope – hope, not optimism.

Since the eighteenth century, the Western world has been nurtured on a belief in progress. Despite all the evidence to the contrary, we have been taught to believe that the world is getting progressively better. Industrial progress, technological innovation, and the rational wisdom of the Enlightenment will produce a world in which the old evils will be left behind. No more fanaticism, extremism, intolerance, but instead sweet reason will prevail.

If you have been watching the comments of some of the world leaders, you may have noticed the idea of universal values – that everyone or at least most people around the world share the same values. That simply is not true. There are many people who do not espouse the same values as Canadians or Christians or even secular people in western democracies. They would not approve of the Charter of Rights or the U.S. Bill of Rights. They do not believe in freedom of speech, or freedom of religion, or in the equality of women. It is a quite different worldview from ours, and some political scholars such as Bernard Lewis and Samuel Huntington refer to it as "a clash of civilizations."

I know... we want to believe we can all get along if we just understand each other better, appreciate our differences, listen to one another and show mutual respect. Sit around the campfire, hold hands and sing Kumbaya, and everything will be okay. Try telling that to a Holocaust survivor, or the victims of terrorist attacks in India, Africa, Asia, Europe and the United States, or the millions of refugees now fleeing the Middle East. ISIS and Al Qaida are not Kumbaya types, especially when they behead Christians and others who do not share their views.

If you think the world is a mess, well, it is. But that does not mean we should become pessimists. Jesus in our Gospel warns us about cataclysmic events. There will come a time, he says, when one of the greatest wonders of the ancient world – the Jewish temple in Jerusalem – will be reduced to rubble. And sure enough, in 70 A.D. – only seven years after the temple was finally completed – it was reduced to rubble by the Roman army. Today hundreds of the stones are still there, still piled on top of one another to make a wailing wall.

The world is on shaky ground, Jesus says. The world may feel like it is out of control, in chaos, with one upheaval after another coming our way. Jesus tells us not to get discouraged because it is the birth pangs of God's kingdom coming into fruition. And that dear people, is where hope comes in.

Hope is not a belief in steady progress, but an unwavering conviction that the world is God's world and that God has continuing plans for it. Yes, there is real evil in this world that needs to be named and condemned. The taking of innocent human life, the wicked violence that shoots people in restaurants and at a concert hall can never be justified or ever excused. Moreover, the invoking of God's name for such ungodly acts is blasphemy.

Hope recognizes that evil exists but insists it does not have the last word. God does. Even when we may not perceive God in the midst of Friday's horrendous events, we still may be absolutely certain of one thing: that evil will not triumph, that justice will ultimately prevail, and that God will vindicate the innocent. Whether today or tomorrow or even at the end of time, God's judgment lies before us, and evil will get its just desert.

When Western Christendom split at the time of the Reformation, and the old certainties no longer proved true, many Christians were at a loss to know where was their security in a tumultuous world. Martin Luther, in reading Psalm 46, took up his pen and wrote one of the great hymns of the Christian faith: *A Mighty Fortress is Our God*. The second stanza of that hymn goes like this:

> *Did we in our own strength confide,*
> *our striving would be losing;*
> *were not the right man on our side,*
> *the man of God's own choosing:*
> *doth ask who that may be?*
> *Christ Jesus, it is he;*

Lord Sabaoth his Name
from age to age the same,
and he must win the battle.[1]

God is with us even in the worst of times. When life is bad, God is still good. When despair seems to have the upper hand, hope still triumphs. When hate seems to have the advantage, love still conquers. When our heart sinks because of a thousand disappointments, God gives us the strength to face another day. When our life is at a dead end, God makes a way where there is no way. In the power of God's love we can face whatever comes our way and still come out triumphant.

The most famous clock in the world is London's Big Ben. It stands by the Houses of Parliament and towers over Westminster Abbey. Big Ben survived the Nazi blitz of London. Not only did it survive, but also its chimes continued to play a tune – a tune that reminded Londoners not to lose heart. The tune is still played today in many churches. It is the tune of "Duke Street" and the hymn is, "I know that my Redeemer lives."

Can you imagine? Enemy aircraft dropping bombs all over London, and yet the tune kept playing, "I know that my Redeemer lives."

God's goodness will triumph over the world's evil. Jesus Christ has defeated evil and death once for all when he died on the cross and rose from the grave. The terrorists already have lost, whether they know it or not. Christ has won the victory.

We may not feel victorious right now. The Middle East is in chaos, refugees flee by the millions, and the forces of darkness seem to be sweeping over the region. No matter – the terrorists of this world have already been defeated. They will not have the last word. They will not extinguish civilization. They will not plunge the world into a new Dark Ages. The Bible says: "The light shines in the darkness, and the darkness did not overcome it" (John 1:3, NRSV).

Keep in mind that whatever happens in our world, whatever tragedies take place, whatever heartbreak afflicts us, whatever sorrow or grief we feel, God reigns. In times of trouble and in times of peace, God reigns. When evil seems to have the advantage over good, God reigns. When truth is on the scaffold and wrong upon the throne, God reigns. Jesus Christ has won the victory; of that we can be sure. And so, we never give up, we never give in, and we never lose heart. God reigns.

Yes, sometimes events can break our heart, but we Christians live in the confidence that truth crushed on earth will rise again. Above all, we stand on the rock-solid foundation of Jesus Christ, who yesterday, today and forever, is our Lord, our Savior, and our God.

November 15, 2015
St. James Westminster Church, London, ON

RACE IN AMERICA

ACTS 10:34-38

Racism is like a virus that affects every aspect of our country, but people with a passion for justice continue to fight against it, and in the power of God's grace, will eventually overcome it. We know that racial reconciliation will not be easy. Nothing worthwhile is ever easy. Still, it is a struggle we must continue to pursue because there can be no peace without justice. Peace and justice will only come together in Christ. As the hymn puts it: "In Christ there is no East or West, in him no South or North, but one great fellowship of love throughout the whole wide earth."[1]

When I pastored a church in Lancaster, Pennsylvania, I thought it the perfect place to live and raise a family. Here, the work ethic was strong, the people were unpretentious, the food was inexpensive, housing was reasonable and the countryside was beautiful. It really did seem like paradise, but not for everyone.

One day our state representative, who was a member of my parish, asked if we would like to join in a dialogue with an African Methodist Episcopal Church in the city. He thought it might be a good idea for a relatively prosperous suburban church and a black inner-city church to come together and share their differing perspectives of the community. At one of our meetings, several members of my parish voiced much the same sentiments about Lancaster that I just shared with you. They loved Lancaster. The members of the black church were not as enthusiastic. Yes, living in Lancaster certainly was preferable to living in Philadelphia… but what about the racism? "Racism?" one of my white parishioners responded, "I've never experienced racism here."

"You're not black," an AME member shot back. "But let me tell you a story. I was in New Holland not long ago interviewing for a job. While I was waiting on the corner for the bus to take me back to the city, a man said to me, 'What are you doing here? Go back to where you came from.' Another person just stared at me like she had never seen a black man before. A third person quietly cursed at me just loud enough for me to hear, as he walked by. That's what we black people face routinely living in Lancaster. Yes, it's a nice place for whites, but it's not always a nice place for black folks."

After the man finished speaking, there was silence in the room. Some of my parishioners were in tears. Others were just stunned. One or two thought the man was exaggerating. Our conversation that night was so emotionally stressful that the two churches never met again. The gap between the city and the suburbs had grown wider. It was like the movie *Grand Canyon* – two different races living in two different worlds, neither really able to understand the other.

Several days later I was at the hospital visiting a parishioner who had suffered a mild heart attack. I told him about the meeting. He wasn't surprised. He said to me, "You know, I am a recovering racist. I didn't call myself a racist but I was a racist because I didn't like black people – why, I don't know. That all changed when I was at a rehabilitation center after my hip surgery. My physical therapist was a black man. He took such good care of me. He washed me. He helped me with my exercises. He was the kindest gentleman I had ever met. As I was leaving the rehabilitation center, I turned to say good-bye to him and lost it. I began to cry. I felt so ashamed of all those ugly feelings I had against black people. I asked for his forgiveness. He looked at me for a moment, and then said, 'God bless you. You're my brother.'"

That dear man not only gave me permission to share his story, but he himself shared it with several members of the parish who were able to move beyond seeing only outward differences to affirming a common humanity. We all learned a lesson in our contact with the AME church. People, no matter who they are or where they come from, are precious children of God – all of us, no exceptions.

I remember a priest hearing a racist comment from a teenager. He turned to the boy and said, "Why don't you treat human beings as human beings?" It is common sense to treat people as people, regardless of who they are, or how they look, or the color of their skin. Yet history is marred by prejudice against people we perceive as different from us.

After the day of Pentecost there arose the question, "Who will compose the church?" Jews, of course! The promises of God are for Israel. However, in Acts 10, the apostle Peter has a vision of a great sheet being lowered from the sky with all sorts of animals in it. Apparently these animals were forbidden for Jews to eat based on the dietary laws. And yet, Peter hears a voice say, "kill and eat" (Acts 10:13, NRSV). When he protests that he has "never eaten anything that is profane or unclean," the voice responds: "What God has made clean, you must not call profane" (Acts 10:15, NRSV).

Peter came to see that the vision was not about unclean food, but unclean people. He is directed to meet the Gentile Cornelius and baptizes him and his entire household. The church could have become a sect within Judaism, a gathering place for disgruntled Jews alone. But no, the promise of God was sent to the outsiders, to the Gentiles. Acts 10:34 is the key verse in the story: "Then Peter began to speak to them: 'I truly understand that God shows no partiality, but in every nation anyone who fears him and does what is right is acceptable to him" (NRSV).

Peter is declaring that God treats people equally, regardless of race, nationality or ethnic origin. And yet, there seems to be some kind of built-in resistance to people who are different from us. We may not be born that way, but over time we take on the characteristics of our culture, our history, our upbringing, our way of life. We tend to identify with people like us and to differentiate ourselves from people unlike us. One common way for us to distinguish ourselves from other people is by race or ethnicity. We may not be foolish enough to hurt people, but don't we identify our group as superior to all the others, maybe not consciously but in the decisions we make and the persons we choose to have around us? We don't say we are superior – that would not be polite – but isn't that what we think?

The twentieth century may quite possibly be the most murderous in all of history because of the belief that those who do not share my race or faith, do not share my humanity. At best they are second-class. At worst they forfeit the sanctity of life itself. They are less than human; outside the circle of humanity or civilization. From this mindset flowed the violence between Muslims and Hindus in India, Catholics and Protestants in Northern Ireland, the jihads, the pogroms, the genocide in Rwanda and the Holocaust that murdered six million Jews as well as many others.

America has never had a Holocaust, though some scholars think our treatment of Native Americans comes close to one. Even without a Holocaust, we have had slavery. It is hard for us to imagine how truly awful was the institution of slavery in the

United States. If any of us know about the design of slave ship used to transport captured Africans to America, you realize how inhumane conditions were on those ships. Slaves chained together in incredibly cramped compartments so that they could not even stand upright throughout the voyage across the Atlantic.

James Michener in his novel *Chesapeake* gave an accurate description of slave ships. They were so horrific that most respectable people could not even bare to tour them. William Wilberforce used tours of slave ships to educate people about the horrors of slavery. His efforts paid off. England abolished the slave trade in 1809 and slavery itself in 1833 – all without a shot being fired. In the United States it would take a Civil War and over 600,000 dead to finally end slavery in the nation.

How could people who were otherwise good and decent human beings, such as Thomas Jefferson, Andrew Jackson, Henry Clay, John C. Calhoun and every President prior to the Civil War justify slavery? The underlying rationale for slavery was that black people were not fully human. The Founders of the United States enshrined in the Constitution that slaves were to be counted as three-fifths of a person. That is how they were counted in the census.

On March 6, 1857, the United States Supreme Court issued its infamous *Dred Scott Decision* which affirmed the right of slave owners to take their slaves anywhere in the United States, even if the state or territory prohibited slavery. The Court held that Dred Scott was not free based on residence in either Illinois or Wisconsin because he was not considered a person under the United States Constitution. Dred Scott was the property of his owner, and property could not be taken from a person without due process of law.

After the Civil War, the ratification of the Thirteenth, Fourteenth and Fifteen Amendments declared that slaves were free citizens with the right to vote. Reconstruction sought to undo the effects of slavery in the South. However, Reconstruction ended in 1877, and soon enough slavery was replaced by segregation – both *de jure* and *de facto* – in the South and North. In *Plessy v. Ferguson*, the Supreme Court in 1896 upheld the constitutionality of racial segregation laws for public facilities if the segregated facilities were equal in quality, a doctrine known as "separate but equal."

Plessy v. Ferguson would usher in segregated schools, segregated lunch counters at restaurants, segregated trains and buses, and even segregated toilets and water fountains. Schools for black children were invariably run down and dilapidated, and never equal to white schools. Only with the Supreme Court decision in *Brown v. Board of Education* in 1954 did the Court acknowledge that "separate but equal" was unconstitutional.

When Barack Obama was elected President, even those who did not vote for him, celebrated that a black man had become President. For many of us, perhaps naively, we thought his election had ushered in a trans-racial America. Sadly, that has not been the case. The vestiges of slavery and segregation remain embedded in our nation and it will take a concerted effort to embark on a program of restorative justice that bridges the racial divide.

It is not for me as a preacher to propose any political solution to the problem of race in America. What I do know is that we need a transformation of values, a change of heart, what Christians term "conversion." As Episcopalians we should reflect again on our Baptismal Covenant to "strive for justice and peace among all people and respect the dignity of every human being."[2] The Catechism tells us that the mission of the Church "is to restore all people to unity with God and each other in Christ."[3] These two statements give us our role as Christians in dealing with racial issues: we are to be reconcilers, healers, bridge builders, peacemakers and advocates for justice. Each of us in our own way can bring a little more light, a little more love into our world, but we have to act. In common law, silence implies consent. To be silent in the face of injustice is to consent to it, and that Christians must never do.

I will always admire my father. Dad and mom were supporters of the civil rights movement at a time when many of our neighbors were uncertain about it. Back in the 1950s, many neighborhoods in New York City, especially Brooklyn, Queens and Staten Island were solidly populated by one dominant ethnic or racial group: Irish, Italian, German, Jewish, Black or Hispanic. The idea of integration outside the workplace made people feel uncomfortable.

My parents weren't activists, but they always treated people fairly, and never disparaged anyone because of their race or color of their skin. Dad's beliefs were rock solid, and that was made clear to me in 1957 when I was a boy. Dad was a supervisor of an industrial plant in Brooklyn when he was asked by the owner of the company to take two of his workers with him to Arkansas to do electrical work on a newly constructed plant.

My father took his two best men – Ruben a black man and Gomez who was Puerto Rican. When they arrived in Arkansas, the plant manager said to my father, "Joe, you can stay and do the job, but your two companions will have to go back to New York. We don't work with colored people here. This is an all-white work force."

My father replied, "If my men don't work with me, then I don't work either. I'm going back to New York. Get someone else to do your job."

That decision cost my father's company a great deal of money, but dad never regretted it. When he returned from Arkansas, I asked about his decision, and he said to me, "Son, you just do what's right, no matter the cost."

My father knew what was right. In that action of his – returning to New York with his men – my father taught me one of the greatest lessons a parent can teach a child: Always do what's right and never, ever, bow to injustice.

(By the way, when my father died, Ruben and Gomez were honorary pallbearers at his funeral.)

My father taught me about justice more by the way he lived than what he said. A quiet man, humble and in no way self-assuming, he had a moral compass about right and wrong that he passed on to his son. It's been said that we have to learn to hate, but it's also true that we can learn to love. My father taught me that better way.

Race in America is an issue that doesn't seem to want to go away. The country is still living with the vestiges of slavery. Good people will disagree on specific actions, but we should never forget that among the world's races, God shows no partiality. Every human being is a precious child of God, without exception. Call nothing that comes from God unclean.

January 9, 2005, revised June 7, 2020
St. Bartholomew's Church, Poway, CA

THE HARD TRUTH

AMOS 8:1-12

Preachers comfort the afflicted and afflict the comfortable. The prophet Amos does the latter and calls the nation of Israel to repent of its unjust practices to the poor. God has a preferential option for the poor, and economics has a moral component that we as a society ignore to our peril. President Calvin Coolidge once said, "The business of America is business." In light of the text from the prophet Amos, we might say, "The business of God is business." God cares about economic justice as much as personal morality and religious doctrine. This text is God's notice to us. We have been warned. William Wilberforce, in the debate on slavery in the British Parliament said: "You may choose to look the other way but you can never say again that you did not know."

When my daughter Allison was young, one of her favorite movies was Walt Disney's *Pollyanna* staring Haley Mills. If you have seen the film, you may remember there is a stern minister played by Karl Malden, who Sunday by Sunday preaches a steady diet of fire and brimstone to his congregation. Eventually he realizes that what he has been preaching is wrong. And so, he announces to the congregation that he intends to preach on every happy text in the Bible, which he estimates should take him about sixteen years.

Happy texts – texts that proclaim God's unconditional love for us, that assure us of God's forgiveness when we sin, that give us the hope that our final destiny is with God – these texts are all part of scripture. However, whether we like it or not, there also are texts that call us to accountability, demand our responsibility, and bring a word of judgment. We may not like these texts, but they are in the Bible, and they have to be addressed.

Today we encounter such a dark, foreboding text. It is not a happy text. It is the kind of text that makes us squirm. It comes from the prophet Amos. For much of his life Amos was a farmer living in the southern kingdom of Judah until God called him to be a prophet to the northern kingdom of Israel. He is prophesying anywhere from twenty to fifty years before the complete destruction of Israel, and what he has to say is very harsh.

Amos declares: "The end has come upon my people Israel… The songs of the temple shall become wailings… the dead bodies shall be many…" (Am. 8:2-3, NRSV). Israel will face the consequences of its own sin. Death and destruction will abound. When Amos spoke these words, Israel was in the midst of a severe famine. Amos tells them that they should start worrying about a famine of the word, a time when God falls silent and refuses to speak to the people.

What has prompted God to threaten judgment upon the people? Is it defective worship, or a failure to keep dietary laws, or matters of personal morality? Are the people maintaining their devotional practices, praying regularly, and fulfilling their offerings to God?

Actually, it is none of these things. God is upset about economics – how business is being conducted. "You trample on the needy and bring to ruin the poor of the land" (Am. 8:4, NRSV).

The marketplace is corrupt, the monetary exchange corrupt, business is exploiting the poor and favoring the wealthy. There is "deceit with false balances, buying the poor for silver and the needy for a pair of sandals..." (Am. 8:5-6, NRSV)).

The poor have been victimized by the rich. Although a prosperous nation with a seemingly bustling economy, the gap between rich and poor has grown ever wider, making the poor the virtual slaves of the rich, and forcing people into ever deeper debt that they can never climb out.

The preaching of Amos is unsettling for us today. God will allow Israel to be destroyed over economics – business practices that have gone wrong. What might this mean for us?

There are some of you who might actually think that Christianity is a "spiritual" religion. Some people get very upset when the church dares to speak on matters of economics or social matters.

Back in the early 1960s, Pope John XXIII published his encyclical *Mater et Magistra* – Mother and Teacher – which called into question the justice of the economies of developed nations. William Buckley, a noted American conservative responded with an article in the *National Review* titled, "Mater Si, Magistra No."

Like William Buckley, many of us may want the church to know its place and stay there. Keep religion to "spiritual" matters, and stay away from economics, politics or social issues. The underlying assumption is that the church should deal with other-worldly matters – almost a kind of Gnosticism that makes a sharp demarcation between the spiritual and the material.

However, Christianity is not a spiritual religion. The Archbishop of Canterbury William Temple observed that "Christianity is the most materialist of the world's religions" – materialist because in Christianity "the Word became flesh" – this is a religion concerned with the flesh and blood matters of life, including money. Sometimes we wish the church really could be more "spiritual" but no, God cares about how we make and spend our money, the way we live our lives, and the impact on other people and the environment.

I knew a couple that had retired from Bergen County, New Jersey to Lancaster County, Pennsylvania. Housing prices in their part of New Jersey were extremely high, but Lancaster County prices were more modest. The couple sold their home in New Jersey for an enormous profit and then proceeded to build a six-bedroom home with three floors in Lancaster. It was just the two of them, both in their early seventies. Instead of living in a more modest house that might better be suited for two aging persons, this couple decided to build the mansion of their dreams. When I asked why they chose to build such a large house at their age, the answer came back, "Because we could." Whether it was realistic or wise was another matter.

Most of us understand that because something can be done, does not mean it should be done. You and I can do many things in life, some of which are terribly unhealthy, while others would deplete our savings, or simply be reckless and irresponsible. Even when we can afford to do something, does not mean we should do it. That is where ethics, moral values, good stewardship and spiritual discipline come into play.

A successful CEO drove himself relentlessly in the pursuit of profits for his company. He was a Type A personality driven to succeed at any cost. Eventually he had a heart attack in which he came perilously close to dying, but he managed to recover his health. When he was asked what he had learned from his experience coming face to face with his mortality, his answer was, "I learned I didn't spend enough money." At first, the interviewer thought he was joking but he was deadly serious. He said that after his bypass surgery, he vowed never again to drink wine that cost less than one hundred dollars a bottle.

I wonder if Amos would be angry with that CEO, or the couple from New Jersey, for that matter. How we spend our money, how we make our money matters to God. Sunday worship matters but so does our checkbook, our investments, our spending habits. Sunday morning we give God one or two hours, but what about the other 166 hours of the week?

Many Americans resist thinking that their finances matter to God. If you earned the money, have the money, why shouldn't you spend it the way you want – after all, it is your money. What's wrong, if you can afford it, to eat the best food, drink the best wine, and fly in a private jet. If you can afford it, why not?

One of the greatest scandals in American business today is executive compensation. Yes, CEOs who make money for their companies deserve to be well paid, but how much is enough? Federal Reserve chairman Alan Greenspan has spoken about "infectious greed" in American corporate leadership. *Business Week* has pointed out that while rank-and-file wages increased over the last decade by just 36 percent, pay for executive officers climbed 340 percent. The magazine commented, "When CEO's can clear $1 billion during their tenures, executive pay is clearly too high."[1]

Take the case of Al Dunlap, former CEO of Scott Paper. According to *Business Week*, Dunlap personally accrued $100 million for 603 days of work at Scott Paper (that's $165,000 per day), largely by slashing the workforce, cutting the research and development budget in half, and artificially growing the company in preparation for sale. He made money but thousands of his workers were out of a job. Did his conscience bother him about what he had done? Not at all! After selling off the company, Dunlap wrote a book about himself, with the title *Rambo in Pinstripes*.[2]

Or, how about the antics of Bethlehem Steel before the company went bankrupt? Bethlehem Steel built a twenty-one-story office complex to house its executive staff. At extra expense, it designed the building more like a cross than a rectangle – a design that accommodated the large number of vice-presidents who needed corner offices. In his book *Crisis in Bethlehem*, John Strohmeyer described a fleet of corporate aircraft, used for taking executives' children to college, and transporting families to weekend hideaways. He described a world-class eighteen-hole executive golf course, an executive country club renovated with Bethlehem corporate funds, and even how executive rank determined shower priority at the club. Bethlehem Steel did not decline in the 1970s and 1980s because of imports of technology. It declined and eventually died because its corporate culture was decayed from within.[3]

Back in the 1980s, when I ministered in Bethlehem at the Episcopal cathedral, I had occasion to ask a former Bethlehem Steel executive about the practices of the company. He answered, "These are business matters, not religious or moral issues." To him, it was not a moral issue how Bethlehem Steel used its resources; it was guided purely by economics. It certainly did not seem to him like a religious issue. And yet, in light of today's scripture, Bethlehem Steel's stewardship was miserable.

Bethlehem Steel and Al Dunlap are not the exceptions, because the problem in American business is systemic. According to *Fortune*, in 2002 the average U.S. CEO earned 282 times what the average worker did. In 1982 the ratio was forty-two to one.[4] In Japan and Germany, the ratio today is fifteen to twenty to one. *Business Week* quotes Plato, who suggested that no one in a community should earn more than five times the income of an ordinary worker, and Peter Drucker, who in the 1980s argued that no leader should make more than twenty times the lowest-paid employee.[5]

Moral responsibility in business is in short supply these days. We are living in a ruthless business culture of Social Darwinism: capitalism without moral restraint is disastrous. No less than the distinguished British business philosopher Charles Handy can cite St. Augustine that profit is a means to an end, not an end in itself, and to take the opposite view "is one of the worst sins." A society of selfishness, Handy warns, "is doomed in the end, to destroy itself."[6]

Amos says that God cares about business. God, in fact, is angry at Israel over economic abuses. The country is rotting from within because of a callous indifference to the poor. We seem to have gotten away from the belief that faith and life are connected to one another; that how we worship on Sunday is related to the other six days of the week. We have compartmentalized our lives. Over here we are doing business. Over there, one or two hours a week, maybe a few minutes each day, we are religious. The various compartmentalized worlds never meet. We may be baptized but we have never baptized the economics by which we do business.

Thomas Tewell, who at the time was Senior Minister of the Fifth Avenue Presbyterian Church in New York City, had a number of members who worked on Wall Street. They were smart, savvy people who knew how to make money, but sometimes they could forget how their Christian faith should be connected to their business practices. Tewell would remind them of the meaning of their baptism, citing Will Campbell that baptism is a radical act of obedience to God. It is an act of saying "no" to the values of the culture and "yes" the values of God's kingdom. When we are baptized, we are called to a quite different bottom line.[7]

When Amos tells Israel to shape up and reform their dastardly business practices, he wasn't trying to destroy their economy. He was saying that business is all well and good, but there are limits you must put on your behavior. God's law is at work in the universe. You do not break that law. You only break yourself upon it.

Years ago the theologian Reinhold Niebuhr wrote a book titled *Moral Man and Immoral Society.* He observed that human beings tend to see themselves as moral, decent people in their private lives, but they do not always act that way in their public roles. In the Bible, however, the private and the public are one. There is no sacred and secular. Economics is as spiritual as worship. In the Book of Amos, the Bible is very specific about economic wrongdoing. When economics go wrong, God gets angry.

I remember asking an Anglican bishop from Uganda what he thought is the greatest challenge facing the church in North America. He responded by saying the greatest challenge in America is materialism. Here, there seems to be so much of everything. Christianity does not do well in such a climate. Where life is filled with so much, there is not enough room for God to get in. Money is always the problem, according to scripture, never the solution.

Why is money the problem and not the solution? Admittedly, money can do enormous good, but it can also corrupt the soul, which is why Jesus warns us: "You cannot serve God and wealth" (Lk. 16:13, NRSV).

On this sunny July day, we hear a harsh word that is meant to provoke rigorous self-examination in each of us. Where will we go after this service of worship? What concerns will consume us? What responsibility do we have for the poor and the less fortunate in our society? How much of our income do we give to charity? How have we voted in recent elections? Have we voted our own self-interest, or have we shown a concern for others?

You may have come to this Eucharist looking for a word of comfort, for peace, calm, and reassurance. You may have expected the preacher to speak about one of those "happy texts" like the minister in *Pollyanna*. Many Sundays that is what is offered. This Sunday, though, what is offered is a hard truth. God cares about economics, business and the stewardship of our resources. God cares how wealth is produced, distributed and used. Many of us think of ourselves as honest, decent people, and no doubt we are. Today God wants us to think about a darker side to our lives and to the nation: greed, materialism, and a callous indifference to the poor and marginalized. It is not too late for any of us to act with courage and live by what is true and right and good.

July 18, 2004
St. Bartholomew's Church, Poway, CA

GOD'S NEW ECONOMY

LUKE 16:19-31

The gap between the inner cities and the wealthy suburbs is a growing problem in America. They are two different worlds which never seem to come together. In Luke's Gospel of Lazarus and the rich man, Jesus challenges this kind of separation. The challenge is to be in relationship with those it is all too easy to ignore. The great danger is for the abnormal to become normal — to hear about shootings in the inner city, or see people sleeping on the streets, or living in decrepit housing and eating unhealthy food, and thinking that is normal. The church's task is not just to provide charity but to advocate for justice — not just to feed the poor in soup kitchens but to advocate for a day when soup kitchens are no longer necessary. Pope Gregory the Great declared: "When we attend to the needs of those in want, we give them what is theirs, not ours. More than performing works of mercy, we are paying a debt of justice."

When I was a young priest in the Diocese of Quebec, one of my clergy colleagues was from England who had served in the mission field in Jamaica before coming to Canada. One summer this priest and his son went to visit the University of Chicago, where his son was thinking of attending school. When he got back to Quebec,

I asked him what he thought of Chicago. His answer stunned me. "The slums and poverty," he said to me. "There were areas of the city with impressive houses and beautiful tree-lined streets, yet right next to these neighborhoods, just a short distance away, were incredible poverty and run-down housing that reminded me of Jamaica." This priest was no anti-American. He admired many things about our country, but he just could not fathom how great wealth and great poverty could exist side by side.

The United States is a nation of contrasts. There is enormous economic disparity in our country. The wealth is obvious. The United States is the home to at least 300 billionaires and almost 9 million millionaires.[1] In the last year alone, the number of millionaires jumped a staggering 14 percent. That means that one out of every 128 Americans can claim membership in the millionaire's club. Moreover, in the two decades leading up to the year 2000, the number of American households with incomes over $100,000 went from 2 million to over 9 million.

For many Americans, things are looking good. Unemployment is down, the stock market is steady, and the economy seems to have rebounded from recession, even with the constant threat of terrorism hovering over us. Materially, Americans are a blessed people. However, with wealth comes a loss of soul, which is why Jesus warns about wealth so often in the Gospels.

Money can corrupt us, compromise us, and above all, isolate us from other people. The more we have, the more detached we become from those who have not. Oh, it may not be a calculated move. We simply get drawn into new priorities. That big house demands more attention. The new car needs washing. And how inviting that sailboat seems after a busy week at work! So, brick by brick we build walls between our comfortable worlds and the struggles of those outside. This is certainly noticeable right here in Southern California with all our gated communities, but it is even more prevalent in Third World countries.

In my last parish I had a parishioner who was transferred to San Paulo, Brazil by Ford Motor Company. When he and his family returned to Pennsylvania for a visit, they shared with me the incredible disparity between rich and poor in San Paulo. They lived in a nice house in one of those executive compounds that are guarded day and night. However, every day on his way to the Ford Motor plant, he would pass neighborhoods with people living in shanties. At first, this man admitted being shaken by the sight of such poverty, but over time he got used to it, until what seemed initially so abnormal became normal.

That is the danger, isn't it, that the abnormal will become normal?

New York City was my home for the first thirty years of my life. In the 1960s and 70s there was far more poverty in the city, and especially street people who lived on sidewalks and near public buildings. During that time, I learned to take street people for granted. I cannot even remember the exact time I first encountered street people, but I was shocked that anyone would have to live on the street. Over time, though, I got used to these people. The sight of someone walking around town with a shopping cart of clothing no longer bothered me, and eventually the homeless became as commonplace as skyscrapers. I would hurry past them and try not to make eye contact. After all, I was a busy person with places to go and things to do. And you know something? There came a point in my life when I did not even see these people anymore, because they were now so much a part of the landscape. The abnormal had become normal.

That is what may be happening to us as we hear about the gun violence in our inner cities. The Cabrini Green projects in Chicago is one of the most violent areas in the country. Shootings in the southside of the city are common, as they are in many inner cities. Not only do many young black men get shot and killed, but also children and teenagers. What a tragic loss of life! However, over time reports of murders in the inner cities do not seem to bother us very much. If you hear the reports of gun violence over and over again, week after week, you get used to it. The abnormal becomes normal.

We in the suburbs are not affected by gun violence to the extent that it affects the inner cities. We keep a safe distance from those violent communities. We live, shop, and maybe even work in areas that are relatively pleasant, clean and safe. Some of us live in gated communities that give us an extra sense of security. Or we build walls around our houses that ensure privacy and safety. We have security systems that monitor our homes. If you have the money, you can insulate yourself fairly well from the violence of other communities.

In light of all the economic disparity and social problems of our nation, it is tempting to build ever higher walls, ever more fortified compounds, to keep us protected from encountering the reality of people from the other side of town or the other side of the border. Walls give us security and block us from seeing people not like us, people who make us feel uncomfortable or even threatened.

In our Gospel today, Jesus tears down the walls we build. He suggests that to be an authentic human being is to be in relationship with other people. No one can be truly human who is isolated, cut off, and separated from the rest of humanity. Human beings are created for relationship.

The seventeenth century Anglican divine John Donne wrote these words: "No man is an island, entire of itself: every man is a piece of the continent, a part of the main; if a cloud be washed away by the sea, Europe is the less. Any man's death diminishes me, because I am involved in mankind; and therefore, never send to know for whom the bell tolls; it tolls for thee."[2]

John Donne wrote eloquently of the individual's essential connection to the whole of humanity. Jesus makes this point in telling the story of the rich man and the beggar, Lazarus. It is not that the rich man is a bad person because he is rich, or that Lazarus is a good person because he is poor. What is important about this story is that Lazarus was right outside his doorstep in plain view for him to see day-in and day-out.

This is a story about contrasts – riches and poverty, heaven and hell, compassion and indifference, inclusion and exclusion. The lines are clear; the issue is focused. There is a great chasm between the two, in this life and in the next. The point here is that Jesus wants us to overcome the great divide that exists among all of us – to reconcile these relationships before the chasm is fixed.

In our Gospel story, Jesus makes it easy for the rich man to give. He needs only to look as far as his own doorstep. Jesus does not ask us to do the exceptional. He asks only that we look around us, do the ordinary, respond to daily life; share our time, talents and money in service to others. In giving this way we are the beneficiaries of our own good works because we open ourselves to receive the graciousness of God.

I knew a pleasant woman who was raised in a privileged household and lived a comfortable life with her husband in one of the most beautiful suburbs in Pennsylvania. And yet, she didn't seem to have any passion for anything beyond her bridge game. Nothing else seemed to matter to her.

Then one day, as she and her husband were driving on a rural road, he started to feel chest pains, pulled the car to the side, and died of a massive heart attack.

The woman could simply not accept her husband's death. She stopped playing bridge, rarely spoke with friends, and, in effect, became a recluse. She felt sorry for herself, feeling that she had nothing left to live for.

One day a friend asked her to help out at a local soup kitchen. She initially refused, but eventually agreed to go once. While she was serving food to the people with whom she would ordinarily have no contact, she began to notice their faces. They were people just like her, only these people were hungry, couldn't afford to buy food, and needed a meal. She began to realize there was more to life than just her.

That experience got her involved in Bread for the World, which is an organization dedicated to feeding the world's hungry. She volunteered one day a week, then two days, with an additional day helping at the soup kitchen. I asked, "What prompted you to become so involved?" She said, "I used to feel sorry for myself that my husband died too young. But I was shocked to learn that most men in the developing world die much younger – because of hunger, disease and violence. My husband over-ate, but these people starve. We had plenty of money to eat at the best restaurants, but these people don't have enough money to eat a healthy diet. We drank fine wine, but these people drink dirty water. We had excellent health care, but these people rarely if ever see a doctor. That's the real tragedy in the world."

All of us had better take a second look at our poor brothers and sisters, not just in the developing world but right here in our own country. We better act now, because Jesus warns us of a great reversal to come: a time when the hungry will be filled with good things and the rich sent empty away. The day will come when each one of us will stand in the presence of God to account for how we have lived our lives. And then it will be too late to go back.

So long as we live and breathe, we have another chance to get things right. We don't have to accept, much less tolerate, the abnormal as normal. Perhaps we might begin by acknowledging, with Millard Fuller, the founder of Habitat for Humanity, that "God's love extends to everyone – with a preferential concern for the poor."

One thing is certain: none of us can remain unchanged in the face of the Gospel. In God's new economy Jesus shows us another way to live: to be connected to each other in some essential way and to give ourselves on behalf of the poor and have-nots of the world. Let those who have ears, hear.

September 26, 2004
St. Bartholomew's Episcopal Church, Poway, CA

THE MYTH OF MORE

MARK 8:27-38

Human nature, being what it is, we always seem to want more. The problem is, we never know when to stop. We are like the prominent financier who had made hundreds of millions of dollars. He was asked, "How much is enough?" He thought for a moment and then said, "Just a little bit more." The obsession with "more" only leads to a sick and unfilled life. Enough is never enough. Jesus teaches us a better way. He tells us you find your life by losing it. You secure your life by giving it away. Abundant life comes to us not by having more stuff but doing more good. When we are in God's will, everything has its proper place. Jesus tells us: "But strive first for the kingdom of God and his righteousness, and all these things will be given to you as well" (Mt. 6:33, NRSV).

John Thain worked his way up the corporate ladder to become the President of the New York Stock Exchange. Then, in late 2007 he accepted the position as head of Merrill Lynch and Company, one of the leading investment firms in the world. Merrill Lynch was in trouble because of its foray into mortgage backed securities and derivatives, and Mr. Thain was brought in to save the company.

What John Thain did instead was spend his time renovating

his office. According to the *Globe & Mail*, with Merrill Lynch losing billions of dollars, he hired famous designer Michael Smith at a cost of $800,000 to be his decorator. He purchased area rugs worth $131,000, and an antique credenza and guest chairs costing $87,000. He spent $35,000 on a commode and $1,400 on a wastepaper basket. All toll, the renovation of his office cost more than $1.2 million.

But those totals pale in comparison to the money Merrill Lynch lost under Thain's leadership – $27 billion in 2008.

On the brink of insolvency, and with enormous pressure from the federal government, Merrill Lynch was acquired by Bank of America to thwart off bankruptcy. John Thain was out of a job.[1]

There have been many books and articles written about the financial meltdown of 2008, what were the causes and who was to blame. I suspect there are still more chapters yet to be written – chapters about greed, hubris and the sheer arrogance that put the world on the brink of economic collapse. Yes, there was a financial meltdown, but even more seriously, there was a moral meltdown. To be fair to John Thain, he is only one of many such culprits, and certainly not the worst.

In today's Gospel, Jesus tells us that if we persist in trying to secure our lives, we will lose our lives; and that only if we are willing to lose our lives will we be able to save them.

God's economy is entirely different from the world's economy. According to Jesus, the more I think of myself, the more I want for myself, the more I take for myself, the more I try to secure myself, then the more miserable I am going to be. I will never make enough or have enough or feel secure enough to experience contentment.

However, it is equally true that the more I share myself with others, the more I think of others, the more good that I do in the world, the more I expend my life for causes greater than myself, then the happier I will be – more contented, more satisfied, more fulfilled in life. The truth is: abundant life comes to us on the way to someone else. If I pass it on, I live. If I keep it to myself, I die.

Some of us may know the name Michael Milken. He was a Wall Street financier who specialized in high yield bonds, commonly known as junk bonds. Michael Milken was an intense individual, whose obsession in life was making money, and lots of it. You may remember the movie *Wall Street* starring Michael Douglas who played a character based on Michael Milken. In the movie, he gives a talk to the students at the Harvard Business School and tells them, "Greed is good."

Well, greed proved not to be so good for Michael Milken. In 1989 he pled guilty to felony charges for violating U.S. securities law. He was sentenced to ten-years in prison, fined $600 million, and permanently barred from the securities industry. While in prison Milken was diagnosed with prostate cancer. The diagnosis changed his life. He had a conversion and renewed his Jewish heritage. He resolved that once out of prison he would use his money to benefit humanity just as he had used it to benefit himself.

After his release from prison, he set up the Milken Family Foundation to fund medical research into curing melanoma and prostate cancer. In the November 2004 edition, *Fortune* magazine called Milken "The Man Who Changed Medicine" – his work in medical research had become that influential. Today Michael Milken continues to do good work, but that has not hurt his net worth, which as of 2018 is $3.7 billion.

It happens, doesn't it? You receive the gift of life by sharing it with others. You make a better world for others and you end up making the world a better place for yourself.

There is, however, a corollary to this truth: For if we save our life by giving ourselves, it is also possible to lose our life by hoarding ourselves. It would be a tragedy for any of us to look back on our life feeling regret that we could have brought more life and love into this world than we did. We could have made this world a better place by our living in it, and instead we ignored the needs of the world and thought only of our own needs. We are going to regret that we didn't do more with the one and only life God has given to us.

Jerry Levin was one of the most powerful media executives on the planet, serving as CEO of Time Warner for ten years, until he was publicly castigated into retirement in the wake of a disastrous merger with another company.

Now his life was falling apart, not just professionally but personally. In 1997 his son Jonathan, a young New York City public school teacher, was robbed and killed by a former student and an accomplice. So, Jerry Levin found himself dealing with the death of his career and the death of his son. His life was literally unraveling before him.

He and his wife moved out of New York to run Moonview Sanctuary in Santa Monica, California, which assists battered executives and their families get their lives back together. Jerry Levin looks back on his life at *Time Warner* and shakes his head. In an interview he admitted: "I finally realized that the intensity of what I was doing, even though in a sense it seemed to be an all-powerful position, was taking a terrible toll on my own soul."[2]

What an awful thing to think you are gaining the whole world and discovering instead that you are really losing your own life? The world says hold on tight. Don't let go, but cling to your life like it's yours to save.

Jesus says something quite different. He tells us that you can find your life by losing it. You can secure your life by giving it away. It's a risk, to be sure, but no greater risk than desperately holding on to your life and in the end losing everything.

You may think that if you give your money to God, you will

lose it. You may think that if you give your time and talents to God, you will lose them. You may think that if you give yourself wholly to God, you will lose the only thing that you really possess. Don't believe it! What we give will be returned to us many times over. How can I say this? Jesus tells us: "For those who want to save their life will lose it, and those who lose their life for my sake, and for the sake of the Gospel, will save it. For what will it profit them to gain the whole world and forfeit their life?" (Mk. 8:35-36, NRSV).

During my time as rector of various parishes, I have been blessed to have clergy on staff of immense integrity and generosity. I think of John Baldwin who was my deacon at St. Thomas Church in Lancaster, Pennsylvania. John was an executive at Armstrong Flooring who took early retirement to train as a deacon. He spent the rest of his life at St. Thomas caring for the sick and elderly and helping with administration. He could have spent his time at the country club playing golf during the summer and being a snowbird in the winter, but he chose instead to serve and give generously of himself. John is now in heaven serving in some capacity, because at the center of that man's life was a servant's heart.

Then there was Father Ned Kellogg. Ned was an Annapolis graduate, a Captain in the United States Navy, and the commander of a nuclear submarine. At some point in his life, Ned heard the call of Jesus to become a priest. He retired from the Navy, went to seminary, got ordained and did whatever jobs the bishop asked him to do, often going to the poorest churches in the diocese. When he died a few years ago, I thought to myself that as he entered the gates of heaven, Jesus was there to greet him with joy.

When I was in university, I got acquainted with a middle-aged Jesuit scholastic studying for the priesthood. Jim Thompson had been an executive with a New York advertising firm. "Why did you leave such a lucrative job to become a Jesuit?" I asked. He replied, "One day at the office I realized that any moment, I could keel over dead. And what did it mean? I decided to walk away from the job, do part-time work, and the following year I entered the Jesuits. I feel better than I have in years. You see, it feels good to be free."

Jim saved his life by losing it, he secured his life by letting go. He died all too early in life, but in his last years as a Jesuit priest he touched the lives of many – another good and faithful servant of Jesus.

The truth is, when we lose ourselves, we find ourselves. When we serve Jesus, we experience freedom. When we take that leap of faith, God reaches out and embraces us with everlasting arms. Abundant life comes to us on the way to someone else. Salvation is always received by sharing it with others. So, take to heart the words of Jesus: "For what does it profit them to gain the whole world and forfeit their life?" (Mt. 8:36, NRSV).

September 16, 2018
Church of the Nativity, Scottsdale, AZ

HOW CAN I LOVE IN A
WORLD LIKE THIS?

ACTS 2:1-11; JOHN 20:19-23

This Pentecost Sunday sermon was written after the death of George Floyd and the civil unrest in Minneapolis. Americans were shocked by Mr. Floyd's death, especially his crying out, "I can't breathe" while the police officer continued to hold his knee on Mr. Floyd's neck. How do Christians live in a world where evil happens, and yet we are called to love? We need to be realistic yet resolved. Christian realism doesn't deny there is evil in the world but it insists that in the power of Christ's love the forces of darkness shall not prevail. We know that not everyone will appreciate the good works we do. Still, Christians never stop trying to bring a little more love into the world because that is what followers of Jesus do. Second Thessalonians 3:13 exhorts us: "Brothers and sisters, do not be weary in doing what is right" (NRSV).

I was speaking with a neighbor recently, and we got into a discussion about my early days as a lawyer before I went to divinity school to become a priest. I told her I was a labor lawyer in a firm that represented the International Longshoremen's Association. The firm allowed lawyers to take a few pro bono or low bono cases, and I particularly enjoyed trial work as a criminal defense attorney.

The neighbor then asked me, "Were the people you represented nice?"

I told her, "Of course not."

She was shocked by my candor, and said, "But how could you represent those people?"

I tried to explain to her that an attorney serves as an advocate for his or her client, committed to providing competent legal representation consistent with the Code of Professional Responsibility and the Rules of Evidence. The defense attorney does not have to prove the defendant innocent; it is the prosecution that must prove the defendant guilty. My job as a defense attorney was to poke enough holes in the prosecution's case that guilt could not be proven beyond a reasonable doubt. That's all I had to do, nothing more, nothing less.

I told the woman, "You have to remember: the jury or judge is not finding a defendant 'innocent' but 'not guilty' – not guilty beyond a reasonable doubt. That is not a moral judgment; it is a legal one. 'Legality is not morality,' as protestors against the Vietnam War would often remind their elders."

I am not sure my neighbor agreed with me. The idea of a "bad" person being acquitted disturbed her, even if the prosecution could not prove its case. I understood my neighbor's concern. In the best of all possible worlds, every 'guilty' person would be convicted and every 'innocent' person would be acquitted. Of course, it doesn't work like that. The world is a very imperfect place.

Years ago, there was the film, *The Big Chill*. In it a young female attorney tells how she went to law school and then joined the public defender's office. She did it because she wanted to fight for the poor and the oppressed. But she was shocked to discover that most of the people she represented in court were rotten people – and guilty as blazes. Disillusioned but enlightened, she soon abandoned her service to them.

Hers was not the Christian way. The Christian has a deeper realism about human nature. The Christian knows service is not based on response. Nor is the Christian surprised when the poor and oppressed turn out to be sinners like everyone else.

Jesus never told his disciples that everyone was nice. He said to love everybody, but his ground was not that everyone was lovable. What he said was to love our enemies. Impossible, you say. Yes, it is impossible unless you have the Spirit of God working within you. Jesus knew we would have enemies. He knew people would be nasty or manipulative or cruel – he was no romantic. He expected his followers to live and serve even the nasty people, and he gave them the Holy Spirit to do what is humanly impossible. That is the Christian difference. Christians love the unlovable, even if we don't always like them.

One of the great American cases of the late twentieth century was the *National Socialist Party of America v. The Village of Skokie*.[1] In 1976, the Nazis wanted to march through Skokie, Illinois which happened to have a large number of Jewish residents and Holocaust survivors. For very understandable reasons, the village tried to prevent the Nazis from marching in Skokie. After the village authorities voted to deny the Nazis a permit, the Nazis sued, claiming their First Amendment rights to freedom of speech and expression were being violated.

Popular sentiment was on the side of the village of Skokie, but the law was on the side of the Nazis. There are numerous Supreme Court opinions that uphold the right to express unpopular opinions. In an often-quoted dissenting opinion, Justice Oliver Wendell Holmes wrote, "If there is any principle of the Constitution that more imperatively calls for attachment than any other it is the principle of free thought – not free thought for those who agree with us, but freedom for the thought that we hate."[2] Years later, Justice William Brennan would write for a unanimous Supreme Court that we have a "profound national commitment to the principle that debate on public issues should be uninhibited, robust and wide open…. That commitment was made with the knowledge that erroneous statements are inevitable in free debate"[3]

The Nazis won the right to march and hold a rally in Skokie. What is particularly interesting, though, is that one of the attorneys for the Nazis was Jewish – Professor Alexander Bickel of Yale Law School. In fact, much of the American Civil Liberties Union legal team supporting the Nazis were Jewish lawyers, who while hating the Nazis and their warped ideology, still defended their rights under the Constitution.

Lawyers are like that – we may not always like our clients, but we defend their rights, whether in criminal court where they are entitled to a fair trial, or in civil court when their constitutional rights are being challenged for expressing unpopular opinions.

I believe that this is exactly what Jesus would do. After all, he is our redeemer on earth, dying for us, taking all the sin and evil of the world upon himself, saving us who could not save ourselves. Jesus is now our advocate in heaven, pleading for us before the throne of God. "He is able for all time to save those who approach God through him, since he always lives to make intercession for them" (Heb. 7:25, NRSV). In a way, he is our defense lawyer, the sinless one pleading for sinners. We are certainly not perfect before God, yet God declares us "Not Guilty!" Martin Luther termed this being sinners yet justified. That is the good news of our faith – we don't get what we deserve before God, but something far better – salvation, grace, mercy and forgiveness.

A young Legal Aid lawyer in New York City was defending a man charged with felony assault and robbery. The man had an extensive criminal record, and with the state's "three strikes and you're out" law, he faced considerable prison time if convicted. The evidence against him seemed insurmountable. Several eyewitnesses to the crime were prepared to testify against him.

As the trial was about to get under way, the young lawyer noticed that his client was tense. In his effort to calm the man, the lawyer said, "Don't worry. I'm here to ensure that you get justice in this court."

A look of horror came on the man's face, and he said, "It isn't justice I want from this court. It's mercy!"

I don't know whether the man received mercy from the court, but I do know that mercy is what God gives us continually. Mercy and grace are perhaps the two most important words in the Christian vocabulary. They are similar in nature, but different in emphasis. Mercy is not getting what you deserve; grace is getting what you don't deserve.

When I was in divinity school, I remember Archbishop Ted Scott, the then Primate of the Anglican Church of Canada, speaking to us at a class in Wycliffe College. The first question he asked of us was this: "Can you tell me what John 3:16 says?"

Immediately every hand in class went up – we all knew the answer: "For God so loved the world that he gave his only Son, so that everyone who believes in him may not perish but may have eternal life" (Jn. 3:16, NRSV).

"Good," said Archbishop Scott. "Now, can you tell me what John 3:17 says?" Not one hand was raised. We looked at each other dumbfounded. Archbishop Scott then recited the verse: "For God did not send his Son into the world to condemn the world, but in order that the world might be saved through him" (Jn. 3:17, NRSV).

"Imagine," Archbishop Scott said, "God does not want to condemn any of us. God wants to save us, each and every one of us, no exceptions. Why is that? The Bible says because God loves us."

It's grace, all grace. God keeps on loving us because God is a loving God. We seek to limit that love, but God never does. With God there are no conditions, no limits. God just keeps on loving because that is the nature of God. Archbishop Scott was right: God is not out to condemn anyone but to love everyone, not some of us but all of us.

One of the great misconceptions fostered by our liberal entertainment and news industries, whether on television or in films, is that the poor and oppressed are beautiful, lovable people who always have our sympathy. They are the ones who have never been given a fair chance in life or have never had a real break. This is the secular illusion our culture is fed.

What about the unlovable, ugly people who have had a chance, and more than one break? These are the people who can't seem to make it in life, or who don't want to make it, or who don't want our help. What do we do about them? We can discard them like we discard our garbage, or we can love them – love them not for what they are, but for who they are – children of God.

I learned this when I was in college at Fordham University in New York. A group of students would volunteer at the Catholic Worker Houses of Hospitality in lower Manhattan. The Catholic Worker movement was founded by Dorothy Day, an ex-Episcopalian who converted to Roman Catholicism after living a rebellious life as a Communist during the 1920s and early 1930s.

After her conversion, and for the next fifty years of her life, Dorothy Day spent helping New York City's downtrodden. Caring for them, feeding them, sheltering them, asking nothing in return, she started the Catholic Worker movement which now has shelters throughout the United States.

When she died, her biography was titled, *A Harsh and Dreadful Love*, for so it was. It was love that overflowed with compassion and generosity, a Spirit-filled love that gave and did not count the cost. It was love that gave love to the unlovable in the name of the God of love.

The love that Dorothy Day showed to others is the kind of love that I have tried to live out in my life as a priest and lawyer. The world is not perfect. People are not perfect. Sometimes even when you do your best, people will let you down, disappoint you, maybe even turn against you. After all, if people turned against Jesus, what makes you think they won't turn against you? We need to love, but we also need to be realistic.

On this Pentecost Sunday, as America is dealing with yet another killing of a black man by a white police officer, we Christians need to love and pray for the family of George Floyd that justice may prevail. Love and pray for the protestors who cry out for justice. Love and pray for the police and the National Guard who are called to maintain some semblance of order in a chaotic situation. And yes, love and pray for Derek Chauvin, the police officer charged with the death of George Floyd. He, like all of us, is entitled to the presumption of innocence until proven guilty in a court of law.

Finally, I would ask us all to pray that this horrible tragedy will be the catalyst for an honest dialogue about race in America. A question that needs to be asked is, "If George Floyd was white, would the police officer have treated him in the same way?" He might have been handcuffed, or even tasered, but he would not have been forced to the ground with the police officer keeping his knee on Mr. Floyd's throat even as he cried out, "I can't breathe!"

Race in America is our Achilles heel, and we need to address it boldly, courageously and honestly. People born into poverty in our country, especially black people in our inner cities, have far less of a chance of going to the right schools, getting the right education, maintaining their physical and mental health, obtaining well-paying jobs and becoming solid members of the middle class. They are the victims of racial bias, both conscious and unconscious. If you are not black, you may not notice it, but it exists and needs to be confronted. As a nation, we have our work cut out for us.

St. Paul says: "If God is for us, who is against us?" (Rom. 8:31, NRSV). The news in our country can drive us to despair. It is good, then, to be mindful of the Christians who have gone before us and have triumphed over trials and tribulations far worse than what we are now experiencing. They knew – and we must know – that in the power of Christ's love the forces of darkness shall not prevail.

May 31, 2020
Online, Peoria, AZ

CHRISTIAN CIVILITY IN
A COARSE CULTURE

ROMANS 12: 9-21

In his book Civility, Yale Law School Professor Stephen Carter wrote: "Something horrible has happened to civility. We can no longer hold political discussions without screaming at each other, so our democracy is dying." Professor Carter is correct. Partisan politics and political vitriol are leading to polarization unprecedented since the Civil War. We have a hard time accepting people who differ from us politically, giving them the benefit of the doubt, or attempting to understand what they are saying or why they are saying it. We think our way is the only way, and therefore everyone else must think exactly like us, or else they are not only wrong but evil. We need a healthy dose of humility, that truth is greater than our understanding, and reality is more complex than we comprehend.

The world has changed since I was ordained back in 1983. One big difference is the coarsening of our culture. There is more vulgarity, a sharpness of language and tone that was not as common years ago. People find it harder to find common ground, live with differences and be civil to one another. Our culture has become shrill, acerbic, more acrimonious, and less willing to compromise.

Take politics in the United States, for example. Candidates running for President have called each other names, using schoolyard taunts and shouting over one another in television debates. Language unimagined in a presidential campaign is now common. Where is the respect for one another or the conduct becoming the dignity of seeking the highest office in the land?

Regrettably, the same ugliness in politics has affected the church. I was a Deputy to the 2003 General Convention of the Episcopal Church. What shocked me was the un-Christian behavior exhibited by some of the deputies, who refused even to share in the Eucharist together. Friends became enemies, relations became strained, and suspicions about one another mounted, and all because of one issue – whether to ratify the election of Gene Robinson as the Bishop of the Diocese of New Hampshire.

There is a new harmony taking place in the Episcopal Church, but only because several hundred thousand members left the denomination. That cannot be God's will for the church. Surely there must be a better way for Christians to come together, pray together, stay together, and rise above their differences. As Bishop Michael Marshall put it, the church is a group of people who have nothing in common, except Jesus Christ, in whom we have all things in common.

So, how do we deal with division, disagreement and even dissension both in our politics and the church? How can we avoid needless polarization in which nobody wins, and everybody loses? Is there a way to keep our civility in a coarse culture? Here is what I try to keep in mind when a potentially polarizing issue comes my way: First, I don't know it all. Second, the world is less than perfect. Third, the remedy to vitriol is kindness.

I don't know everything and neither do you. In this life, at least, we pursue the truth continually, but we never claim to possess it definitely. It was Oliver Wendell Holmes writing to philosopher William James who said: "The great act of faith is when a man decides he is not God." In other words, human beings are fallible creatures prone to error. None of us has full and absolute truth. "For now we see in a mirror, dimly," (I Cor. 13:12, NRSV) wrote St. Paul. That makes listening to differing voices crucial to our understanding of any political or social issue. Even if our opponents are wrong, they may have something important to tell us. St. Augustine said that every error may have some truth. In being attentive to the truth of others we may rethink or even strengthen our own understanding of an issue.

In the end, we may believe we are right and our opponents wrong. We can try to change their minds, but we cannot control their choice. We need to know our limits and limitations. Quite frankly, none of us know everything, so we shouldn't act as if we do. Each of us is just a speck in the universe, finite, mortal and fallible, which makes humility something to cultivate.

No one has expressed this better than President Abraham Lincoln in the fiery struggle of the Civil War. Prior to the war, there were Protestant ministers of both the North and South making their case for and against slavery, citing the same Bible and claiming the same authority for positions directly contrary to each other. In his *Meditation on the Divine Will* in September 1862, President Lincoln wrote: "The will of God prevails. In the great contests each party claims to act in accordance with the will of God. Both may be, and one must be, wrong. God cannot be for and against the same thing at the same time. In the present civil war it is quite possible that God's purpose is something different from the purpose of either party."[1]

Lincoln's meditation should be read regularly by the most devoted partisans who simply cannot believe that their opponents have any views of merit. A humble person is one that examines his views, scrutinizes them rigorously, believes they are correct but is open to revision as evidence and arguments warrant.

You don't know everything, so stop acting like you do. Get on with living a humble but faithful life. The truth is, there are no absolute, clear-cut answers to all the complex questions we face today. Only the fanatic sees the world in black and white. Most of us understand that no one has the full truth and that we are all prone to error. We can only do our best, as God gives us the light to see the right.

The second lesson, "The world is less than perfect" can help to reduce the complaining we do. If you live in the world, things are going to go wrong all the time. Toilets overflow, car troubles happen, sprinkler systems fail, and you may even get an audit from the IRS. That's life. And because all of us are mortal, our bodies' age and ache, our hair turns gray, we get sick, have this problem or that, and then we die. Life is like that. God never said you won't have problems, or that you will always get your way, no matter how right you think you are. As the song put it, "I beg your pardon / I never promised you a rose garden."

Catholics understand this better than Anglicans. Their spirituality views life as a "vale of tears" where the joys and pains of being human go hand in hand. There is no perfection in this life – not even in the church. People do things that break our hearts and sap our strength. The history of the Church is filled with corrupt and even brutal Popes, Cardinals, Bishops and Kings. Even at the local level, every parish has its own "war" stories to tell.

When I was studying divinity at Trinity College, many of us looked to George Herbert as the model priest we all sought to emulate. Herbert was a seventeenth century Anglican divine whose book on the *Country Parson* shaped the Anglican way of parish ministry – a sane, balanced, and eminently moderate way of life, not too stressful but prayerful and pastoral.

The trouble is: what George Herbert wrote is not true. It wasn't true then and it isn't true now. No one considering parish ministry should ever think there is anything sane and balanced about it. Maybe that's why there is now a book out with the provocative title: *If You Meet George Herbert on the Road, Kill Him.* Ministry is tough and not for the squeamish, the insecure or the faint of heart. It takes perseverance, stamina and a thick skin to ward off the inevitable complaints, criticisms and attacks that come our way.

Of course, tough times don't happen just to priests but to every one of us. Teachers, lawyers and other professionals experience similar challenges. The point is not to grumble or complain but to accept the fact that we live in a less than perfect world. I am not perfect, and neither are you.

The third lesson is in some ways the most important: the remedy to vitriol is kindness.

Woody Guthrie, the folksinger, told a story about a banker who went to a farmer to foreclose on his property during the Great Depression. The banker asked if the farmer could pay what he owed, and the farmer said he just didn't have the money. In that case, said the banker, I must foreclose on your farm. The farmer asked for more time, which the banker was reluctant to give him, but then he said, "Look, I just got a glass eye. If you can tell my glass eye from my real eye, I'll let you have another week."

The farmer carefully looked into one eye, then the other. Finally, he said, "The left one is your glass eye."

"You're right," said the banker, "but how did you know?"

"It was easy," said the farmer. "It was the only eye with any twinkle of human kindness."

Kindness is in short supply these days. I am amazed at all the mean-spirited comments I read on Facebook any time someone makes a political statement. Even more shocking is that I know some of the respondents. They are nice people, pleasant to be around, but on Facebook or Twitter they turn from Dr. Jekyll to Mr. or Ms. Hyde. Why does social media bring out the worst in us? Are our political passions so intense that we have stopped being decent human beings? Even in the church the internet and telephone often are used for gossip, rumor mongering and disparaging our fellow Christians. Where is the kindness that the church, above all other institutions, should be witnessing to the world?

I am the first to admit that kindness is not easy to practice. It takes discipline, resolve, forbearance and a steadfast commitment to live out the Sermon on the Mount that Jesus taught, especially the beatitude: "Blessed are the merciful, for they will receive mercy" (Mt. 5:7, NRSV). Here is how I try to practice kindness.

First, I try to give people the benefit of the doubt. Or, as Indra Nooyi, the President of Pepsi-Cola advised "assume positive intent." People may not mean what they say, or they may mean something quite different from how you understand them. So, we need to listen, listen, listen, and strive to put the best interpretation on what others say. Always be quick to affirm and slow to condemn. Give people the benefit of the doubt unless there is clear and compelling evidence to the contrary.

Second, I try to focus on the substance of the argument rather than to attack the person. The difference here is between "I think your argument is incorrect because..." and "You're an evil person with an even worse opinion." Discuss issues but don't attack people. Unless there is clear proof to the contrary, never impugn the motives of anyone, even if you disagree with their viewpoints or actions.

Finally, I ask God to help me see others the way God views them. We all have our struggles in life. I know people who feel life has cheated them because their marriage ended, or their job was not as fulfilling or successful as they hoped. You never know the struggles of another person. Often a gentle word or a warm compliment can be immensely helpful. You can do a great deal of good by just being considerate, smiling instead of expressing displeasure, extending a little friendship, going out of your way to do just one nice thing, or saying one kind word. And who knows, by your act of kindness you may turn an enemy into a friend.

In this time of political and cultural upheaval, we should all read Romans 12:9-21 at least once a week. There is much wisdom in that passage, especially in dealing with enemies and political opponents. Remember that God loves your enemies and political opponents as much as God loves you.

You may recall the German Lutheran Pastor Martin Niemoller who was imprisoned by Hitler. When he was released from prison, he said: "It took me a long time to learn that God is not the enemy of his enemies." Wise words from a wise pastor, after all, if God can love his enemies, maybe we can too.

All this does not mean you cannot disagree with people, or express disapproval over their actions, or even engage in heated debate. Of course you can disagree and disagree strongly. Just keep practicing kindness. Treat one another with respect. We all are children of God. This is basic stuff for Christians, but essential if we are to live together as one community, one country and one church.

Refuse to get down in the mud and throw barbs and curses at one another, demeaning and disparaging others simply because they hold a different politics or religion or even lifestyle. Is it not possible for us to accept our differences while affirming our common humanity that all people are made in God's image?

There is a story about a man who tried to save the city of Sodom from destruction by warning the citizens, but the people ignored him. Some cursed at him. Others laughed at him. Still others threw stones at him. One day someone asked, "Why are you bothering with these people? They will not listen to you. You can't change them."

"Maybe, I can't," the man replied, "but I still shout and scream to prevent them from changing me."

We need to prevent the culture from changing us. We must stand for what Christians have always stood for – human dignity, a common humanity, and a belief that all people are made in the image of God. We need to hold firm to our Christian faith, our values and beliefs, even as the culture becomes more politicized and intolerant, more vulgar and coarse in the way people treat one another. If we have enough humility to know that we don't know everything, and if we have enough realism to accept that we live in a less than perfect world, and if we try to practice kindness even when we think we have been wronged, then the light of God will shine through us and there will indeed be hope for our country and our world.

May 29, 2016
St. James Westminster Church, London, ON

PART FIVE

HOME FIRE: CHURCH LIFE

In the last chapter of the last book of his monumental seven volumes, *The History of the Christian Church*, Kenneth Latourette summed up his work in this way: "Always the Church seems to be dying yet lives." Having completed his survey of twenty centuries of ebbing and flowing, of triumph followed by failures of faith, nerve and will, this wise man went to the heart of the matter: the church lives because it remains the place where the deepest needs of human beings are heard, understood and acted upon.

For all its flaws – and there are many – the church endures and thrives because it continues to have the concerns, the fears and the milestones to which the love of God alone is an adequate response. The church is the one and only institution in the world that affirms God's amazing grace and unconditional love in Jesus Christ for every human being, no exceptions. We sometimes try to limit that love, but God never does.

At a time when the church is one competing voice among many in North American culture, the preacher should focus on Jesus. Yet, preachers get in trouble when they speak about Jesus. I say this from firsthand experience. In one parish I served, an irate parishioner came up to me one day and said, "You've got to stop preaching this Jesus! You're driving me crazy!" Well, maybe Jesus needs to disturb our peace of mind, challenge our complacency and make us feel uncomfortable. After all, if Jesus is at the heart of being a Christian, then we need to make room for him in our lives and in our churches. That may make people feel uneasy, but there is no way of avoiding it if preachers want to see their congregants become disciples of Jesus.

With all the talk of church growth (and decline) these days, the church will flourish only if it is faithful, relevant and authentic in the work of the kingdom of God, keeping Jesus at the center of faith and life. Jesus needs to be the center of everything we are and everything we do as Christians, because without him we cannot succeed, but with him we cannot fail, even if "results" do not come as we hope or expect.

Expanding Your Circle of Love was preached at my church in Lancaster, Pennsylvania, and dealt with a common challenge for Episcopalians: How do we expand our circle of love to include people not like us? This is a difficult issue in most churches, especially where members think of themselves as friendly. The question I posed is: Friendly to whom? Do church members move beyond their comfort zone or do they stay with their own kind of people?

The Heart of Priestly Ministry is a sermon preached at an ordination to the priesthood. Churches have bought into a competency model of ministry. They want and expect their clergy to be competent practitioners of ministry, and there is nothing wrong with that. However, what is often missing is Jesus. Unless Jesus is at the center of every priest's life, the ministry will not bear any lasting fruit.

Your Ordination to Ministry is based on the Reformation doctrine of the priesthood of all believers. Every Christian by virtue of baptism is ordained to ministry. Though we may have different roles, and different functions, we all are ministers of God, sharing in the one priesthood of Christ, and called to love and serve the world in his name.

Satisfying the Hungers of the Heart is a seeker-sermon on the Eucharist. The focus is not on the real presence of Christ in the bread and wine, but on the twofold action of every Eucharist: grace and faith – God's acceptance of us and our commitment to God.

The Courage to Change Your Mind was preached before divinity students at Huron University College in London, Ontario. Religion can often get stuck in the past, unable to change and adapt to changing circumstances, and even become rigid, static and inflexible. And yet, as the sermon shows, God changes his mind, and therefore so should we.

God in a Changing World deals with our changing experience and understanding of God. As the context of our culture changes, so the content of our theology changes. God is not a fixed idea but an ever-changing concept. We see this reflected in church architecture, where modern design reflects a differing understanding of God from previous generations.

The Power and Majesty of Music was preached in one of the foremost music churches in Canada as part of the Elora Music Festival. How could there not be a sermon on music when dealing with the church? Music may be the greatest proof that God exists – for through music people have experienced the presence of a loving, awesome, comforting God who inspires us, lifts up our spirits, soothes our souls, and draws us to a holy realm. This sermon celebrates the role of music in all the triumphs and tragedies of our lives.

Overcoming the Religious Spirit deals with rigidity and inflexibility in the church. Christians are all familiar with the seven last words of the church: "We never did it that way before." That may be true, but the Spirit stretches us to move beyond our comfort zone and forge new paths for Christ's sake. When religion gets in the way of love, that is never a good thing.

The Call to Discipleship is a challenge to mainline churches to stand out from the culture rather than always affirming it. The Episcopal Church has traditionally been more comfortable blessing culture than challenging it. This sermon questions that way of thinking. Christians may not always be popular with the culture but we must always be faithful to Jesus.

Turning Points is a sermon I preached two weeks before my official retirement from parish ministry. It is a reflection on the three cardinal beliefs that have shaped and guided my ministry – Jesus, the Way, the Truth, and the Life; Human Dignity as the foundation of law and ethics; and All-Inclusive Love as the hope of the world

EXPANDING YOUR CIRCLE OF LOVE

MATTHEW 9:9-13

Christian maturity is moving beyond ourselves and even our friends and family, and reaching out to others as Christ reaches out to us. Stepping out of our comfort zone is difficult for the best of us. We prefer the safe and familiar, and to love the people who love us. However, the love of Jesus is not only for people we know and like, but for strangers and those we may find difficult to love. How wide should we expand our circle of love? As wide as the love of Jesus. As St. Bernard put it: "The merciful are those who are quick to see truth in their neighbor; they reach out to others in compassion and identify with them in love, responding to their joys and sorrows in the lives of others as if they were their own..."

Heather and I were at a prominent New York City church to attend a worship service on the Sunday after Christmas. The service was magnificent featuring a men and boys choir. After it was ended, we decided to attend the coffee hour, which was held in a large, ornate room. The men were dressed in jackets and ties, the women wore dresses or skirts, blouses and holiday sweaters.

Coffee and tea were poured from beautiful silver pots onto cups of fine china. There were delicious sweets and sandwiches, and holiday napkins of the finest quality. The furniture in the room consisted of elegant wooden tables and chairs, leather seats, and wood paneling on the walls. If you didn't know any better, you might think you were in nineteenth century Victorian England.

Being somewhat of an anglophile, at first I thought I was in paradise. Soon enough, however, I realized it was an inferno. Heather and I were visitors. We wanted to meet some of the people and thank the clergy for such a beautiful worship service. No one, though, absolutely no one bothered to talk to us. We stood by ourselves alone. Some people looked at us, but quickly turned away. I caught the attention of one of the assistant clergy. He looked at me for a brief moment and then quickly went elsewhere. It was as if we did not exist, or worse, no one cared whether we existed – not one person in the room bothered to exchange a smile or say hello. When we left the room, my wife and I speculated, "Were we dressed the wrong way? Was there something about us not right? Did they think we were beggars?" We would never know the answer to those questions because we never returned to that church.

A few years after our visit, when I was serving as a priest in the Diocese of Bethlehem, Pennsylvania, I had a conversation with the bishop about my experience in that church. He told me that he had taken his family to New York to see the Christmas show at Radio City Music Hall. They planned it so that the family could attend church before going to the show, and they chose the very same church that Heather and I had attended. Sure enough, said the Bishop, no one talked to them either. They were totally ignored at the coffee hour. I felt relieved and told the Bishop, "Well, at least that church is an equal opportunity discriminator!"

This story is both funny and sad. It is hard to imagine churches today being snobby and elitist, but a few continue to exist, and not just in the Episcopal Church. There are people on the margins, people with tarnished social reputations, or of the wrong economic class who are of no interest to some churches. If you have money, prominence or position, they will treat you royally, but if you have nothing to offer them, or what you do offer is not what they want, those churches will much prefer you go elsewhere.

In our Gospel today, we meet a tax collector by the name of Matthew. At the time of Jesus in ancient Israel, tax collectors working for the Roman government were some of the most hated people in the community. Most of these tax collectors were Jews who preyed on their own people, acting as extortioners to squeeze whatever money they could from people who were already poor. The Jewish people looked upon tax collectors as traitors, chiselers, and utterly dishonest and disreputable.

Matthew was one such tax collector. He is the least likely person for Jesus to invite to join him. And yet, Jesus invites Matthew to become his disciple. The Bible says that Matthew "got up and followed him" (Mt. 9:9, NRSV).

One might question the judgment of Jesus. Why pick a tax collector as his disciple? Jesus, however, doesn't stop there. He goes to Matthew's house for a dinner party and surrounds himself with some of the most disreputable people in the neighborhood – the rich and infamous.

The one thing about Jesus is that he is always reaching out to the most unlikely people to bring them into his circle of love. He reaches out to ostracized and marginalized women, to the unclean, to fishermen, to Samaritans, to no-good tax collectors, to sinners of every kind and even to pagans. After the day of Pentecost, the church is prodded by the Spirit to reach out to the Gentiles, to people of different races and ethnicities, and to the ends of the earth. It is painful to be stretched, and all too easy to be comfortable, but as followers of Jesus we are called to draw the circle wide.

Some people have a circle so small and restricted that it includes only themselves. I term this the circle of self – the world revolves around them. There is actually a philosophy that promotes self-centeredness. It was popularized by the writer Ayn Rand in novels and books. It is called Objectivism which has as its core virtues "ethical egoism" and "rational selfishness." Take her novel *Atlas Shrugged*, for example. The main character, John Galt, is a relentless self-server who lives for himself and absolutely no one else. His is the type of personality where the world revolves around "me" – my self-interest, my comfort, my well-being, my success, my legacy. Such people are obsessed with achievement for themselves and care nothing for others, except as others benefit them. If there is no more use for a person, the person is dropped, either from the firm or as a friend. I have noticed this kind of personality in clergy, university professors, military officers, politicians and business executives. There was even an ad that appeared in a business magazine several years ago that read: "In the end cunning and ruthlessness will overcome ability and youth."

In the end this self-centered lifestyle will fail us. It is a myth to think you can live a happy, contented life if you allow the world to revolve around you. At some point, there will be a day of reckoning when you realize that you have missed out on the most important things of life.

Maturity is moving beyond the circle of self to include others. However, human nature being what it is, we tend to include in our circle only people who share our views and values. We might call this the circle of friends.

We tend to like people who are like us. We socialize with people like us. We live in neighborhoods with people like us. We even worship with people like us. You may remember what the Episcopal priest, Malcolm Boyd wrote in his book *Are You Running With Me, Jesus?* He said that 11:00 a.m. Sunday morning is the most segregated hour in America. Sadly, he was probably right.

One thing I have noticed about Episcopalians: we are all very similar in our lifestyle and values. We are primarily a group of middle and upper middle-class professional people who are relatively comfortable with our lives. It is hard to reach out to people outside of our class; to understand and befriend those we perceive to be below us or removed from us in some way.

When I served at the cathedral in Bethlehem, Pennsylvania, I relished my time there, and I especially loved the people. They were some of the kindest, most decent human beings I have known. The cathedral was on the south side of Bethlehem near Lehigh University, the Bethlehem steel mills, and in a neighborhood becoming increasingly Hispanic with mostly low-income homes. The cathedral, on the other hand, attracted the majority of its members from either Saucon Valley with its beautiful country club, or members came from the north side of Bethlehem, which was very middle class, white and educated. Several Bethlehem Steel executives attended the cathedral, but I wasn't familiar with any Bethlehem Steel workers at the church. There was a definite caste system at work in Bethlehem, certainly not deliberate, since most cathedral members would consider themselves socially liberal, tolerant people, with several members involved in New Bethany social ministries. However, as far as church membership went, their circle of love was, intended or not, limited to mainly themselves.

The cathedral is not an exception in the Episcopal Church but the norm. We are a church of the like-minded. Yes, we have some slight differences theologically and politically, but basically we are all the same kind of people, with mostly the same kind of taste. I feel comfortable in such a church, but I cannot get away from the challenge of Jesus who said, "For if you love those who love you, what reward have you? Do not even tax collectors do the same?" (Mt. 5:46, NRSV).

Now I know that some Episcopalians will protest and say, "But we feed the hungry at a soup kitchen, or do this or that social ministry helping the poor." All well and good, but if the people you serve at the soup kitchen were to come to your church on Sunday morning, how would they be treated? Would they be judged for being poor or ill dressed? Would parishioners make comments if they had a bad smell? Would they be shunned? Or perhaps they would be offered a perfunctory greeting but then ignored? I know a church in one large city where a homeless woman came to worship several weeks in a row and no one bothered to talk with her or get to know her. After a few weeks, she just stopped coming.

One of the most dangerous things about a "friendly" church is that it can become inward-looking – focusing on members but ignoring visitors and guests. At coffee hour everyone is busy talking and laughing and having such a good time that no one notices the stranger by the door, or the woman in a wheelchair, or the shabbily dressed man in the corner. Each of these persons is just waiting for someone to come to them and say, "We're glad you're here. Welcome!"

Even the best of us needs to enlarge our circle of love. Jesus calls us to move out of our comfort zone and to reach out to the world he came to save. He wants us to love as he loves, which is a radically all-inclusive love. This love can be difficult. It is a love for our enemies and not just our friends, for our political opponents and not just our political allies, for people who are on the opposite end of the theological spectrum from us, or people of a different economic or social level. Loving such people may be a challenge, to say the least.

I will never forget a Jesuit priest that I knew in New York. He was a kind and gentle person, but fiercely committed to social justice and working with the poor. As he was riding in his car in lower Manhattan, he saw a homeless man who was laying on the street vomiting profusely. It was early evening and he was scheduled to be at a dinner that was being hosted by one of the Catholic auxiliary bishops of the New York Archdiocese. Seeing the man on the street, obviously in need of help, this Jesuit stopped his car, helped the man to his feet, got him in the car, and then drove him to the local hospital. At the hospital he took the man to emergency and stayed with him in the waiting room until he was finally seen by a doctor. Before he departed the hospital, the man asked why he would bother to help him. The priest said, "I guess it's because I'm a Christian, and that's what Christians are supposed to do."

As it turned out, that priest never got to the dinner. His clothes had vomit on them and he stank. He told the bishop, "I don't think you want me at your dinner tonight. I need to go home, shower and change." By that time it was too late for dinner anyway.

I don't know how many of us could demonstrate that kind of love. Honestly, I don't know if I would have stopped the car or not to help that man. I like to think I would have done the same thing, but I don't know for sure. What I do know is that Jesus wants us to become a church that cares for the people beyond ourselves. He wants us to expand our circle of love to become as embracing of others as his love is for us – to lift up rather than to put down, to affirm rather than to judge, to welcome rather than to ignore.

Last Thursday our sexton George came into my office as soon as I walked in the building, and with evident consternation on his face, told me that one of the little boys at the S. June Smith Center here at St. Thomas Church had died last night. Little Joey, four years old, was born a crack cocaine baby in inner city Lancaster.

He was one of George's favorites. He had a big smile and a playful demeanor that hid the pain of his sick and battered body.

Joey never had a chance. So many young people in our inner cities never have a chance. Somehow I have to believe that Christ's church needs families in the suburbs who care deeply about all the children who never have a chance. Somehow I have to believe that if the Gospel means anything in this hurting world, it means that Christ is calling us to expand our circle of love to include all the Joeys in this world.

After I spoke with George, I went to see Joey's teachers to see how they were coping with the news. They didn't say much. What could they say? It was a loss, a real loss, and they felt it. One of the teachers said to me, "You know, Father Gary, sometimes I think no one cares!"

I tried to assure her that many people care, good people in our churches who are just too busy and it is hard to get them to commit, but I know there are many who care!

She looked at me, her dark eyes flashing, and said, "Name just one person who really cares!"

Can I give her your name? Will you tell her that you really care?

June 9, 1996
St. Thomas Episcopal Church, Lancaster, PA

THE HEART OF
PRIESTLY MINISTRY

MATTHEW 16:13-20

This sermon was preached at the ordination to the priesthood of the Rev. Carolyn Richardson who was Assistant for Pastoral Care at my church in San Diego. In my sermon, I focused on the question: Just what makes an excellent priest or pastor? Competency, compassion and character are fundamental, but is there something even more crucial to being a faithful and effective pastor? Jesus said: "I am the vine; you are the branches. Those who abide in me and I in them bear much fruit, because apart from me you can do nothing" (Jn. 15:5, NRSV). St. Augustine said that all pastors should follow Christ the Good Shepherd. "This means," he said, "that Christ should be the shepherd, that they should be shepherds for Christ, shepherds in Christ, not shepherds for themselves, apart from Christ." In the end, what churches need,, whether they know it or not, is a pastor who is sold out to Jesus.

Several years ago, Warren Bennis wrote a book with the provocative title, *Managing People Is Like Herding Cats*. Churches are composed of cats. You know cats: they have a mind of their own. They do what they like. You can't control them or train them very much. Cats do what cats want, whether you like it or not.

That is what makes being a parish priest so difficult. Priests are called to lead church members who have minds of their own, and strong opinions on how a church ought to operate. No wonder there is more conflict in churches today at any time since the Reformation.

Several years ago Roman Catholic vocation directors came out with a list of ten qualities desirable for every priest: understanding, sincerity, humility, respect for people, intelligence, politeness, hope in God, abnegation regarding comfort, will power and zeal. An Episcopal list might include the ability to live with ambiguity, a high sense of tolerance, a wholesome sexuality, a sense of humor, and a pastoral presence.

The Church Deployment Office of the Episcopal Church recommends that priests revise their ministry profile every few years. In working on mine recently, I realized just how much the church has accepted a competency model of priesthood – we expect our priests to be skilled practitioners of ministry – people who are adept in preaching, teaching, pastoral care, administration, church growth, stewardship, social ministry, conflict resolution, and so on. We want visionaries and unifiers who can bring people together in common mission.

I like all that, but what are we missing? Are psychological traits enough? Is a competency model sufficient? Or to put it another way, what is the essential quality we presume of every priest?

I remember as a third-year divinity student meeting Bishop Reginald Hollis of Montreal. We were having coffee in a Toronto café. The first question he asked me was, "Tell me what you think about Jesus?" Frankly, I was stunned that any bishop would ask such a question. I wasn't sure how to answer, but after mumbling that Jesus was my Savior and Lord, I said that the two things I knew for certain was that Jesus loved me and I loved him. At that Bishop Hollis broke into a great big smile and said, "Good!"

Of course, we are all called to love Jesus, lay and ordained, but there is a special imperative for the priest.

Years ago Bishop Fitzsimmons Allison wrote an article in which he argued that the central verse for a New Testament understanding of priesthood is found in Romans 15:16. It is a verse I come back to again and again in my own ministry. St. Paul says that the grace of God was given him "to be a minister of Christ Jesus to the Gentiles in the priestly service of the gospel of God" (Rom. 15:16, NRSV). There it is – priestly service is mediating in one's own person the good news of Jesus Christ to all people. The priest's role is to love Christ, to share Christ, to live Christ, to model Christ, and to witness Christ. Whether in parish or some other kind of ministry, the priest is called to be a thoroughly Christ-centered human being. St. Paul reflected this Christ-centeredness when he wrote in Galatians: "It is no longer I who live, but Christ who lives in me. And the life I now live in the flesh I live by faith in the Son of God, who loved me and gave himself for me" (Gal. 2:20, NRSV).

Yes, we want our priests to be skilled practitioners of ministry, but there is a danger here. We priests can be effective administrators, raise enormous sums of money, practice all the latest church growth techniques, be leaders in the community, work for peace and justice, know how to get publicity for our agendas, but if we don't love Jesus our ministry will prove worthless. Jesus himself reminded us on the night before he died that: "Apart from me you can do nothing" (John. 15:5, NRSV).

And why is that? Simply put, the priest represents the church, and the church stands or falls on the Christ of the church. We see this in today's Gospel. Jesus asked his disciples the question: "Who do people say that the Son of Man is?" (Mt. 16:13, NRSV).

They answered: "Some say John the Baptist, but others Elijah, and still others Jeremiah or one of the prophets" (Mt. 16:14, NRSV).

"He said to them, 'But who do you say that I am?'" (Mt. 16:15, NRSV).

It was Simon Peter who gave the answer that has resonated through the ages: "You are the Messiah, the Son of the living God" (Mt. 16:16, NRSV).

That's the answer, isn't it? "You are the Messiah, the Son of the living God" (Mt. 16:16, NRSV). On that assertion the church stands or falls. Think about it. What makes us Christians? The answer is not beautiful buildings or elaborate liturgies or even pushy preachers. The one who makes us Christians is Jesus. Christianity is Christ. Without Jesus there would be no church, no ministries, no sacraments, no liturgies, no good news.

Other faiths teach about the good and the true, but only Christianity has Jesus. We Christians believe that God came to us in the flesh, as a Jew from Nazareth named Jesus. It is our astounding claim that we look at the Jewish carpenter's son, who was born of Mary, lived briefly, died violently and rose from the dead unexpectedly, and we see as much of God as we hope to see. As Bishop John Robinson put it, "Jesus is the human face of God."

Now we can sympathize with people who look at Jesus and see only a noble teacher, or a great moral example, or even a wild-eyed revolutionary peasant. After all, from the very beginning, Jesus frustrated people's expectations about how a Messiah ought to act. Messiahs – like bishops today – were expected to have power, to take charge, set things right, fix all of our problems, lead confidently, courageously and boldly. Jesus refused to coerce anybody into following him. He refused to dominate or to take up arms. Looking at his life, many people would say that Jesus was one of history's most noble failures.

I notice there are now business books that focus on the

leadership style of Jesus and even make him out to be a CEO of a corporation. I appreciate the effort to Christianize the marketplace, but I can't help but think that if Jesus were a CEO of a major American corporation, he'd be fired for turning the values of the company upside down.

Jesus wasn't a success. He wasn't even a success at being God. He just didn't appear the way people thought God should appear. He wasn't a grand or pompous person, not majestic or powerful, not self-centered or so task-oriented that he neglected the needs of people. He was humble, down-to-earth, putting people first, and with a heart for the least, the last and the lost. If he got angry, it was to the self-righteous, judgmental people who looked down on others, more eager to condemn than to show mercy. He insisted that to follow in his way is to follow in the way of love – to love God and to love our neighbor.

Being a Christian is about following Jesus. Carolyn, as the priestly representative of all of us, is called to remind us of our calling to follow Jesus, no matter how unpopular that may be. As Bishop Robert DeWitt once said, referring to bishops, we are not called to be crowd pleasers.

I realized the truth of Bishop DeWitt's insight when I was a priest at the cathedral in Bethlehem, Pennsylvania. I gave a sermon on evangelism – and judging by the reaction of the people coming out of church that Sunday morning, it must have been the first sermon on evangelism ever preached in that church. One dear woman came up to me and said, "I know you would never want to offend anyone in your sermons, but I was deeply offended by your emphasis on Jesus." And I thought to myself, "Talking about Jesus is tough stuff!"

Part of Carolyn's calling as a priest is to challenge us to develop a relationship with Jesus. Christianity is not primarily a religion, it's a relationship with Jesus. Carolyn as a priest will attempt to model that relationship for us, but we are all called to it, every one of us.

We Christians really believe, not only that Jesus spoke to us, came to us, but that he speaks to us and comes to us even now. Frankly, I have never been able to understand people who say they are Christians but don't believe in the resurrection. Just ask yourself, if Easter had not happened, would anyone now be thinking about Jesus? The Sermon on the Mount, for example, makes no sense without the resurrection. No wonder he had trouble getting his message across to the crowds. Even his disciples did not understand him until after the resurrection. Except for John, they all fled for their lives when he got arrested. It was his resurrection that vindicated his life and teachings. Easter was God saying to us, "When he spoke, I spoke. When he acted, I acted. When you focus on Jesus, you're focusing on me, the one who created "galaxies, suns, and the planets in their courses."

I know this seems an astounding assertion to those who have not experienced it, but Christians believe that Jesus is present with us, walks with us, and is closer to us now than even we to ourselves. And this is what Carolyn will proclaim to us again and again in her priestly ministry as she says a prayer, blesses bread and wine, and declares the forgiveness of our sins – we will discover through her ministry that Jesus is with us. When just two or three of us make Eucharist together, Jesus promises to be there with us: "For where two or three are gathered in my name, I am there among you" (Mt. 18:20, NRSV).

So what qualities do you want in your priest? Competence, compassion and character are all important, but there is one quality above all others absolutely essential for priestly ministry – to love Jesus. My hope and prayer is that Carolyn will be sold out on Jesus – preaching and teaching about Jesus, transforming lives in Jesus, guiding her people to know, love and serve Jesus, and forming disciples of Jesus.

Jesus turned to his disciples and asked them: "But who do you say that I am?" (Mt. 16:15, NRSV). It was Peter who gave the answer that has resonated through the ages: "You are the Messiah, the Son of the living God" (Mt. 16:16, NRSV). Jesus – the personal, powerful presence of God. Jesus – the joy of every Christian. Jesus – the hope of every human being. Jesus is the good news Carolyn as a priest will proclaim to a world desperately in need of good news. For on Jesus, the church takes its stand.

August 25, 2002
St. Bartholomew's Church, Poway, CA
Ordination of the Rev. Carolyn Richardson

YOUR ORDINATION
TO MINISTRY

LUKE 3:15-17, 21-22

Every Christian by virtue of baptism is an ordained minister. For too long the church has had a hierarchical system of the clergy on top and the laity at the bottom – the ministers and the ministered, the rulers and the ruled. Whatever the success of this model in the past; it does not work anymore. Moreover, the model is not biblical and is contrary to the "priesthood of all believers" – a hallmark doctrine of the Reformation. Only as the church reclaims the ministry of the baptized can it unleash its members for ministry. Writing to all members of the church, St Peter writes: "Come to him, a living stone though rejected by mortals yet chosen and precious in God's sight, and like living stones, let yourselves be built into a spiritual house, to be a holy priesthood, to offer spiritual sacrifices acceptable to God through Jesus Christ" (1 Pet. 2:4-5, NRSV).

I was ordained a priest on June 21, 1984 at the Cathedral of the Holy Trinity in Quebec City. The ordination was part of a three-day Synod, so the church was packed with diocesan leaders and ecumenical representatives. As I was encircled by more than 40 priests from around the diocese, Bishop Alan Goodings laid his hands on my head and recited the words from the Canadian Book of Common Prayer: "Receive the Holy Ghost for the office and work of a priest in the Church of God... Whose sins thou dost forgive, they are forgiven; and whose sins thou dost retain, they are retained. And be thou a faithful dispenser of the Word of God, and of his holy Sacraments..." In that act of prayer and the laying-on-of- hands by the bishop I was made a priest forever – a moment that I shall never forget.

Do you remember the time when you were ordained? You are, you know, ordained. You are a minister of the Gospel. In the early rites of baptism, the church made this clear. The newly baptized Christian was given a white robe, symbolic of the new life that was now being lived. Hands were laid on the head, oil was poured on the forehead, and the sign of the cross was made – all symbolic gestures, that the gift of the Holy Spirit was bestowed upon the candidate in the act of baptism. Through baptism the candidate was ordained for ministry in the world.

Most of us now associate the laying-on-of-hands with clerical ordination or perhaps confirmation. Over the centuries, baptism lost its significance as the making of "priests" and became only a rite of initiation into the church. This led many to the unfortunate conclusion that bishops, priests and deacons are the real ministers of the church, and the laity just exists to support the clergy. You may remember the old nineteenth century adage that the role of the laity is to "pray, pay and obey." That, however, is wrong.

Today's Gospel is an account of the baptism of Jesus. When Jesus is baptized, a dove descends, and there is a voice proclaiming Jesus as God's beloved son. Right after this event, Jesus begins his ministry of preaching, teaching and healing – a sign that the reign of God is breaking into the world. The baptism of Jesus is the day of his ordination, the beginning of his ministry.

From the baptism of Jesus, I draw this conclusion: our baptism conveys the gift of the Holy Spirit which commissions us for ministry. We are given the Spirit in baptism so that we might be empowered to participate fully in the ministry of Christ in the world.

On the monthly newsletter of my former parish in Pennsylvania, the masthead read: "Ministers: The Congregation; Rector: Gary Nicolosi." That got it right. All of us are ordained by God to be ministers. Clergy, in the New Testament sense, are not here to do the ministry of the people, but to equip the people to do the ministry. How different this understanding is from the view that the clergy are the paid professionals who minister to a passive congregation content to be served. The New Testament has no such view of ministry.

Of course, we do have different functions. We have different roles. We exercise different gifts, but we are *all* ministers because we *all* have been ordained by the Holy Spirit at our baptism.

I have been blessed to travel around North America teaching and preaching about church growth and stewardship, and in my travels, I have come to know many parishes large and small. I see choirs of all sizes singing their praises to God. I see church schoolteachers and pastoral care visitors and members of the altar guild and ushers and greeters. I see prayer partners and prayer intercessors, people who serve at soup kitchens and homeless shelters and addiction treatment centers and shelters for abused women. I see people that volunteer to work on the Sunday bulletin, or paint a room, or mow the lawn, or help with coffee hour.

I see ministry in countless ways: taking the time to listen to a person in pain or calling the homebound on the phone to let them know someone cares about them. I see people being involved in diocesan work, sometimes traveling long distances without any compensation to fulfill their obligations. I see people making a difference where they work and live, impacting their communities and leaving a more life-giving world.

So, in a way I was wrong. The day I got ordained was not back on June 21, 1984 when I was made priest, or on June 24, 1983 when I was made deacon. The day I got ordained a minister was all the way back on September 10, 1950 when a priest dipped his hand in the font, poured water on my head, and baptized me in the name of the Father, and of the Son, and of the Holy Spirit. On that day, in that act, I was ordained for the work of ministry.

The same is true of you – on the day of your baptism, you were ordained for ministry. One reason why you are in church today is to become more adept at ministry, to gain the skills, insights, and vision needed to be a good minister of the Gospel wherever God has planted you. I, as your priest, preach and teach in order that you might preach and teach wherever you go in the coming week. I, as your priest, am not expected to do all the work of ministry, but I am here to equip you for ministry. My success as a priest is determined by how successful you are as priests – how much you serve others, how much you give of yourself, and how effectively you minister in the world as disciples of Jesus.

Look around you. There is much ministry to be done beyond these church walls. There are all sorts of people in need of ministry: hurting people, hungry people, homeless people, angry people, addicted people, lonely people, empty people, aging people, messed-up people, people who are confused, anxious, afraid, and maybe even in despair. People who yearn for a word of hope – a word that says God loves them, God cares about them, values them, and accepts them as persons of precious worth.

Will they hear that word from you? Think about it. You may be the only Gospel they ever read, the only good news they ever hear. In some mysterious sense, you and I are living, walking Gospels called to share God's love with every person we meet.

And who knows? You may be the one person who draws some lost soul into the kingdom of God and right into the arms of Jesus.

L'Arche is a community not unfamiliar to Canadians because of its founder Jean Vanier. In August 1964 Jean Vanier invited two men who had been living in an institution for people with mental disabilities to share a house with him in a French village. Within a year that little community started to grow, and today there are 132 similar communities in 34 countries, including right here in London, Ontario.

Two years ago, my wife Heather, daughter Allison and I had dinner with the residents and staff at one of the L'Arche homes. After dinner, everyone from the three homes in the community came together for a worship service in the large living room. It was a simple but beautiful liturgy, with residents playing instruments, singing songs, praying and being so attentive to God.

At the intercessions, many of the residents prayed aloud for someone or some cause. One of the staff, a dear woman, announced to the group that she had been diagnosed with cancer and was going to have a breast removed in the next week. She then said that whatever might happen, she trusted God with the outcome. Immediately, after her sharing, everyone in the room, without any prompting, and even the most severely disabled residents, gathered around the staff member to pray for her healing and lay hands on her. As we were driving home after the service, my wife Heather said to me, "What we experienced tonight was a glimpse of the kingdom of God."

She was right. We experienced a community of people bound by their strengths and their brokenness, a community of people who are limping toward the sunrise but know that God loves them, everyone.

Isn't that a church at its best?

When I look back on that night at that prayer service, who was the "priest" in that room? The Presbyterian minister leading the worship had her role. But the residents and staff had their role as well, praying for the young woman with a cancerous breast, laying their hands on her head, hugging her, and blessing her.

The truth is, ministry is not confined to any one person or any one role or any one group or any one church, even if one wears a clerical collar or a purple shirt. By virtue of our baptism, all Christians are ordained for ministry. Wherever there is hurting, we are called to heal; wherever there is suffering, we are called to comfort; wherever there is despair, we are called to offer hope; wherever there is dying, we are called to be life-givers.

So, go on and be the minister God has called you to be, ordained you to be.

January 13, 2013
St. James Westminster Church, London, ON

SATISFYING THE HUNGERS
OF THE HEART

JOHN 6:32-51

Episcopalians refer to a sacrament as an outward and visible sign of an inward and spiritual grace. The Eucharist or Holy Communion is the sacrament commanded by Christ for the continual remembrance of his life, death, and resurrection, until he comes again. It consists of two actions: God's gift to us and our response to God. In the bread and wine of Christ's Body and Blood we receive God's grace by faith – God giving himself to us and our giving ourselves to God. While Episcopalians do not have formal altar calls like some other churches, in a way every Eucharist is an altar call in which we literally walk down the aisle and stand up for Jesus. When the celebrant at an Episcopal Eucharist invites the worshipers to come forward to receive the bread and wine of Christ's Body and Blood, she says the following invitation: "The Gifts of God for the People of God. Take them in remembrance that Christ died for you, and feed on him in your hearts by faith, with thanksgiving."[1]

When All You've Ever Wanted Isn't Enough: That's the title of a book Rabbi Harold Kushner wrote several years ago. You may know what the Rabbi was getting at. We work hard, plot our goals, plan our strategy, and climb the career ladder. We focus on getting the right job, meeting the right people, and joining the right club – all in the pursuit of "success" – only we discover that "success" doesn't satisfy. When we think we have it all, it's never enough.

That's the experience of many high achievers. "When you get to the top, there's nothing there." How many so-called successful people have had that sense of emptiness in their lives? They are at the top of their professions, and yet there is a deep dissatisfaction in their lives. I have known such people, and maybe you have too. They have been climbing the career ladder their whole lives only to discover as they reach the top that they are on the wrong ladder. They have everything, yet they feel like they have nothing. They have no inner peace, no contentment, and no joy in their lives. The result: the satisfaction they so desperately crave becomes as elusive as chasing the wind.

It was to fulfill this emptiness that Christ came into the world. Jesus says, "I am the bread of life..." You can search all over the earth to find that one thing that is missing in your life, but until you feed on Jesus, you will never be satisfied.

Feeding on Jesus comes spiritually by faith but it also is symbolized in a powerful way in the Holy Eucharist. The Eucharist, also called Holy Communion, the Lord's Supper and the Mass, is many things. It is a memorial of Christ's saving love for us when he died on the cross for our redemption. It is a meal in which we receive the bread and wine of Christ's Body and Blood in obedience to Jesus who said: "Do this in remembrance of me" (Lk. 22:19, NRSV).

The Eucharist also is a symbol of human wholeness. It dramatizes both God's feeding and our need to be fed. It communicates God's desire to satisfy our deepest hunger. Jesus says: "I am the bread of life. Whoever comes to me will never be hungry, and whoever believes in me will never be thirsty" (Jn. 6:35, NRSV).

Coming to the Eucharist is much like the boy who came to a church serving hot meals after a flood had devastated much of his town. As he approached the church hall where the meals were being served, the boy told a worker he was from another town, not directly affected by the flood. The tone of his voice suggested that he wanted something to eat but wondered whether he could have any food since he was not a flood victim. The church worker knew there was only one criterion for receiving the food and asked the boy, "Are you hungry?" The boy said he was and then took a hot meal for himself and one for his mother.

That's how God works. There is only one criterion to be fed at the Eucharist – "Are you hungry?" – hungry for relationship, hungry for acceptance, hungry for pardon, hungry for self-esteem, hungry for self-worth, hungry for meaning.

Perhaps that's why the Eucharist has remained such a powerful symbol through the centuries. It is the symbol of human wholeness. It dramatizes God's feeding and our need to be fed. It communicates God's desire to satisfy the hunger of our hearts. "I am the bread of life," Jesus says. "Whoever comes to me will never be hungry, and whoever believes in me will never be thirsty" (Jn. 6:35, NRSV).

There are two movements in every Eucharist: grace and faith. Another way of putting it is to speak in terms of God's acceptance of us and our commitment to God. God's acceptance, our commitment – here is the key to a satisfying life.

The primary movement of the Eucharist is God's acceptance of us. What an incredible thought: total, unconditional acceptance by God! Before God we don't have to be anyone but ourselves. We don't have to hide behind the masks of convention or put on airs or project the person we are not. In a world where it is often hard to be authentically who we are, God accepts us just as we are.

The Eucharist declares God's love for us totally and unconditionally. It's not a matter of good works or even being a good person. It's a matter of accepting the love that God freely gives simply because God loves us.

Consider the flow of the Eucharist: Christ breaks the bread, we eat it. Christ takes the cup, we drink it. The movement is from Christ to us, from what God gives to what we receive, from the God who is love to we who are loved.

So first and foremost, the Eucharist is God's assurance that we are totally and unconditionally loved. The theologian Paul Tillich famously said that the great act of faith is to accept that you are accepted. In the Eucharist we are accepted – just as we are. When we approach the Eucharist to receive Christ's Body and Blood, we affirm that we are loved simply because God loves us.

A middle-aged woman had gone through a difficult divorce after her husband abandoned her for a younger woman. Loneliness and depression were her constant companions. She was always a heavy drinker, but now she started to pop pills to get through the day and then to sleep at night. She began to hate herself because she knew what she was becoming: a lonely, aged, addict.

Then, one day, tragedy struck. Too much alcohol and too many pills took their toll. By some miracle she survived and was soon released from the hospital.

Still on the brink of self-destruction, and with her self-respect in ruins, she decided to visit an old friend who happened to be a priest at a New York City church. When she came to the church, the priest was celebrating a weekday Eucharist. She decided to sit in the back pew and wait until the service was ended.

When the time for communion came, the priest noticed that the woman remained in her seat, weeping. He knew her story. He knew about the divorce, the alcohol, the pills, and her brush with death. When everyone else in the church had received communion, the priest hastened down the aisle with the bread and wine. He put the bread in her hand, whispering gently, "Go ahead. Take it. Jesus loves you. Jesus loves you very much."

Listening to his gentle voice as she looked at the bread, she experienced an overwhelming sense that she was indeed loved by God. It was as if God had pulled her back from the depths. She felt reassured that she was accepted by God, just as she was. And more than that, she no longer felt alone. God was with her. The bread and the wine told her so.

The Eucharist is God's assurance of our acceptance, but it is also a symbol of our commitment. Every Eucharist is a call to decision – either to accept or reject God's love. The truth is, in the face of God's overwhelming love, some of us do not believe. It's not that we don't believe in God, or even in Christ. It's that we don't believe, when confronted with our felt inadequacies, that we are loved – unconditionally loved – by a personal, powerful presence that cares about us.

As a young parish priest on the Gaspe Coast of Quebec, I met a couple from Texas that was searching for the meaning of life. Both were highly educated. One was a university professor; the other was studying to be a medical doctor. Three times a year they would come to the Gaspe from Texas where they would attend church every Sunday – yet they never received communion. Instinctively, they recognized that to stand up, leave the pew and proceed to the communion rail to receive the bread and wine meant a special kind of commitment they were not sure they could make.

When they expressed their hesitancy to me, I told them that communion is the Episcopal version of an altar call – only our altar call takes place every Sunday at every Eucharist when people literally "Stand up for Jesus."

One Sunday, when the church was mostly empty because of a severe snowstorm, this couple rose from their seats, and for the first time, came forward for communion. The moment I put the bread into their hands shall ever remain one of the highlights of my priestly ministry. They had taken seriously Christ's invitation to receive his unconditional love. God's acceptance of them led to their commitment of Jesus.

Years later, when I served as a priest at the cathedral in Bethlehem, Pennsylvania, I had the joy to baptize their child "as Christ's own forever."

And so, we come back to the title of Rabbi Kushner's book: *When All You've Ever Wanted Isn't Enough.* In the Eucharist there is enough – enough grace to live your life abundantly, enough love to sustain you through the tough times, enough power to give you the strength to live for today and to face the future with courage. In the Eucharist, we discover how much we are loved, not because we deserve such love, but simply because God gives it. In the sharing of the bread and wine, we are given a vision of life as it was meant to be – a vision of God among us, within us, and by our side.

One of my favorite films is *Places In The Heart*, for which Sally Field won an Academy Award. The film is set in a small southern town filled with economic distress, personal grief, natural disasters and racial hatred. It is a broken world where people yearn for healing and wholeness. At the end of the movie, the vision comes to fruition in a church's celebration of Holy Communion. As the choir sings Amazing Grace and the pastor reads the scripture (1 Corinthians 13), and as the elements of bread and wine get passed among the people, we notice something surprising, extraordinary, about this celebration. We suddenly see receiving the bread a black man who in the course of the film had been driven out of town, and then a white man who had been shot dead hands the tray to another black man who shot him and was himself lynched. The film ends with this vision of reconciliation and healing, this vision of perfect love that is a hallmark of the kingdom of God.

As we approach the communion rail to receive the bread of heaven and the cup of salvation, let us come as hungry people – hungry for the abundant, satisfying life that only Christ can give. Hungry to put away our inadequacies, failures and faults, and to receive those precious tokens of Christ's redeeming love. We are called into companionship with Jesus who loves us always and forever.

August 10, 2003
St. Bartholomew's Church, Poway, California

THE COURAGE TO
CHANGE YOUR MIND

EXODUS 32:7-14

Nothing is more damaging to Christians than having a fixed, static, and rigid mindset that does not allow for growth and development. In the New Testament, the Spirit is constantly prodding the church to expand its understanding of mission – moving from Jew to Samaritan to Gentile, and from Jerusalem, to the Greek world, and then to Rome. God is constantly calling the church to change, adapt and move forward into new mission fields. In the Hebrew Scriptures, God even changes his mind. So, the question is: If God can change his mind, why can't the church? Cardinal Newman famously stated: "In a higher world it is otherwise, but here below to live is to change, and to be perfect is to have changed often."

Several years ago, I met a friend from college who has since become an Orthodox priest. When I mentioned that I was now an Anglican priest, we began to chat about the similarities and differences between our two churches. My friend said to me, "The trouble with you Anglicans is that you always change your mind. You might say one thing one day, and another thing another day.

305

You lack consistency. We Orthodox are clear on the authority of scripture and sacred tradition. We are unwavering in our teaching. We never change."

I don't know if my friend's characterization of the Orthodox Church is accurate, but over the years I have thought seriously on what he said about Anglicans, and considering our lesson from Exodus, I have an answer for him. Notice what Exodus 32:14 says: "And the Lord changed his mind about the disaster that he planned to bring on his people" (NRSV).

That is an important verse of scripture. Jewish biblical scholar Richard Friedman makes the point that we ought to take this verse seriously as revelation, the very heart of the story.[1] It tells us about the kind of God we have. We have a God who changes his mind.

Yes, I know, we tend to think of God as unchanging and changeless. "Change and decay in all around I see: / O thou, who changest not, abide with me" wrote Henry Francis Lyte in one of the most beloved hymns of the Christian Church.[2] The Scottish pastor and hymn writer W. Chalmers Smith said it more poetically: "We blossom and flourish as leaves on the tree, / and wither and perish, but naught changeth thee."[3]

Nothing changes God. But according to our text from Exodus, God changes his mind by the intercession of Moses. God was about to destroy the Jewish people for their apostasy, but thanks to Moses he relents and changes his mind.

What a God we have here! This is not Aristotle's Unmoved Mover or Plato's Absolute Good. The God of Israel is one who is open to change. God will revise his plans and reconsider his decisions based on his ongoing interaction with those affected.

In our passage from Exodus God wants to destroy the people for their idolatry. Moses intervenes: "'Turn from your fierce wrath; change your mind and do not bring disaster upon your people. Remember Abraham, Isaac and Israel, your servants, how you swore to them by your own self, saying to them, 'I will multiply your descendants like the stars of heaven...'" (Ex. 32:12-13, NRSV). The text goes on to say: "And the Lord changed his mind about the disaster that he planned to bring on his people" (Ex. 32:14, NRSV).

That is amazing. It reveals a God who gets angry, and relents, and keeps on forgiving, repeatedly. You can read the entire history of Israel that way. It is the history of God getting angry at Israel, threatening to do something terrible, and then remembering the covenant he made with Abraham, Isaac and Jacob, and relenting, forgiving, and taking Israel back. What this tells us is that the most essential thing about God is mercy, love, forgiveness and compassion. The distant, immortal, immutable, unchanging, unfeeling God is not the God of the Bible. God may appear that way to those who do not know any better. That God is the God of the philosophers. The God of the abstract idea, the prime mover, the first principle, the ground of being, some idea, some concept – but that is not the God of the Bible.

Now if God can change his mind because his very nature is compassion, love, mercy and forgiveness, then so can we. So can the church. I do not mean change our minds capriciously or arbitrarily, but change them to become more loving, more forgiving, more merciful, more compassionate, more Christ-like.

Over the years the church has changed its' mind many times. John Noonan, a well-respected Roman Catholic scholar and jurist, wrote a book several years ago titled *A Church That Can and Cannot Change*. Noonan argued that the Roman Catholic Church has changed its mind on five key issues over the centuries: marriage, slavery, the death penalty, religious freedom and lending money at interest. It is difficult for us to comprehend, for example, that the institution of slavery was widely practiced and accepted by most Christians until the nineteenth century. Muslim slaves were manning papal galleys until 1800. Jesuits in colonial Maryland owned slaves, as did nuns in Europe and Latin America. It was only at the urging of Protestant Britain that the papacy condemned the slave trade in 1839, and only condemned slavery itself in 1888 after every Christian nation had abolished it.[4]

Whether it wants to admit it or not, the Roman Catholic Church has over the centuries changed its mind on many issues. So have Anglicans. Just think of the religious upheaval at the time of the Reformation. If you were a priest ordained in 1530 and died in 1560, you would have experienced five major upheavals in the church! It would take another one hundred years before liturgy and doctrine would be settled with the 1662 Book of Common Prayer.

Change is still happening. It may surprise us to know that until the second half of the twentieth century no divorced person could be remarried in the church, let alone be eligible for Holy Orders. That, of course, is no longer the case. The church changed its mind – and most of us would say for the better.

The same goes for the ordination of women. One of the strongest opponents of women priests in the Episcopal Church was Victor Rivera, the Bishop of the Diocese of San Joaquin in California. Bishop Rivera not only would not ordain women, but he refused to allow any woman priest to function in his diocese. When his daughter Nedi Rivera was ordained a priest, Victor was not present at the ceremony. However, when Nedi was elected Suffragan Bishop of the Diocese of Olympia in Washington State, one of her co-consecrators was her father Victor. Through his daughter he changed his mind and had come to believe in the rightness of women's ordination.

Did you know that the Anglican Communion opposed birth control until 1930? At the Lambeth Conferences of 1908 and 1920, the bishops voted against any kind of contraception. To them, church teaching was clear – going back to St. Augustine: "Sexual activity… is forbidden except within marriage, where it is allowed only in acts that are open to procreation. Contraception, since it violates the integrity of the conjugal act, is prohibited."[5]

However, in 1930, Anglicanism became the first major branch of Christianity to allow for contraception. Quickly, mainline Protestant churches followed, but the Roman Catholic Church did not. In 1931, Pope Pius XI issued his encyclical *Casti Canubi* which reiterated the long-held prohibition on contraception. That decision was reaffirmed by Pope Paul VI – and it remains official Roman Catholic teaching today.

So, who is right – the church that changed its mind in the face of 1500 years of tradition because different circumstances and new knowledge warranted a different conclusion or the church that adhered to the tradition absolutely, even in the face of a changing world? You be the judge.

The Anglican Church continues to change its mind as it develops a new understanding of sexuality based on experience deepened by empathy. There are many complex questions here, and no simple answers. John Noonan thinks doctrinal development should be based on love, knowledge and insight, and he likes St. Augustine's rule of faith: a true understanding of divine revelation is one that will "build up that double love of God and of neighbor."

Some of you may know that I support Open Communion or allowing unbaptized persons to receive Holy Communion. There is a great deal of controversy about the issue, which makes ongoing conversation important. Someone recently asked me, "How inclusive does the church have to become to accommodate people into it?" I told him that I didn't know the answer to that question, except that it seemed to me God was stretching the church to draw the circle wide – wider and wider – until all people everywhere are embraced in the arms of Jesus who loves without limit and whose mercy is without end. The issue for me is whether the church is able to welcome and accept people with the same love and acceptance as Jesus.

In a church which I served, a mother and daughter came to worship one Sunday. Neither was a Christian, but they had just lost their husband and father, and now they were searching for comfort and a deeper meaning to their lives. They did not know what to expect when they came to the church, but as they sat in the pew waiting for the service to begin, they read in the bulletin: All who seek God are welcome to receive the bread and wine of Christ's Body and Blood. Even if you do not seek God, God seeks you and invites you to his table."

When they read those words, the mother and daughter began to cry. They knew they were home. They experienced unconditional love and acceptance in a way they could never have imagined or expected. When they went to the rail to receive communion, they felt an overwhelming sense of being drawn into something, someone, a feeling they could not articulate until after receiving communion. When I asked them to tell me about it, the mother said that after receiving the bread and wine, she just wanted to cry. They were not tears of sadness but tears of joy. She had an overwhelming sense of being loved. And then, the most amazing thing happened. Although she didn't know much about him, she knew that she believed in Jesus.

Needless to say, a few weeks later, mother and daughter were both baptized.

Changing our minds is not about the church being trendy or fashionable. We should never just go along with the culture. However, it is permissible, and even desirable, to change our minds when that leads us to the church becoming more loving, more compassionate, more embracing of those within and outside our membership. It is desirable to give up beliefs and opinions that no longer make sense because they prevent us from loving other people as God loves them. We should never be so fixed in our beliefs that God cannot melt our hearts and open our minds to the new things God is doing in the world.

We in the Anglican Church may not always get it right, but it always is better to err on the side of being more loving than less loving, more merciful than less merciful, more compassionate than less compassionate. The next time you dig in your heels and draw a line in the sand and refuse to budge on an issue, think twice about it, because if God can change, so can you.

April 7, 2011
Huron University College Chapel, London, ON

GOD IN A WORLD OF CHANGE

EXODUS 3:1-6; JOHN 3:1-16

Christians throughout the centuries have experienced and understood God in different ways, for while God does not change, we do. As a result, how we think about God, worship God, and respond to God will vary with each generation. In a democratic and increasingly egalitarian world, thinking of God as an absolute ruler or king simply does not resonate with many people. God is with us and beside us more than over us and above us. Theology, church architecture and worship reflect this changing understanding of God. None of this should threaten Christians, because a vital and vibrant church is always adapting to changing times. Cardinal Newman famously wrote: "Growth is the only evidence of life."

I remember asking my divinity school professor, "Does God change?"

"No," he replied. "God doesn't change, but our idea of God changes."

My professor touched upon an important point about the nature of religious belief. God doesn't change, but we do. Each generation has a different understanding of God.

Several years ago, the Yale theologian Jaroslav Pelikan wrote the book *Jesus Through the Centuries*. He argued that the same Jesus has been understood differently by different generations in history. In the early church, Jesus the Good Shepherd lays down his life for his sheep. By the time of the Byzantine Empire, Jesus became Sovereign Lord or Pantokrator. During the Middle Ages, he was Judge of sinners. The Reformation saw him as Savior of sinners. The Enlightenment portrayed him as a person of wisdom while minimizing his deity. The Victorians so emphasized his divinity that they sometimes forgot his humanity. In twentieth century liberal Protestantism, Jesus became "the man for others" – a social activist standing against injustice and healing a broken world. To fundamentalists and evangelicals, Jesus was the defender of "traditional" moral values and the revealer of true doctrine. To Latin American theologians, Jesus was the liberator against oppression who fought unjust social systems.

And so, it goes. Each generation has its' own understanding of Jesus. Pelikan's book helps answer a question often asked by Christians: Why are there so many changes in the church? Why can't things just remain the same? If we follow Pelikan's reasoning, the answer is clear: As the context of our culture changes, so the content of our theology changes. Changing culture and changing lives result in a changing understanding of God. Because we experience God differently, we understand God differently. God is experienced and known differently by different generations in different cultural contexts.

Perhaps there is no better display of our changing understanding of God than in church architecture.

Consider the church architecture of the Middle Ages, mainly Romanesque and Gothic. There are the medieval cathedrals and the imposing churches of Europe. Salisbury Cathedral is enough to lift any sagging heart with its long, tall spire pointing heavenwards. The great cathedral of York Minister dominates the

City of York with its massive stone buttresses and towers. Here are churches built to last whose very structures represent stability and security.

That is the way it was in the Middle Ages. The church building dominated the city. Even in rural villages, the parish church was always at the center of the community. In much of Quebec today, one will find an imposing church even in a small village – always the most impressive building in the community. The same was true in Puritan New England and Anglican Virginia. The church was at the center of community life, guiding souls along an earthly pilgrimage to paradise; leading the faithful from earth to heaven.

Our present age is quite different. We still have cathedrals and large churches, but they are sandwiched in between skyscrapers. Churches in the city do not stand out like their medieval counterparts. They no longer impose themselves on our psyche. To some extent, they have even lost their distinctiveness.

In New York City there is St. Patrick's Cathedral; but also the Empire State Building. There is St. Bartholomew's Episcopal Church, Park Avenue but also the Chrysler Building. Churches such as St. Patrick's and St. Bartholomew's represent an architecture which was designed to stand against culture; but contemporary church architecture is designed to blend within culture. St. Peter's Lutheran Church in New York City, for example, was once a magnificent Gothic structure until it was torn down. It has since been rebuilt as part of the Citicorp Building. The church has actually become part of a skyscraper. No longer does it stand alone or possess a distinct identity. Its religious identity has been merged into a secular building.

Megachurches and even smaller conservative and independent churches often have the design of a business park – buildings that in no way stand out from culture but instead reflect culture. These churches are bright, spacious, contemporary, with stadium seating or comfortable chairs, air conditioned and properly ventilated, with excellent sound and lighting systems. The worship space is often referred to as an "auditorium" rather than a "sanctuary" or "narthex." The goal of these churches is to blend with the culture in order to reach the culture.

Look at the churches being built today. The distinction between sacred and secular is broken down. No longer dominating culture, the church is now in the midst of culture. No longer a fortress from the world, the church is now embedded in the world. As a result, church buildings constructed today are not designed to last hundreds of years like medieval churches. In a changing world, nothing is permanent, not even our places of worship.

If you examine contemporary churches and contrast them with the old Gothic, Romanesque and Baroque churches, the differences are startling. In the Middle Ages, churches had long aisles and high altars away from the people. The sanctuary was clearly set apart from the congregation, usually by a rood screen such as still exist in some Episcopal churches. There was a high ceiling and a somber setting which emphasized the majesty and mystery of God. In entering a medieval, or especially baroque church, one's thoughts were immediately lifted to God. Sometimes the experience could be overwhelming.

I shall never forget visiting the Basilica of Notre Dame in Montreal, Quebec. The exterior of that building is not particularly impressive, but the interior is captivating. Every inch of that church – the walls, the ceiling, the floors – is painted in beautiful colors: gold, blue, red... Here is a glimpse of heaven on earth – exactly what its' designers meant it to be.

Modern churches built today are quite different. They are minimalist in their design, almost austere. The altar is usually found in the middle of the church, or at least near the people. Nothing blocks the people from the priest in celebrating the liturgy together. In some churches, movable chairs have replaced pews. Where pews continue to be used, they are usually placed in a semi-circular position to foster greater intimacy among worshippers. The churches themselves tend to be light and bright rather than dark and somber, reflecting an openness to the world and a concern for the human condition.

Some of us may not appreciate or even like modern church architecture, but our aesthetic taste is not the issue. What I want us to ponder is the question: "Why the change?" Why has church architecture changed so radically since World War II? Certainly, God has not changed, but our culture has changed, and with it our experience of God.

The Middle Ages was an age of faith. The modern age is an age of secularism. Our understanding of God today reflects secular culture. And yet, thoroughly secular as we are, we function as Christians in the language of cultures past. The Bible we read, the creeds we affirm, even much of the Book of Common Prayer are the products of the past. If many of us have difficulty understanding their language, it should not surprise us. Religious language has become foreign language. Like any foreign language, it needs to be translated for our times and culture. As true, noble and beautiful as our religious tradition is, the church today is called to adapt to contemporary culture or risk becoming an anachronism.

Take, for example, the difference between the medieval view of the world and our modern one. In the Middle Ages there was sovereign rule – the monarch reigned. Today, at least in western developed nations, there is democratic rule – the people decide. In the Middle Ages, scholastic theology predominated with its highly intellectual and objective approach to God. Today, theologians are more likely to be influenced by psychology and the social sciences. The focus is as much on the emotions as the mind;

as much on the personal as the objective. In the Middle Ages, there was a predominately agricultural society. Today, we live in a technological, informational society. In the Middle Ages, people lived in homogeneous communities. Today, we mostly live in heterogeneous communities, which are multicultural, multireligious and pluralistic. In the Middle Ages, there was a God-centered culture. Today, we are human-centered.

Our understanding of God is different from the past because our world is different. We no longer rely on sole authority figures to govern us. Instead, we are democratic in making our own political choices and decisions. Consensus has replaced divine fiat. In our culture, God is no longer a rule-giver but a bridge-builder, not so much dictating rules of conduct as reconciling people one to another. Pope Francis understands this, which is why he is trying to transform the Roman Catholic Church before it becomes an outdated institution. The triangle of hierarchy is being replaced by the circle of egalitarianism.

Psychology now plays a major role in understanding human beings. As psychological beings, we experience God more through persons than ideas. We think with our feelings as much as with our mind. Living in a technological world, we have a pressing need for intimacy with each other in order to withstand the alienation that threatens. Living in a heterogeneous world, we value pluralism, toleration and equality in a way our forebears did not. We also value autonomy and choice, thinking for ourselves, making our own decisions, living our own way. We tend not to rely on dogmatic pronouncements by authority figures, but on our experience and intuition in determining the truth.

Many of us take for granted that we have the right to choose our religion – or not to have any religion at all. If you don't like the Episcopal Church, you can always become a Roman Catholic, or a Presbyterian, or Methodist, or Lutheran. Or you can be an atheist or agnostic. In America, the choices are endless. We in America take for granted that we have the right to choose or not choose a religion.

However, do we realize how secular an attitude that is? It would have been unthinkable to our medieval forebears to choose one's religion. One could no more choose one's religion than one could choose into the class he or she was born.

Even when our preferences may be for tradition and our views conservative, our attitudes are distinctly secular because we value freedom, autonomy and choice. God has a role to play in our lives, but not the dominant role of the Middle Ages. God, the church and religion are all choices – options among many options in a world of endless choices – that is the secular world. If the church is to be a vibrant force in this world, it needs to come to terms with the appeal of secularism – that God, religion and belief are just more options from which to choose how we will conduct our lives. We are not medieval. We are modern, and I suspect, most of us prefer it that way.

The church functions in a secular culture, and therefore we need to be sensitive in how secular people think and what they value. Secular people, and particularly younger people, value sacred moments more than sacred space. The place of worship matters less than the experience of worship. Buildings matter less than experiences. For many in our culture today, God is more felt than thought, more intuitive than intellectual. In secular culture, experience determines truth. People experience something as true before they believe it to be true. In this culture, God is a lived experience more than an object of belief – within us and beside us more than over and above us.

This may seem baffling to Episcopalians who love their buildings and value the beauty of holiness as much as the holiness of beauty. We want beautiful buildings that inspire the spirit and draw us closer to God. We cannot comprehend why people would want to meet for worship in a business park, or an auditorium in a steel building that seems more appropriate for a warehouse than a church. And yet, in our secular culture, sacred moments trump sacred spaces. It isn't the building but the experience that matters.

So, how do we respond to this secular challenge? The Christian doctrine of the Trinity gives us an answer. For just as God is a community of persons united in one Godhead, so the church is called to be a community of love united under one God.

The Trinity speaks to our deepest need – the need to belong to a community of love. We need to belong because we need to experience the nearness of God in our lives. We need the assurance that God is present in the here and now of everyday living. We need to affirm that in our increasingly impersonal world there is still a personal God who cares for us with unconditional love, and that this love can be experienced in the community Christians call the church. In a changing world, love is a permanent value.

The greatest sign that the living God is present among us is in the love we share as Christ's church in the world. This is the love which celebrates diversity rather than fears it. This is the love which seeks out the best in people rather than brings out the worst. This is the love which reaches out to others rather than shuns them away. In this secular age, more impressive than our cathedrals and church buildings, our liturgy and music, is the love which binds us together. Such love attracts, affirms and builds up people, healing their hurts and lifting their spirits to the God who already loves them always and forever. This is the love which gives us the assurance that in this secular world, God is still the center of our being who draws us into community.

I heard a story about a young girl who was serving as an acolyte for the first time in her church. In the sacristy she put on her white robe and was briefed by one of the senior acolytes about her role in the worship service. Seeing that she seemed a bit nervous, the priest went up to her and said, "Don't worry about making a mistake." Without a moment's hesitation, the young girl replied, "Oh, I'm not worried, because church is the one place you can make mistakes and it's still okay."

That young girl had it right. The church is a community where you can make mistakes and still feel loved, forgiven and accepted. The church is people bound together by their strengths and their brokenness, people who are limping toward the sunrise but know that God loves them, everyone. The church is people becoming alive together in Jesus, praying together, loving one another, supporting each other, finding faith and reaching out to others.

A sign over an Italian hotel which once served as a hospital had the words: "To heal sometimes, to comfort often, to care always." I can't think of a better description of any church, no matter its architecture, ancient or modern. That's the kind of love every church should express, whether it is a small country church or a large urban cathedral.

Buildings have their importance but people are always more important. It isn't the beauty of a building but the love of the people that ultimately matter. If we as a church fail in love, we fail in all things else. If we seek to love, we cannot fail. In this secular age, God is to be found in a community of love or not at all.

June 14, 1987
Cathedral Church of the Nativity, Bethlehem, PA

THE POWER AND
MAJESTY OF MUSIC

PSALM 150; REVELATION 5:11-13

*Choral Morning Prayer and Evensong are worship services in
Anglicanism in which music plays a prominent role. It is not
uncommon for church choirs to sing the Canticles – the Song of
Zachariah (Lk. 1:68-79), the Song of Mary (Lk. 1:46-55) and
The Song of Simeon (Lk. 2:29-32) as well an offertory anthem.
Occasionally someone may complain, "I didn't come to church
to hear a concert but to worship God." That misses the point of
biblical worship which gives a central role to music and singing.
Think, for example, of Psalm 150 with its references to musical
instruments or Psalm 149 which begins: "Praise the Lord! Sing
to the Lord a new song..." (Ps. 149:1, NRSV). Music may be
the greatest proof for the existence of God. It surely is a way in
which people have been drawn to God or become convinced of
God's existence. I myself was drawn to the Episcopal Church
at a service of Choral Evensong at Washington's National
Cathedral. In a church with such beautiful music, I thought,
God is surely present. But the power of music extends beyond
the church. Even secular and contemporary composers bring us
nearer to God, instill in us a desire to work for justice and peace,
and draw us closer to one another.*

Here we are in one of the most pre-eminent music churches in Canada, in the middle of the world-renown Elora Music Festival and having just listened to one of the great choirs in North America. So, it seems fitting this day to reflect on the power and majesty of music, in our lives and in the church.

Let me begin with a story. When I was a freshman in a Catholic prep school, one of my courses was in music appreciation. We began by studying Gregorian chant. That led to Palestrina, Gabrielli and Bach. With each class I was being drawn into the enchantment of music and feeling pulled ever closer to God.

And then, one day, we came to Handel and his great *Messiah*. Somewhere as we heard "The Glory of the Lord shall be revealed, and all Flesh shall see it together..." I had what I can only term a mystical experience in feeling the power and presence of God. I knew at that moment God existed; convinced not by logic but music. When we came to the Halleluiah Chorus, I imagined that Handel himself had gone to heaven to bring us such a gift. Nothing outside of some kind of divine revelation could account for it.

There is power in music, isn't there? St. Augustine preached: "He who sings prays twice." An old Jewish proverb says: "When the Messiah comes there will be singing." Read the Book of Revelation and the angels and saints in heaven always seem to be singing and praising God. In the Hebrew Scriptures, the Book of Psalms is Israel's hymnal – expressing praise, thanksgiving, lament, sorrow, anger and confession... all the host of human emotions are present in that one book. The last of the psalms – Psalm 150 – is about praising God through music. How fitting indeed!

Music has the power to give us hope when we are threatened by despair, to help us face the future with faith, to provide assurance that despite all the awful things happening in our world, God is with us always and forever.

One of the most beautiful pieces of music ever composed – and you don't have to be a Roman Catholic to appreciate it – is Franz Schubert's *Ave Maria*. I have known that piece of music since I first heard it as a young boy, and it has comforted many an aching heart. Years ago, I was asked to visit an elderly woman in the hospital several days before Christmas. Her house had caught fire and she was suffering from burns throughout her body. From her hospital bed she could hardly move because of the pain. And yet, this dear woman said that what kept her going was singing in her mind Schubert's *Ave Maria*. The prayer itself gave her strength but the music lifted her spirit and made her more able to bear the pain of her burns. Schubert's *Ave Maria* is in Latin, but many of us know the prayer in English:

> *Hail Mary, full of grace,*
> *the Lord is with thee,*
> *blessed art thou among women*
> *and blessed is the fruit of thy womb, Jesus.*
> *Holy Mary, Mother of God,*
> *pray for us sinners,*
> *now and at the hour of our death. Amen.*

As it turned out, the dear woman died a short while after I visited her, but I am almost certain she was praying the *Ave Maria* when she took her last breath.

Former New York Mayor Ed Koch died this year. He was a character, but I loved the man. On several occasions he shared that his favorite song was the Catholic hymn, "Be Not Afraid" by Bob Dufford. Now Ed Koch was Jewish, but as mayor he attended many a Catholic funeral for a police officer gunned down in the line of duty or a firefighter who lost his life trying to save others. At many of those funerals, "Be Not Afraid" was sung. Mayor Koch said that if his rabbi would give permission, he would have the words of that hymn on his gravestone, because they helped him get through some of the darkest days in his life.

> *Be not afraid*
> *I go before you always*
> *Come follow me*
> *and I will give you rest.*[1]

In the Book of Isaiah, the prophet gives an image of heaven and earth rejoicing at the return of the Jewish people from exile: "Sing, O heaven, for the Lord has done it; shout, O depths of the earth; break forth into singing, O mountains, O forest, and every tree in it! (Isa. 44:23, NRSV). As if to highlight the occasion of Israel's return to the promised land, Isaiah repeats the call to sing and rejoice: "Sing, for joy, O heavens, and exult, O earth; break forth, O mountains, into singing!" (Isa. 49:1, NRSV). This section of Isaiah, commonly called Second Isaiah, was written after the destruction of the Kingdom of Judah and the exile of the Jewish people to Babylon. Now the time of exile is over and the people are returning to their homeland. For the Jewish people this is a great time to rejoice, and so they sing.

For Christians, heaven is our permanent homeland. When we enter that place of eternal promise, there will be singing. I once spoke with a parishioner who told me he did not like singing in church. I good-naturedly replied: "If you read the Book of Revelation, there will be plenty of singing in heaven. So, you better get used to it."

Singing as a way of praising God is what you do in heaven. Maybe that's why almost every Christian church has singing.

Whether you are a Roman Catholic singing "Here I am, Lord," or a Lutheran singing "A mighty fortress is our God," or a Baptist singing "To God be the glory," or an Anglican singing, "Praise, my soul, the king of heaven," there isn't a Christian church anywhere that doesn't sing to God. Even Quakers, who may not sing in their meetings, sing outside their meetings. After all, if Jesus is in our hearts and the Spirit in our lives, then shouldn't we want to sing about it?

After the September 11, 2001 attack on the United States, Americans were numbed, panicked, and frightened. I was rector of a church in San Diego at the time, and I remember having to call all the staff together – it was a large multi-staff parish – and try to calm everyone down to focus on ministering to our members. People were in tears. On Tuesday afternoon we changed the entire worship service to deal with the horrible reality of the nation being attacked and thousands of people dead. New lessons, new sermon, new hymns, new anthem – all designed to comfort those who mourn and strengthen the fainthearted and lift up those in despair. Because my parish had a number of active and retired military among the members, especially in the Navy, on Sunday we sang the Navy hymn, "Eternal Father, strong to save." I can tell you, there wasn't a dry eye at any of the services as we sang that hymn.

> *O Trinity of love and power,*
> *Thy children shield in danger's hour;*
> *from rock and tempest, fire and foe,*
> *protect them wheresoe'er they go;*
> *thus ever more shall rise to thee*
> *glad hymns of praise from land and sea.*[2]

Yes, sometimes the only thing you can do is sing. Music allows us to express our deepest heartfelt emotions when there are no words adequate to utter.

There's another thing music does for us: it draws us together in ways where otherwise we would remain separate.

When I served in the Diocese of San Diego – Heather, Allison and I were always invited to the annual diocesan Cursillo Christmas party, which was held at a parishioner's home. After everyone had enjoyed the eggnog and holiday treats, the group of about 80 people would gather around the piano and begin singing Christmas carols. And then, something almost magical would happen. As we sang together, there grew this feeling of being an extended family, even though people in the room had deep theological differences that were splitting apart the Episcopal Church. For that one night there was no "them" and "us;" no liberal or conservative, no progressive or traditionalist. We were united in song praising our great God as we sang together, "O come, all ye faithful, joyful and triumphant...O come, let us adore him, Christ, the Lord."

Yes, when we sing, we sing as the family of God. I have often wondered why God created us with voices that are so different. The soprano can hit such high notes; the bass can get so low. But then we blend our voices into one glorious sound. To me, it easily qualifies as proof of God's existence. Why would blind evolution give us such a gift? It makes no sense. Music calls us together into one beautiful family. At Christmas we sing "Hark the Herald Angels Sing" and I believe the angels sing with us. At Easter we sing, "Jesus Christ is risen today" and I know that Jesus lives, and one day we shall live with him.

Music allows us to express our deepest feelings. Music draws us closer together. And most importantly of all, music speaks to us of God.

The great Swiss reformed theologian Karl Barth once said

that it was impossible to hear Mozart and still not believe in God. Echoing Barth, a parishioner once said to me, "I haven't been to heaven, but I have heard Bach." Music lifts our hearts to a realm beyond all imagining. You don't have to think about God when you listen to the music. You simply experience God in the music.

Charles Gore was the scholarly Bishop of Oxford. One evening he attended a concert in which the orchestra had played a Brandenburg Concerto. His almost unconscious comment on the music showed he had encountered glory: "If that is true, everything must be all right."

How many times have we come home after a hectic and maybe even rotten day at work, sat in a comfortable chair and listened to our favorite music? What a powerful effect music can have on us, calming us, relaxing us, and even healing the hurts we may be experiencing. One person I know had a particularly exhausting day teaching in his high school. After an early dinner he went to his study and listened to all nine of Beethoven's symphonies. The next morning, he was ready to face his students once again.

Music lifts us up, guides, strengthens and sustains us. Think of all the civil rights marchers in the American South during the 1950s and 60s. Notice they always sang a song to keep strong, to keep together, to withstand the water cannons and cattle prods and night sticks. "We shall overcome" they sang – and they did overcome, proving stronger by far than their adversaries.

Keep that in mind next time you struggle with your own challenges – as doubt or despair or disappointment come your way. Never forget that there is a God who took on all the evil powers of this world and won – a God who conquered death itself, and therefore can conquer whatever difficulties may come your way.

Music speaks to us of this God. That's why music has always been part of the church. Even people who say they are "spiritual but not religious" will listen to Gregorian chant or appreciate

Anglican Evensong or download a popular artist who sings "On Eagles' Wings." What logic or persuasion or argument cannot do, music does. It draws us to an encounter with God.

Toshi Seeger, the wife of the folk singer Pete Seeger, died this month. In reading her obituary in the *New York Times*, I recalled just how much the music of Pete Seeger meant to me, especially growing up in the tumultuous years of the 1960s and 1970s. One particular song that Seeger sang has become one of my personal favorites, and I was delighted that the Anglican Church of Canada chose to include it in the updated *Common Praise* hymnal. The song dates back to the nineteenth century New England Shakers. These Shakers knew so well that music has the power to keep us going when we want to give up, and to give us the courage to face whatever comes our way.

> *My life flows on in endless song*
> *above earth's lamentation.*
> *I hear the real though far-off hymn*
> *that hails a new creation.*
> *No storm can shake my inmost calm,*
> *while to that rock I'm clinging.*
> *Since love is lord of heaven and earth,*
> *how can I keep from singing.*[3]

Whatever song may have touched your life, I hope you'll sing it with gusto. Let it stir your soul, strengthen your spirit, and draw you ever closer to God.

July 28, 2013
St. John's Anglican Church, Elora, ON

OVERCOMING THE RELIGIOUS SPIRIT

MARK 7:1-8, 14-15, 21-23

One of the most insidious forces in the church is the religious spirit which makes the rituals, practices and laws of religion more important than loving people at their own level of need and understanding. Anytime the church is more focused on outward forms, legal mandates and church structures than on its mission to obey the Great Commandment and the Great Commission, it will decline not only in members but in energy, passion and spirit. It will lose its first love, Jesus, and focus instead on itself. The church is not an institution to be preserved but a movement of Christ in the world – a community of love with a mission to build a civilization of love. No wonder St. Augustine could say: "Love and do as you will."

I was greeting people at the church entrance after a glorious Easter morning service. The choir and congregation had just finished singing the Hallelujah Chorus from Handel's *Messiah*. "Christ is risen" echoed throughout the church as people began to leave the building. Everyone had smiles on their faces and Christ in their hearts. Except one woman. She looked at me sternly and said,

"Why was there no confession of sin in this service?" I explained that on Easter Sunday it is appropriate to leave out the confession since the focus of our worship is on resurrection and new life. That explanation did not satisfy her. "I am very upset," she said. "You priests are always changing the service. Just stick to the Prayer Book." And with that she left in a huff.

One of the most common criticisms of the church is that we always seem to focus on the trivial, the inconsequential and unimportant matters rather than what is at the heart of Christian faith. To the people outside the church, we look silly. They see and hear about us attending church, believing in Christ, and receiving the sacraments. But then they see us majoring on the minors, making form more important than substance, outward show more important than spirit, being more focused on ceremony and ritual than adoration and praise. It is this kind of religion that comes under attack in today's Gospel.

Jesus and his disciples were eating a Sabbath meal. Some of the strict Jews noticed that the disciples had not washed their hands with proper religious ritual before they ate and challenged Jesus as to how religious he really was. So they asked: "Why do your disciples not live according to the tradition of the elders, but eat with defiled hands?" (Mt. 7:5, NRSV). Jesus reacted with anger and said: "Isaiah prophesized rightly about you hypocrites, as it is written, 'This people honors me with their lips, but their hearts are far from me, in vain do they worship me, teaching human precepts as doctrines'" (Mt. 7:6-7, NRSV).

In the time of Jesus a religious person might hate his neighbor with all his heart, and he might be full of envy and jealousy and concealed bitterness and pride, but that did not matter as long as he carried out the correct hand-washings and observed the correct laws about cleanness and uncleanness.

A religious spirit takes account of people's outward actions;

but it takes no account of their inward feelings. A person may well be meticulously serving God in outward things and bluntly disobeying God in inward things – and that's hypocrisy.

Jesus could not stand that kind of religion. For more than 2,000 years the problem of the religious spirit has not gone away.

There is a kind of person for whom faith is a set of dogmas and regulations. Rather than a religion centered on relationships, it is a religion centered on rules. It is principle for the sake of principle. It is all the lips, not of the heart. These are profoundly serious religious people but according to Jesus, people with a serious problem. So... what is wrong with the religious spirit?

First, it is not a religion of God. It is something centered in human activity – not divine activity. "You abandon the commandment of God and hold to human tradition" (Mk. 7:8, NRSV). These people are concerned more with the way one worships than with worship itself; with the right form regardless of the right spirit; with the right words rather than with what the words mean.

I began my ministry in the Diocese of Quebec where there were several joint Anglican – United Church of Canada parishes. Ministers from the two denominations would alternate in parishes every few years because neither the Anglicans nor the United Church members were large enough to go it alone.

In one remote parish, the congregation became deeply split over the shape of a proposed communion table. Anglicans wanted one kind of table, United Church members another. The divisions became so deep that the Anglican priest then serving the parish had to resign – and all over the shape of a table!

Here was a church divided – in the name of religion.

One of the most-unpleasant church disputes I have ever encountered was an Altar Guild meeting. Guild members hotly debated where the bread box and cruets of wine and water should be placed on the credence table. Some wanted it one way, others wanted it a different way. The discussion got so heated that one woman walked out furious; she just could not stand the bickering and pettiness any longer.

Here were Christians divided – in the name of religion.

A parishioner of a prominent church told me about his former rector who insisted on using red vestments on Christmas Eve, even though the liturgical color appointed is white. This parishioner was so upset by what the priest had done that he left the church – he just could not accept that the priest used the wrong color. He only returned when the priest retired from the parish. I pointed out to this person that before the nineteenth century Anglicans did not have colored vestments. There were no stoles or chasubles, red, white or whatever. That surprised him but he still could not accept what the priest had done. To him it was a cardinal sin to use red rather than white at Christmas.

Here was a person angry at a fellow Christian – in the name of religion.

I have encountered parents who have refused to attend their daughter's wedding because she was being married in a different church from theirs. I have seen the same phenomenon with the ordination of a priest whose mother of a different church refused to attend the ceremony. This is dividing the family and denying their daughter – in the name of religion!

Jesus knew that true religion is not a matter of rules; it's a matter of relationship – a relationship with the God who knows the heart of a human being, knows what a human being thinks and feels – a God who desires to forgive our sins and heal our hurts and love us and be our friend. The problem Jesus had with people who have a religious spirit is they knew nothing of that kind of selfless love – they have missed it, and their religion had kept them from it.

So first: the religious spirit is not a religion of God, but second, the religious spirit raises the wrong issues. In our Gospel reading, the issue raised by the Pharisees is trivial. It was not about the nature of God, or who Jesus was, or how a person can find and know God. It was about washing your hands in the proper way! It was principle for the sake of principle.

Certainly, all of us have admiration for people who hold strong principles and refuse to compromise on an issue of conscience. What we must be sure of, however, is, are we emphasizing the right issue?

When I was in Lancaster, Pennsylvania, I heard the story of an old-time Mennonite bishop who was having difficulty with some women under his spiritual care. The Mennonite bonnet had strings which were used to tie the bonnet under the chin. Some women (and this may be shocking to sensitive ears) decided not to tie their bonnets, but to let the strings dangle. The bishop remarked, "Honestly, I just don't know what this world is coming to!" Here was a church leader with strong principles but the wrong issue.

Tying your bonnet may not be a serious matter, but sometimes there are serious matters that the church ignores at its peril. In 1917, while the Bolshevik Revolution was being violently waged in the streets of St. Petersburg, the Holy Synod of the Russian Orthodox Church was meeting in a grand palace – debating the shape of liturgical vestments. Of all we know of that synod, the issue of the shape of vestments was hotly debated – but not a word about the social conditions in Russia! People were protesting in the streets, the government was on the brink of collapse, but synod members were concerned about vestments. The members of the synod had strong principles but the wrong issue.

True religion gives churches and their members a sense

of balance in life, common sense, not principle for the sake of principle, but principle for the sake of people.

So first: the religious spirit is not of God. Second, it raises the wrong issues. And third, the religious spirit creates a kind of personality that is incompatible with the personality of Jesus.

What Jesus found in the Pharisee is a personality that is cold, negative, holier-than-thou – often judgmental and always right. In contrast, Jesus, and those who follow him are warm, open, positive people – our religious experience being one of liberation, not enslavement – one of understanding, not of judgment – not always having the right answers but knowing the right, true God.

Several years ago, there was a news report about a Roman Catholic priest who refused communion to anyone who did not conform to his dress code. His bishop removed him from the parish. The priest's appeal to Rome was rejected, not because standards of dress do not matter, but because refusing communion is a judgment on a person's heart which cannot be made based on clothing. True holiness has always been a matter of the heart, a right relationship with God by faith. Externals may matter, but it is the heart that counts most.

So, how does the church overcome the religious spirit? It is simple, really. When we have the same love and acceptance for others that God has for us, when we make love the priority and everything else secondary, when we act in the spirit of Jesus and claim the freedom of the Gospel, then the religious spirit will give way to a life-affirming, life-giving community of love. When love supersedes law, and when relationships are more important than rules, then we know we are moving in the way of Jesus.

When I was a young priest in upstate New York, I had a parishioner who was a former Quaker. She was now a baptized member of the Episcopal Church. One day she came to me and said that her mother would be visiting from Delaware, and would

I be open to giving her Holy Communion. Then she said: "My mother is a Quaker, and Quakers do not have sacraments. So, my mother is not baptized, but she is a committed Christian."

This was the first time I had to deal with an unbaptized person seeking to receive Holy Communion. The canons or laws of the Episcopal Church state that only baptized persons shall receive communion. Would I violate the law and accommodate a dear woman who wanted to receive Holy Communion with her daughter? I thought for a moment, and then said: "Of course, I will give your mother communion. And I will tell her how delighted we are to have her as our guest."

On Sunday morning, the mother and daughter received communion together, and it was a great blessing for the both of them.

Did I do the right thing? It depends on whether law or love is our priority. Law has its place but love always triumphs. After all, the fundamental religious question is not about church-going, or even about which church you belong to. The fundamental question is: How is your heart towards God and your fellow human beings?

September 2, 2018
Church of the Nativity, Scottsdale, AZ

THE CALL OF DISCIPLESHIP

LUKE 14:25-33

Since the Reformation there has been a difference among churches between those that insist on a conscious decision to accept Jesus as Savior and Lord, and those that practice infant baptism and believe that becoming a Christian is a matter of growth and development – a process of journeying in faith more than a momentary decision. Today both sides are coming together in recognizing a need for discipleship. Churches want people who are not just Christians in name but intentionally follow in the way of Jesus. Being a Christian is not a nominal decision but a life-changing one in which we resolve to take up our cross and follow Jesus, even if that means putting our lives on the line. A prayer attributed to St. Ignatius Loyola reflects the heart of a disciple: "Dearest Lord, teach me to be generous. Teach me to serve you as you deserve; to give and not to count the cost; to fight and not to heed the wounds; to toil and not to seek for rest; to labor and not to ask for reward, save that of knowing that I am doing your will. Amen."[1]

This summer I visited St. Benedict's Monastery in Snowmass, Colorado. The Cistercian monks there live a very demanding life. They start praying at 4:15 in the morning, have seven periods of prayer a day, work on their ranch or make crafts, eat a vegetarian diet, and live a regimented life with emphasis on silence, austerity, prayer, poverty, simplicity and obedience.

I asked one of the monks why life at the monastery was so rigorous. He said that St. Benedict viewed the monastery as "a school for the Lord's service," and although the life was incredibly rewarding for those who were called, it also was very demanding, and deliberately so. Benedict knew that following Jesus as his disciple meant being willing to live a very disciplined life. Discipline and discipleship go together, the monk said to me.

We at Advent live in a very different world from those monks. We have responsibilities to our families, in our communities, and with our church.

I remember Bishop Mark Dyer, who was a former Benedictine monk and my bishop in the Diocese of Bethlehem, telling the clergy that as parish priests we should never try to be monks. Our duties are to our families, to our parishes, and to the diocese. It would be unrealistic for us to pray the same seven-fold Daily Office as monks. Jesus, Bishop Dyer told us, is not calling us to leave the world. He is calling us to be disciples in the world. The question is, "How do we live as disciples of Jesus with integrity?"

The most obvious answer is that we carry our cross. Jesus says: "Whoever does not carry the cross and follow me cannot be my disciple" (Lk. 14:27, NRSV). To be a disciple of Jesus means to carry your cross.

We all have our crosses to bear, don't we? I know people who are caregivers to their spouses or even to their parents. I know parents who care for their special-needs child. I know elderly folks who are dealing with health issues or struggling to remain mobile. If we are in the workforce, we sometimes have to make a choice between doing the right thing and keeping our job. Sometimes we are called to speak out against injustice even if that is deemed impolite. You don't laugh when someone makes a racist or sexist joke. You give your money to worthy causes. You volunteer to help the poor. In so many ways, personal, professional and social, we witness as disciples of Jesus.

In my home office, I have a picture of a lawyer in Vietnam being escorted out of the courthouse in handcuffs with a squad of police surrounding him. It is April 2011 and attorney Cu Huy Ha Vu is being escorted to prison to serve a seven-year sentence after being convicted of spreading propaganda against the state. You see: Cu is a human rights lawyer and that makes him a threat to the Communist government of Vietnam.

As an attorney, I try to keep abreast of the lawyers and judges under siege around the globe simply for doing their job. Because they believe in the rule of law and human rights, they endure harassment, surveillance, and intimidation. Many experience detention, prosecution, torture, imprisonment, and even death.

Some two hundred lawyers are imprisoned in Vietnam alone. In China, more than 300 Chinese lawyers have been ensnared in the government's "709 crackdown," which was launched in July 2015 and continues to this day. In what has been termed a "war on law," Chinese lawyers have been summoned for questioning, kidnapped by secret police, detained in prisons, tortured, tried, convicted and sentenced without due process on charges trumped up by the state. No wonder the people of Hong Kong are rebelling in the streets – they know what awaits them.

In the Philippines, lawyer Ben Ramos was gunned down on the street, targeted for his pro bono work representing political prisoners and dissidents. He was the thirty-fourth lawyer to be assassinated for human rights since President Duterte took office in June 2016.

I could go on.... in Saudi Arabia, in Turkey, in Iran, in Bahrain, in Swaziland and other African and South American nations, lawyers and judges have been imprisoned for defying their governments and upholding the rule of law.

None of them chose to be arrested or go to prison. They could easily have gone along with the system, and not rankled government officials. They were not looking to carry a cross, but their conscience dictated otherwise. They had a belief in justice and the dignity of the human person that made them willing to risk their freedom and even their lives. That's what it means to carry your cross. You stand up for justice. You stand up for righteousness. You stand up for Gospel truths against the principalities and powers of the world. It's not easy, I know, but that's what it means to be a disciple.

So, first, carry your cross – whatever that cross may be in your own life. Second, strive to give your whole self to Jesus, even when that moves you beyond your comfort zone. In our Gospel Jesus says: "So therefore, none of you can become my disciple if you do not give up all your possessions" (Lk. 14:33, NRSV). That's a tough statement, I know. What could that possibly mean in our situation? After all, we have bank accounts, investment portfolios, homes, and cars.

If you have been following the plight of the migrants on our southern border, the one thing you might have noticed is that these people come with the clothes they are wearing, whatever bags they can carry and the little amount of money they may still possess – and that's it. They bring nothing else. They have nothing else. Whatever else they had, they left behind. And why do they leave everything behind trying to get into America? For freedom, for a better life, to ensure that their sons will never be forced into a gang and their daughters will never be used as sex slaves. These people are willing to give up everything for the freedom and security that America offers.

That's the way it is for disciples of Jesus. Disciples are willing to sacrifice everything for Jesus just as refugees and migrants sacrifice everything for freedom. That's the point of this vivid hyperbole: "Whoever comes to me and does not hate father and mother, his wife and children, his brothers and sisters, yes, and even life itself, cannot be my disciple" Lk. 14:26, NRSV). "Hate" here doesn't mean despise. It means putting God first; making God a priority in our lives; resolving to be in God's will, no matter the cost or the consequences.

Some of us may recall the Martyrs of Libya. In February 2015, twenty-one Egyptian Coptic Christians working in Libya were captured by ISIL terrorists and threatened with death unless they converted to Islam. To their credit, not one of them was willing to abandon the Christian faith to save his life. As each was being beheaded, their last word before dying was to pray the name of Jesus. The press rarely reports these stories, but Christians are the most persecuted religious group in the world, and the persecutions are intensifying.

As a young priest, I used to think that if the church is going to grow in North America, we need to make Christianity easy – not too many requirements. Don't hassle people or demand too much of them. The Episcopal Church has been good at this. You know what they say about the Episcopal Church compared to the Roman Catholic Church: twice the fun and half the guilt.

I used to think that "Christianity light" was the way to go, but not anymore. I think we are making the Gospel too easy and not expecting enough from our people. We pitch everything to the lowest common denominator. Maybe we need to rethink our church strategy. Most people understand that if there is anything that can provide meaning and significance to our lives, it will not come easy. It will not be three steps offered without cost. It will not come cheap. It will be something that will challenge us and demand something of us. We will have to give something, even sacrifice.

When I served a parish in Lancaster, Pennsylvania, one of the neighboring churches was a very conservative Presbyterian church. This church adhered to the Westminster Confession, taught Puritan theology and practiced strict church discipline, including having members sign-in at worship so church officials would know who was absent. The Session would even discipline members who engaged in notorious public misconduct. We Episcopalians shook our heads in disbelief that any sensible, modern human being would want to be a member of that kind of church. And yet, the church grew and grew and grew, with one building campaign after another, and worship services packed to capacity.

One young man, a member of the church, had just gotten back from a mission trip to Haiti where he helped build a medical clinic. He paid for his entire trip and was planning to go again next year. I asked him why he was a member of the church? He said to me, "I need structure and discipline in my life, and this church has it. They are not afraid to speak the hard words of Jesus, hold people accountable and call people to discipleship."

I found what the young man said unsettling. Then, I thought, "Maybe what he wants is to be a Christian."

Following Jesus is not easy. It demands something from us; it has a cost. At times, it is downright difficult. It involves obedience, sacrifice and self-discipline. None of these things are fashionable these days, and yet people want something to live for that is greater than them. Some give their lives for their country in the military. Others work as teachers in the inner city or depressed, rural areas. Some volunteer for the Peace Corps or to work with migrants at our border. I am amazed by their willingness to give of themselves, to engage in work that is tough, difficult, but in some sense very rewarding.

Can you hear Jesus calling you to be his disciple – to take up your cross and strive to give your whole self to him? It's not easy, I know. It may demand from you not less than everything. But perhaps, in your life and mine, you are still drawn to him and to what he says to us and how he expects us to witness to him. Jesus comes asking us to pay the price. In our better moments, we are just dying to pay the price, just dying.

Several years ago, the Episcopal Church circulated a film on stewardship. It was about a clown who was trying to be a follower of Jesus. He did all sorts of things that people on the street found silly, foolish, absurd. And yet, each act of kindness somehow reflected the upside-down kingdom of God. Some folks thought he was weird but that did not matter to the clown.

The last scene in the film finds the clown in a church. He wants to make an offering to God but he doesn't have any money. He gave all his money away helping people. So what can he do? He sees a huge collection plate, takes it to the front of the altar, puts it down on the floor, and steps into it himself.

September 8, 2019
Church of the Advent, Sun City West, AZ

TURNING POINTS

1 CORINTHIANS 13; JOHN 14:1-6

I suppose all clergy reflect on their ministry before retirement. Apart from building campaigns and church plants, it is often difficult to determine just what we have accomplished. So much of ministry is intangible, personal and difficult to quantify. While we can look at the growth of church budgets, the number of new members, and any campus expansion, what really matters are the lives transformed in Jesus, the faithfulness of our preaching and pastoring, and how we have reflected God's love, compassion and truth in our lives. In this sermon, preached two weeks before my retirement, I reflected on three turning points that have shaped my life and ministry: Jesus as the Way, the Truth and the Life; Human Dignity as the foundation for law and ethics; and All-Inclusive Love as the hope of the world.

Periodically we face pivotal moments that define our lives. They are turning points that shape who we are and how we act in the world. I want to tell you about three of those turning points that have shaped my life and ministry as a priest.

The first turning point occurred when I was a college student at Fordham University in New York. I had gone to Catholic schools most of my life, and I even was considering becoming a

Jesuit priest. I was studying philosophy at the time, and for some reason, I began to have doubts about Jesus. The Gospel of John has Jesus claiming: "I am the way, the truth and the life. No one comes to the Father except through me" (Jn. 14:6, NRSV).

But was that true? Could I be so sure of Jesus that I would be willing to stake my life on him? Did I have the courage to follow Jesus, even if that meant sacrificing my own comfort and security? What if Jesus was mistaken? What if the Gospel was not true? What if the entire Christian faith was a fraud? In that case, I would be wasting my life following Jesus.

Thankfully, there were several professors at Fordham who helped me through my intellectual difficulties, the greatest of whom was the philosopher Dietrich von Hildebrand who lectured monthly at the university. His father was the noted German sculptor Adolph von Hildebrand and his mother was quite learned in the humanities. Although nominal Lutherans, neither of his parents were believers.

As Dietrich von Hildebrand told the story, one evening at dinner when he was a young boy of about eight years old, he spoke about Jesus to his parents. He said that his friends had told him that Jesus was God. "Was it true?" he asked.

"Of course not," his parents assured him. Jesus was a good man, a moral teacher, but certainly not God.

As he went to bed that evening, young Dietrich was restless, unable to sleep. In his room on the wall was a crucifix – a relic of a bygone era and a symbol without any meaning for his parents. For some reason, young Dietrich got out of bed and stared at that crucifix. He kept his gaze on the broken body of Jesus hanging on the wood before him. It seemed like an eternity that he just kept staring at that crucifix, but finally with tears in his eyes he cried out, "Yes, you are God!"

"Yes, you are God!" When I heard those words from von

Hildebrand, they completely changed my thinking. I do not know why or how, but at that moment I had this deep inner assurance that Jesus was indeed God. What saints and scholars, theologians and ordinary folk have believed about Jesus is indeed true. Jesus is the Son of God, the Word made flesh, the Way, the Truth and the Life – the foundation of the church's faith and of my faith.

Now, thirty-three years a priest, I cannot imagine life without Jesus. He is the basis for everything I have done as a priest, every Eucharist I have celebrated, every sermon I have preached, every person I have ministered to, baptized, married, buried and counseled. Nothing in the priestly life, or for that matter in the Christian life, makes any sense without Jesus being who the church says he is. The Nicene Creed puts it succinctly: "...God, of God; Light, of Light, Very God, of very God; Begotten, not made; Being of one substance with the Father; Though whom all things were made..."[1] On this faith Christianity stands or falls – there is no middle ground, no compromise. This is the faith of the church.

I remember a story that the former Bishop of Norwich Maurice Wood shared when he came to Canada many years ago. He told of a fine young Church Army captain with inoperable cancer. As they talked of Christ, and of suffering and death, the captain smiled and said: "Bishop, this is no time for doubting."

I think those words apply to us in the church today. This is no time for doubting. It is a time to trust Jesus – to accept him as Savior, to obey him as Lord, and to believe in him as God Incarnate – God become human. Yes, Jesus is the Way, the Truth and the Life. I am a committed Christian because I believe in Jesus.

The second turning point in my life happened in law school when I was taking a course in jurisprudence taught by Professor Aaron Schreiber. Professor Schreiber was not only a lawyer and an accomplished scholar but also a rabbi. I became Professor Schreiber's assistant and through him studied the legal theory of Yale Professors Myres McDougal and Harold Lasswell who defined law as "policy science." According to Professors McDougall and Lasswell, the purpose of law is to promote human dignity – an inclusive term that affords people the freedom to achieve power, wealth, respect, well-being, affection, skill, rectitude and enlightenment.

That notion of human dignity became a guiding principle for my own life – and when the 1979 American Prayer Book was authorized, to my delight, there in the Baptismal Covenant was the promise to "respect the dignity of every human being."

Of course, as Christians, we take the notion of human dignity one step further and say that every human being is created in the image of God and is therefore deserving of respect. No human being should be considered as a cog in a machine, or an expendable unit of labor, or a means to an end. All human beings have intrinsic value and worth, no matter their race, age, gender, nationality, ethnic background, disability or sexual orientation.

I have learned over the course of my life that the struggle for human dignity and the expansion of human rights is a never-ending process because there will always be social and political forces that want to squelch both. However, they are destined to lose. God is on the side of the poor, the oppressed and the marginalized. When we advocate and work for justice, and build a more equitable and humane society, we are on the side of the angels.

Jesus the Way, the Truth and the Life – and Human Dignity as the foundation for law and ethics –these two core beliefs have been central to my life.

There is, however, one more – the belief that All-Inclusive Love is the hope of the world. We seem to be trying to build higher and higher walls these days, and not just at the American southern border but in our own personal lives. Yet, I agree with

Robert Frost: "Something there is that doesn't love a wall."[2] We shouldn't be building walls but breaking them down. As a Christian I believe that no one is outside the pale of God's love, absolutely no one. If the world is not ready for this idea of All-Inclusive Love, then it is up to the church to show the way. The church must always reach out and minister to all sorts of people and say, "There is a place for you here!" The church should always be willing to draw the circle wide so that no one is left out or shut out. In this, we mirror the kingdom of God.

As a priest who has served in many different kinds of parishes over the years, I have come to recognize that the church is a body of wounded people, men and women with troubled minds and burdened consciences, all loved by God. The church is a community of people bound together by their strength and their brokenness who are limping toward the sunrise, but know that God's love claims them, everyone.

When I was rector of a church in Pennsylvania, a couple asked to meet with me during the week. They came to my office, sat down and got right to the point: "Would you be willing to welcome our family into your church?"

I was taken aback by the question, so I said, "" Come again."

They repeated, "Would you be willing to welcome us into your church?"

"Of course," I said. "Why would you ever think otherwise?"

"Well, it's like this," they said. "We have a mentally disabled autistic son. We have gone to several churches in the area, and in each one we have been asked to leave because the church could not handle our son in the Sunday school. They said he was too challenging, too disruptive, and too hard for the teachers. We've been given all sorts of reasons why we need to find somewhere else to worship."

As they were speaking, my heart went out to them. Most

couples would have given up on the church long ago, but not them. They really believed in Jesus and they wanted a church that would act like Jesus.

I said to them, "I have a daughter with Down syndrome. I know it is not easy for us parents with special needs children. Doors get slammed in our faces all the time, but the one place we have a right to expect an open door is in the church. Here's my promise to you: I'll do everything within my power to see that your son is fully welcomed into this church."

And their son *was* welcomed. So were several other special needs children and adults who became part of the church family. In fact, the parish made hospitality to persons with special needs one of its primary ministries.

When the new education wing was built, the parish invited the S. June Smith Center for special needs children to use our facilities during the week – at no cost except to cover expenses. About forty special needs children came to the church campus each day for programs in the morning and afternoon.

Word spread that the parish was a safe and welcoming place for children with disabilities. The parish began to grow in members and receive donations for special projects, such as a state-of-the-art playground. Eventually the parish would host a second school – Veritas Academy – a Christian elementary school that specialized in the classical method of education. We had special needs children in one wing on the campus and children learning Latin and studying Aristotle in another. What a wonderfully diverse church family it was – a place of grace where everyone was welcomed with open arms.

This is the church at its best – accommodating people at their own level of need and understanding, meeting them at their own stage in life, responding to their hurts, being sensitive to their experiences, and offering a warm welcome to all – "a place of grace" for everyone. This is a church that blesses rather than curses, affirms rather than condemns – a church that counts people in rather than kicks people out – a church for everyone willing to live with grace towards everyone in need of grace. In fact, in this kind of church the only way to be excluded is for you to exclude yourself.

I know the church must maintain standards of faith, morals and discipline. We can't be an "anything goes" kind of church and have credibility in the culture. And yet, I believe from the depths of my being that before the throne of God, we will never be judged and found wanting for loving too much, only for loving too little. If we err, let it be on the side of love.

With all the talk of a wall between Mexico and the United States, did you know there is a wall in heaven? Every morning St. Peter would find a horde of undesirable aliens whom he was certain he had never admitted through the official border crossing. Some had never been baptized, some were ignorant of the Bible; many were damaged souls who would never qualify under the vetting process.

St, Peter decided he would investigate how these illegal aliens were getting into heaven. So in the darkness he prowled about the border wall, trying to determine how these folks were sneaking in. At last he discovered a dark corner where a few bars had been removed from the wall since the last inspection an hour before. A crowd of refugees and migrants were steadily creeping in. He rushed at them with indignation, but was amazed to find Jesus there, welcoming them as they crossed the border. Peter then realized that getting into heaven was not a matter of merit but mercy, not grit but grace, not law but love. None of the folks deserved to get into heaven. Some were never baptized. Others were not quite orthodox in their religious views. And still others had lived less than ideal lives. All of them were miserable sinners. And yet, they were God's special friends and welcomed anyway.

Three turning points: Jesus as the Way, the Truth and the Life; Human Dignity as the foundation for law and ethics; and All-Inclusive Love as the hope of the world.

These are the three beliefs that keep me going when I get discouraged. They recharge me when I get exhausted. They assure me that I am not wasting my time or energy when results are not immediate or even when there is a setback.

Years ago the mystical Jesuit priest paleontologist Teilhard de Chardin wrote words that have resonated with me throughout my ministry. They give me the hope that even in the worst of times love with triumph. He wrote: "Someday, after mastering the winds, the waves, tides, and gravity, we will harness for God the energies of love, and then for a second time in the history of the world, man will have discovered fire."

May it be so, dear God, may it be so!

June 5, 2016
St. James Westminster Church, London, ON

ENDNOTES

INTRODUCTION

1 "A sermon preached by John Venn in 1806 upon the anniversary of the departure of a group of missionaries to Africa." *Celebrating the Saints*, compiled by Robert Atwell (Norwich: Canterbury Press, 1998) 224.

PART ONE
BUILDING THE FIRE: TRANSFORMING LIVES IN JESUS

1 Margaret Craven, *I Heard the Owl Call My Name* (New York: Dell Publishing, 1973) 38-39.

PART TWO
KINDLING THE FIRE: EXPLORING FAITH

GOD, SECULARIZATION AND THE NEW ATHEISM

1 "A Nation Living in Sin." *MacLean's*, July 7, 2008, 55.

2 Matthew Stewart, *The Courtier and the Heretic* (New York: W.W. Norton, 2006) 29.

3 Walter Kaufman, *Hegel: A Reinterpretation* by Walter Kaufman (New York: Anchor Books, 1965) 268.

4 Matthew Arnold, *Dover Beach and Other Poems* (New York: Dover Publications, Inc., 1994) 86.

5 Jennifer Michael Hecht, *Doubt: A History* (San Francisco: Harper San Francisco, 2003) 371.

6 Christina Rosetti, "In the bleak midwinter." *Poems of Grace: Texts of The Hymnal 1982* (New York: Church Publishing Incorporated, 1998) 112.

7 See A.J. Ayer, *Language, Truth and Logic* (New York: Dover Publications, 1952).

8 Christopher Hitchens, *God Is Not Great: How Religion Poisons Everything* (New York: Warner, 2007); Richard Dawkins, *The God Delusion* (New York: Houghton Mifflin Company, 2006); Sam Harris, *The End of Faith: Religious Terror and the Future of Reason* (New York: W.W. Norton & Company, 2005).

9 Richard Dawkins, *The God Delusion*, 31. In my analysis of the New Atheism, I have relied on a series of articles titled, "The New Atheism." *America*, May 5, 2008, 12-29. See also John Haught, *God and the New Atheism* (Louisville: Westminster John Knox, 2008); Alister McGrath, *Dawkins' God* (London: Blackwell Publishing, 2005) and Kitty Ferguson, *The Fire in the Equations* (Philadelphia: Templeton Foundation Press, 1994).

10 Graham Greene, *The Power and the Glory* (New York: Open Road Integrated Media, 2013) Kindle Edition.

11 David Edwards, "Reasons for Faith." *Church Times*, September 12, 1986, 14.

12 Betty Stafford, "Letter to a Reluctant Atheist." *America*, April 14, 2008, 17-18.

13 *Maclean's*, January 14, 2008, 15-16.

14 Maltbie Babock, "This is My Father's World." *The Book of Common Praise* (Toronto: Anglican Book Centre, 2000) Hymn 600.

15 Francis B. Sayre, Jr., "The Mystery and the Miracle" preached at Christ Church, Cambridge, Massachusetts on August 4, 1991.

16 Thornton Wilder, *Our Town* (New York: Perennial Library, 1957) 45.

UNDERSTANDING HEAVEN

1 Walter Isaacson, *Steve Jobs* (New York: Simon and Schuster, 2011) 570-71.

INTO THE DARK

1 T.S. Eliot, "Four Quartets, East Coker, III." *The Complete Poems of T.S. Eliot* (London: Faber and Faber, 1969) 180.

RISING ABOVE YOUR PAIN

1 Thornton Wilder, *The Bridge of San Luis Rey* (New York: Library of America, 2009) 192.

2 *The Book of Common Prayer* (New York: Oxford University Press, 1990) 466.

THE CASE FOR RELIGION

1   Richard Dawkins, *The God Delusion* (Boston: Houghton Mifflin Company, 2006) 1-2.

2   Sandi Dolbee, "In God's Name." *San Diego Union-Tribune*, November 9, 2001, E1,4.

3   John Henry Newman, *Difficulties of Anglicans*, Vol. 1 (London: Longmans, Green and Co., 1897) 239-240. Hitchens, in the debate, cites this passage as being in Newman's *Apologia Pro Vita Sui*.

PART THREE
FANNING THE FIRE: THE SPIRITUAL JOURNEY

SPIRITUALITY 101

1   Hugh Montefiore, *OH God, What Next?* (London: Hodder and Stoughton, 1995).

THE MYSTERIOUS MIRACULOUS GOD

1   A.J. Ayer, "What I Saw When I Was Dead." *The Sunday Telegraph* (London, U.K.), August 28, 1988.

THE MYSTERY OF UNANSWERED PRAYER

1   *Manual of Prayers*. James D. Watkins, editor (Rome: Pontifical North American College, 1995) 250-251.

THE HUMAN PARADOX

1   Sonia Saraiya, "Hilary's Humility Moment: A rabbi walks into a Town Hall and asks a question you'd never hear in the GOP debates." *Salon.com*, February 4, 2016.

2   *The Book of Alternative Services* (Toronto: Anglican Church of Canada, 1983) 586.

MY JESUS MOMENT

1   *The Book of Common Prayer* (New York: The Church Pension Fund, 1986) 718.

REACHING YOUR FULL POTENTIAL

1   George Mannes, "How Should You Measure Success?" *Money*, October 2012, 100. Note: Professor Christensen died on January 23, 2020.

GET OUT OF THE BOAT

1   Ben Stein, *How Successful People Win (Carlsbad, CA: Hay House, 2005) ix-xix.*

CHOOSING WHO WE BECOME

1   Bishop Theodore Schneider shared this story at a June 2007 Kirby Smith Stewardship Conference in Hershey, Pennsylvania.

PART FOUR
THE WORD ON FIRE: CONTEMPORARY ISSUES

CROSS-CENTERED LIVING

1   Martha Beck, *Expecting Adam* (New York: Three Rivers Press, 2011) 212-216.
2   Robert Bolt, *A Man for All Seasons*, (London: Bloomsbury Press, 1960, 2013) Act II, Kindle Edition.
3   *Celebrating the Saints: Daily Readings for the Calendar of the Church of England.* Robert Atwell, editor (Norwich: Canterbury Press, 1998) 227.
4   I am indebted to Justice Antonin Scalia's talk on, "Not to the Wise – the Christian as Cretin" in *On Faith: Lessons from an American Believer* (New York: Crown Forum, 2019). Justice Scalia praises Thomas More as someone in a prominent position who put God first, even at the cost of losing his life. Justice Scalia, like Thomas More, was a Christian who could stand contrary to culture while fully engaging in it – a model for all of us who seek to live out our Christian commitment in the world.

THE MOMENT TO DECIDE

1   *Manual of Prayers*, James D. Watkins, editor (Rome: Pontifical North American College, 2011) 236.
2   James Russell Lowell, "Once to Every Man and Nation." *Common Praise* (Toronto: Anglican Book Centre, 2000) Hymn 587.

WHEN THE WORLD FALLS APART

1   *Manual of Prayers*, James D. Watkins, editor (Rome: Pontifical North American College, 2011) 251.

2   Martin Luther, "A Mighty Fortress is Our God." *Poems of Grace: Texts of Hymnal 1982* (New York: Church Publishing House, 1998) Hymn 687.

RACE IN AMERICA

1   John Oxenham, "In Christ there is no East or West." *The Hymnal 1982* (New York: The Church Pension Group, 1982) Hymn 529.

2   *The Book of Common Prayer* (New York: Oxford University Press, 1990) 306.

3   Ibid. 855.

THE HARD TRUTH

1   Edward M. Welch, "Justice in Executive Compensation." *America*, May 19, 2003, 8-9.

2   Jim Collins, *Good to Great* (Harper Business, 2001) 28-29.

3   Ibid. 138.

4   Matthew Boyle, "When Will They Stop?" *Fortune*, May 3, 2004, 123.

5   Welch, 9-10.

6   Robert Heller, *Charles Handy* (London: DK Books, 2001) 69,77.

7   Thomas Tewell, "Ministering to the Business Community." *Theology Today*, October 2003, 353.

GOD'S NEW ECONOMY

1   Since the sermon was originally preached in 2004, the number of billionaires has increased to 540 with a net worth of about 2.4 trillion dollars. Millionaires also have increased to over eighteen million.

2   John Donne, *Devotions Upon Emergent Occasions* (New York: Vintage Spiritual Classics, 1999) Chapter 17, 103.

THE MYTH OF MORE

1   "Big bonuses, costly commodes: Thain out of B of A." *The Globe and Mail, Report on Business*, January 13, 2009, 1-5.

2   *Business Week*, July 14, & 21, 2008, 23-24.

HOW CAN I LOVE IN A WORLD LIKE THIS?

1 *National Socialist Party of America v. The Village of Skokie*, 432 U.S. 43 (1977).
2 Dissent by Justice Oliver Wendell Holmes in *United States v. Schwimmer*, 279 U.S. 644 (1929).
3 *New York Times v. Sullivan*, 376 U.S. 254 (1964).

CHRISTIAN CIVILITY IN A COARSE CULTURE

1 Abraham Lincoln, *Meditation on the Divine Will*, September 1862 (abrahamlincolnonline.org /speeches.meditat.htm).

PART FIVE
HOME FIRE: CHURCH LIFE

SATISFYING THE HUNGERS OF THE HEART

1 *The Book of Common Prayer* (New York: Oxford University Press, 1990) 338.

THE COURAGE TO CHANGE YOUR MIND

1 Richard Friedman, *The Hidden Face of God* (New York: Harper Collins, 2001).
2 Henry Francis Lyte, "Abide with Me." *Common Praise* (Toronto: Anglican Book Centre, 2000) Hymn 24.
3 Walter Chalmers Smith, "Immortal, Invisible, God Only Wise." *Common Praise* (Toronto: Anglican Book Centre, 2000) Hymn 393.
4 John T. Noonan, *A Church That Can and Cannot Change: The Development of Catholic Moral Teaching* (University of Notre Dame Press, 2005).
5 Cardinal Avery Dulles, *The New World of Faith* (Huntington, Indiana: Our Sunday Visitor, 2000) 87.

THE POWER AND MAJESTY OF MUSIC

1 Bob Dufford, "Be Not Afraid" (Portland, OR: Oregon Catholic Press, 1975).
2 William Whiting, "Eternal Father, Strong to Save. *Common Praise* (Toronto: Anglican Book Centre, 2000) Hymn 567.
3 Robert Lowry, "My Life Flows On in Endless Praise." *Common Praise* (Toronto: Anglican Book Centre, 2000) 401.

THE CALL OF DISCIPLESHIP

1   *Manual of Prayers*, James D. Watkins, editor (Rome: The Pontifical North American College, 2011) 321.

TURNING POINTS

1   *The Book of Common Prayer 1962 Canada* (Toronto: Anglican Book Centre, 1962) 71.
2   *Robert Frost's Poems*, Louis Untermeyer, editor (New York: St. Martin's Paperbacks, 2002) 95.

ABOUT THE AUTHOR

Gary Nicolosi has been called "a man on fire" - not wildfire out of control nor a fire that consumes. Rather, he burns with a fire that forges the armor of faith for living in a tough world.

Growing up in Brooklyn, New York, young Gary never imagined himself as a priest or preacher until in the sixth grade at military school. There he had an experience in which Jesus became real to him in a way he could not deny. From that time on, he has had a passion for Jesus that has been the hallmark of his ministry as a priest.

After military school, Gary attended St. Francis Prep in Brooklyn, New York, Fordham and Georgetown Universities, and Temple University Law School. A member of the New York Bar, he practiced labor, criminal and constitutional law in New York City. In 1980 he took, in his words "a giant leap of faith," and left law practice to study for the priesthood at Trinity College, University of Toronto. Some of his law colleagues thought he was being foolish to abandon his successful career, but a voice spoke to his heart – a call from God to drop everything, enter divinity school and dedicate his life to God, Christ and the Church.

On St. John the Baptist Day, June 24, 1983, Gary was ordained at the Cathedral of the Holy Trinity in Quebec City, Canada. In stark contrast to life as a New York City lawyer, Gary was assigned five small churches on the rural Gaspe Coast of Quebec. His car often got stuck in the snow as he traveled from congregation to congregation. At times, he flew in a tiny plane to the Magdalene Islands to lead worship services for churches without a priest.

Over the course of his thirty-seven years of ordained ministry, Gary has led rural, suburban and urban congregations in both the United States and Canada, served as Canon for Ministries at the Cathedral Church of the Nativity in Bethlehem, Pennsylvania, and as Congregational Development Officer in the Diocese of British Columbia. He received his Doctor of Ministry from Pittsburgh Theological Seminary in 1997. Under his leadership St. Bartholomew's Episcopal Church in suburban San Diego County grew from 1,200 to over 2,300 members, making it one of the largest Episcopal churches on the West Coast.

Through his diverse pastoral ministry, Gary Nicolosi demonstrated extraordinary insight into reaching people who were on a spiritual quest for meaning in their lives. His dynamic preaching connected the church and the culture, the religious and the spiritual, the sacred and the secular. He describes his overriding passion like this: *to transform lives in Christ, connect the Gospel to culture, and grow the Church.* He has shared his insights on bringing people to Christ with clergy and congregants in 28 dioceses across North America and in 2009 led a church growth seminar for Canadian Anglican and Lutheran bishops.

A current resident of Peoria, Arizona, Gary served as interim rector of the Church of the Nativity, Scottsdale for twenty-one months, and remains active in the Episcopal Diocese of Arizona where he currently serves on the Clergy Disciplinary Board. He is a member of the New York Bar, the American Bar Association, the Federal Bar Association, ASISTA, the Federalist Society, and licensed to practice in the federal immigration and veterans courts. He is a prolific author of hundreds of articles, and leads seminars and workshops on evangelism, church growth, stewardship, congregational development and preaching. He can be contacted at desertglorysermons@gmail.com.

Gary is married to Heather Bruce Nicolosi and they have one daughter, Allison, who has Down syndrome.

CPSIA information can be obtained
at www.ICGtesting.com
Printed in the USA
LVHW011433110521
687107LV00005B/50

9 781664 213050